Place and People

Mr. Clarke, currently on leave from the University of Hawaii, is now a Research Fellow in Human Geography at The Australian National University, Canberra.

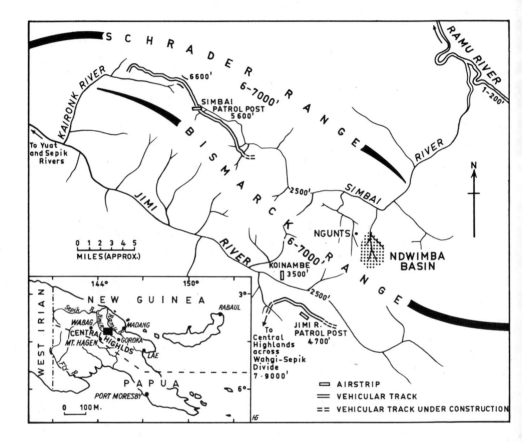

SCHRADER RANGE

KAIRONK RIVER

RAMU RIVER
1·200'

6600'

BISMARCK 6-7000' RANGE

SIMBAI
PATROL POST
5600'

To Yuat
and Sepik
Rivers

JIMI

RIVER

2500'

SIMBAI
RIVER

N

NGUNTS·

NDWIMBA
BASIN

6-7000' RANGE

KOINAMBE
3500'

2500'

0 1 2 3 4 5
MILES (APPROX.)

To
Central
Highlands
across
Wahgi-Sepik
Divide
7·9000'

JIMI R.
PATROL POST
4700'

NEW GUINEA

144°   150°   3°

RABAUL

WEST IRIAN

Sepik River
WABAG   MADANG
CENTRAL HIGHLDS
MT. HAGEN   GOROKA
Fly   LAE

PAPUA   6°

PORT MORESBY

0   100 M.

K5

⬭ AIRSTRIP
══ VEHICULAR TRACK
══ VEHICULAR TRACK UNDER CONSTRUCTION

Place
and
People

AN ECOLOGY OF
A NEW GUINEAN COMMUNITY

William C. Clarke

UNIVERSITY OF CALIFORNIA PRESS
BERKELEY, LOS ANGELES, LONDON 1971

UNIVERSITY OF CALIFORNIA PRESS
BERKELEY AND LOS ANGELES, CALIFORNIA
UNIVERSITY OF CALIFORNIA PRESS, LTD.
LONDON, ENGLAND
COPYRIGHT © 1971, BY
THE REGENTS OF THE UNIVERSITY OF CALIFORNIA
INTERNATIONAL STANDARD BOOK NUMBER: 0-520-01791-9
LIBRARY OF CONGRESS CATALOG CARD NUMBER: 78-126764
PRINTED IN THE UNITED STATES OF AMERICA
DESIGNED BY DAVE COMSTOCK

Contents

Illustrations

Tables

Preface

As with any persisting group of organisms, a community of people must in some ways adapt to the conditions of the place where they live. Within and beyond their adaptation, all peoples also modify their parts of the face of the earth. By these truisms are expressed what have been two principal themes in studies of the links between place and people: the influence of the environment on man and the effect of the man on his environment. Partisans urging the predominance of the extreme of either theme—that the environment determines man or that man can come close to manipulating freely the passive, even if limiting, environment—have both enjoyed periods of ascendancy; but it is now only rarely that either viewpoint is held up as the sole means of illumination. With the dissolution of these simpler faiths has come a recognition of the interchange between man and environment, neither of which is considered to act on the other in a unilinear way; instead, both are thought of as parts of an ensemble where cause and effect are but interacting elements in an ever-changing plexus of process and event.

In recent years investigators concerned with such interactions between the human habitat and human, or cultural, behavior have frequently termed their studies "human ecology" or "cultural ecology"—thus formally marking out a field of interest that extends into the traditional subject matters of both anthropology and geography. This book, which results from a reworking of my PhD dissertation in geography, had its genesis in such an interdisciplinary concern when, as a member of an anthropological-geographical research project titled "Human Ecology of the New Guinea Rainforest," I spent close to a year among the Maring-speaking people of New Guinea during 1964 and 1965. This joint research project was a continuation of a more strictly anthropological study, "Culture and En-

vironment in the New Guinea Rainforest," that was initiated
by the anthropologist A. P. Vayda. He, together with four
graduate students in anthropology, had carried out investiga-
tions among the Maring in 1962 and 1963.

One of the major objectives of the anthropologists' project
was said to be "the analysis of the cultural adaptation of a
primitive horticultural population to its environment." To this
end the anthropologists gave their special attention to certain
features of Maring ritual and social behavior that seemed to
have ecologically adaptive functions. To date, the major out-
come of their work has been Roy Rappaport's *Pigs for the Ancestors* (Rappaport, 1967b). The collaborative work that the
project's geographic members, John M. Street and I, carried out
in 1964 and 1965 was proposed because the anthropologists
believed that they lacked sufficiently precise information on
Maring environment and land use for the full development of
some of their hypotheses—for instance, that the fission and
fusion that occur frequently among the small local groups of
Maring might serve to adjust man-land ratios that had become
adaptively unfavorable. To meet the anthropologists' need, Dr.
Street and I devoted five months to a survey of the agriculture,
climate, and conditions of the vegetation and soil in the territories of several Maring communities, some of which had relatively little land in proportion to the size of their population
and some of which had extensive tracts of unused land available. We hoped by this means to provide the anthropologists
with useful information about the degree to which human use
had altered the natural environment of the territories of several
Maring communities; this information, in turn, could provide
a basis for judging varying degrees of population pressure. After
making the aggregate survey with Dr. Street, I remained alone
in the Maring area mostly with a single group known as the
Bomagai-Angoiang, whose territory, which I named the
Ndwimba Basin, Dr. Street and I had visited twice during our
work together. It is with the ecology of that small community
of 154 persons that this study is concerned. In my writing my
principal purpose is to describe the structure, functioning, and

trends of the ecosystem in which the Bomagai-Angoiang are now the dominant organisms. The meaning of the concept "ecosystem" is developed at the beginning of Chapter 2 and in Appendix A.

Almost inevitably, the major task of an attempt to transmute a dissertation into something approaching a generally readable book is to cut out some of the overload of fact and theory and to translate professional jargon into more widely understood language. To this end I have shortened the theoretical buttressing and the statement of field problems that served as an introduction to my dissertation; further to spare those readers not interested in such matters, I have appended this shortened version as an epilogue (Appendix A), rather than placing it at the beginning of the book. In the main text I have condensed some descriptions, particularly those of plant communities, and I have tried to make clear any technical terms that I have used. In Appendixes B, C, and D I have abbreviated the details relating to the use of plants and animals by the Bomagai-Angoiang. Readers seeking more information on these matters are referred to the original dissertation.

During my field investigation I received support under a grant from the National Science Foundation. Andrew P. Vayda, Professor of Anthropology at Columbia University, was Principal Investigator. Further financial aid for field research and travel within New Guinea was granted to me by the Agricultural Development Council. The Department of Human Geography, Research School of Pacific Studies, the Australian National University, provided cartographic and typing services.

For their enlightening criticism I am grateful to Clarence Glacken, Carl O. Sauer, and James Anderson—all members of my dissertation committee at the University of California at Berkeley. Further, to Dr. Sauer I owe my original interest in geography as a field of study.

The anthropologists A. P. Vayda, R. Rappaport, C. L. Vayda, and A. Rappaport—all fellow members of the Maring project—were generous with their comments and ideas. The geographer John Street, who was with me in the field for six months, provided much wise counsel and unfailingly good companionship.

Identifications of plant and animal specimens were made by Harold E. Moore, Hobart M. Van Deusen, R. E. Holttum, Benjamin Stone, Harold St. John, Thomas Whitaker, J. Linsley Gressitt, and John Womersley and his staff at the Botanical Gardens at Lae in New Guinea. H. C. Brookfield, R. and S. Bulmer, I. Hughes, and R. G. Robbins freely shared information and ideas on the peoples and environments of New Guinea. H. E. Gunther's cartographic skills are evident in the maps. The following persons were especially helpful in the field: G. Carter, M. Brown, and A. Noblet, all patrol officers of the Territory of New Guinea; Fann Sibut, the clerk of the Simbai Patrol Post; R. McCormac, the agricultural officer of Madang District; the staff and associated personnel of the Anglican mission at Simbai; Herbert Bapera, then of Gai; and Aindem and Men of Kwiop who served well as interpreters and about my camp. As for the Bomagai-Angoiang themselves, I only wish that they could know the extent of my appreciation for their friendship, tolerance, and help.

Note on Orthography and Usage of Pidgin English and Maring Words

Words in Pidgin English or my translations of words from Pidgin English or Maring into colloquial English are enclosed by quotation marks. Except for proper nouns, words in Maring are italicized. The letters that I use to represent vowels as usually sounded by Bomagai-Angoiang Maring have the following approximate equivalents in English:

a as in *a*rm	*o* as in *o*ld
ai as in *ice*	*oi* as in *oi*l
e as in *debt*	*u* as in f*oo*d
i as in *see*	*ə* as in c*a*thedral

The prenasalized syllabic consonants that occur before initial *b*, *d*, or *g* I represent by *m* or *n*; thus in the place name Ndwimba the *n* is pronounced in the same way as the African town of Ndola. Maring words that I spell with an initial *t* begin with a sound, always pronounced with a slight flap, that to my ears was interchangeably English *l*, *r*, or *t*. The other consonants that I use in spelling Maring words have the usual English values. I use an apostrophe to indicate a glottal catch.

An aerial photograph of the vicinity of the Ndwimba Basin taken from 25,000 feet May 21, 1959 (approximate scale, 1:44,000). The line encloses the contiguous zone currently inhabited and cultivated by the Bomagai-Angoiang. (1) Gardens of the Fungai clan. (2) Ndwimba Creek. (3) These lightly colored trees are high-elevation *Pandanus* species on the crest of the basin's southern wall. (4) Uninhabited arable land on the route to Kumoints. (*Photograph available by the courtesy of the Director, Division of National Mapping, Department of National Development, Australia.*)

CHAPTER ONE

First Impressions

> We knew for long the mansion's look
> And what we said of it became
> A part of what it is . . .
> —WALLACE STEVENS *

After reaching the Territory of New Guinea, a traveler from the outside world must make his way toward the Ndwimba Basin [1] either from Madang, a seaport on the north coast, or from a town of the Central Highlands, usually Mount Hagen. From these relatively developed parts of the territory the traveler sets out for the heavily dissected and only recently explored series of mountain ranges that for so long isolated the capacious upland valleys of the Central Highlands from the lowland Ramu Valley and the northern coastal region. (See frontispiece.) Although the beginnings of roads stretch out from both the highlands and the north coast, at present the traveler's only means of modern transport into the mountains near the Ndwimba Basin are small aircraft, which can land at the short, grass-covered airstrip at either the Jimi River Patrol Post, which is at a place called Tabibuga in the Jimi River Valley, or the Simbai Patrol Post near the headwaters of the Simbai River. [2] From either of these outposts of Australian administrative con-

---

* Reprinted with permission of Alfred A. Knopf, Inc., from "A Postcard from the Volcano" by Wallace Stevens in *The Collected Poems of Wallace Stevens* (New York: Alfred A. Knopf, Inc., 1969), p. 159.

1. The name Ndwimba Basin is of my own coinage. On maps and in government patrol reports, the Ndwimba Basin as well as the adjacent area to the west is known as Ngunts (or Gunts) or as Sipapi (or Tabapi), which is the native name of the Bomagai land on which the government rest house is built in this vicinity.

2. Since I left New Guinea, another airstrip (shown on Map 1) has been opened in this region at the Anglican Mission Station at Koinambe, and a road connecting the Jimi River Patrol Post with the Central Highlands has been completed.

trol the traveler can ride for a few miles by vehicle over earthen roads now being built by levies of local native people; but for most of the two-day journey to the Ndwimba Basin, he must go on foot over narrow walking tracks.

If the traveler has flown into the Jimi River Patrol post, he must go northward to reach the Ndwimba Basin. First he descends into the steep-walled inner valley of the Jimi River; then, after crossing the river on a swaying suspension bridge of vine, he climbs for more than 4,000 feet up the south wall of the Bismarck Range, first through the tall forest near the river, then through the gardens, grassland, and secondary forest and woodland of the inhabited middle slopes, and last into the uninhabited and cloud-pervaded montane forest that caps the higher parts of the range. From the Bismarck's narrow crest— in this vicinity about 7,000 feet in elevation—the traveler descends a thousand or more feet among the wet, mossy trunks of the montane-forest trees before again entering inhabited mid-elevation slopes where he encounters the walking trail that leads eastward from the Simbai Patrol Post to the Ndwimba Basin.

If the traveler has flown into the Simbai Patrol Post, his route to the basin will lead him down the Simbai Valley from the upper valley, where extensive grasslands manifest much human activity, through the partially grassy middle valley, on to the region of the Ndwimba Basin, which has almost no grassland and beyond which to the east along the north side of the Bismarck Range lies a great stretch of almost uninhabited forest.

Because the Ndwimba Basin's inhabitants and their immediate neighbors do live here on the edge of settlement and because they have a reputation for rusticity, they are sometimes spoken of by people who reside farther up the Simbai Valley as "men at the tail of the snake." In many ways the intended implication of this designation is apt. Certainly, the people of the Ndwimba Basin are isolated both from European influences [3] and from densely populated native regions where the

---

3. Six young men of the basin were recruited in 1962 to "go to the beach" as laborers on coconut plantations. Five of them returned

environment has been strongly affected by human occupation. Moreover, living on the edge of an empty and apparently primary forest, the people of the Ndwimba Basin seen like pioneers, with land to spare—and they have the backwoodsman's technically simple agriculture. Also, the people who live in and near the Ndwimba Basin are among the last people of the Simbai and Jimi valleys to have been contacted by white men; it was in 1958 that an Australian government patrol entered this previously unexplored part of the Bismarck Range. The Australian journalist Gavin Souter accompanied this patrol and later, in his book *New Guinea, The Last Unknown,* described the patrol's encounter with a small group of natives who had never before seen white men (Souter, 1963:235–236):

In 1958 I accompanied a patrol into the Bismarcks, a range of mountains whose green rococo folds of rain forest form the northern wall of the Jimi Valley in the Western Highlands District. Two years earlier a patrol had been attacked in this valley by 200 bowmen, and had been obliged to shoot ten of its attackers. A patrol post was then established at a place called Tabibuga, and by 1958 most of the valley was well under control. The only people not yet visited by the patrol officer at Tabibuga were a group known as the Gants, and it was with these people high up in the Bismarcks that my patrol hoped to make contact.

After two weeks of more or less comfortable walking on patrol roads and native tracks, we climbed an almost vertical slope of mud and tree roots for three hours, crossed a ridge of moss forest at 6,000 feet, and then jolted downhill beside a hectic, nameless stream

---

in February 1964 after their two-year contract had expired. They brought home knowledge and goods (blankets, wooden suitcases, cigarette lighters, small knives, cotton clothing) from the outside world. However, so far their experience has not much altered the way of life in the basin. Because they were all young and bachelors when they returned, the status gained from travel and association with the Europeans still did not give them authority equal to that of the older "big men." Moreover, because the older men had cleared land for the laborers' mothers while they were gone and also had helped the laborers reestablish gardens when they returned, the laborers are still obligated to the older men. Thus, though the young men who did leave seem to lack respect for dietary taboos and for the men who stayed "in the bush," they have not yet spoken strongly for change.

which our guides said would lead us to a rendezvous they had
arranged with the Gants. After descending between steep walls of
forest for four hours, we heard some shrill calls in the distance
which were quite unlike the yodelling practised around Tabibuga.
Ten minutes later we met the Gants: they were standing beside a
waterfall, about forty little men in grass sporrans and plumes and
possum fur, and some of them were so nervous that they held each
other's hands for comfort.

They led us to a campsite named Gunts, called their women
and children out of the bush, and presented the patrol with two live
pigs trussed to poles. After returning this compliment with steel
hatchets and salt, the patrol officer, Barry Griffin, addressed the
Gants in Pidgin English. Our interpreter relayed the speech in his
own place-talk which, although not identical with that of the Gants,
was intelligible to them. "I am the Kiap," said Griffin. "I am the
Government. I have built a house at Tabibuga, and I look after all
the people who live there. Many times I have heard you Gants
people mentioned, and you have interested me. Now I have come
here to your place, and I see all you men, women and children
gathered to meet me, and I am pleased. You are all dressed up in
your finery, and I am pleased. The reason I have come is that I want
to tell you something very worth while. What I am going to say to
you, you must take in properly. This talk of mine must go right inside your head, and it must stay with you, and you must give it
much thought."

When Griffin had finished telling the Gants that they must no
longer kill or steal, and that they must help the Government build
patrol roads, the time was 5.30 P.M. and the sun had almost set.
But there was still time to lower the Australian flag which had been
hoisted beside our tents earlier in the afternoon. As the flag slid
down its bamboo pole Griffin came to attention and saluted; his
police slapped the butts of their bayoneted .303s, and the poor
bewildered Gants stood gaping.

The people described by Souter as the Gants were members of the Fungai-Korama clan cluster,[4] whose territory lies

---

4. I use "clan cluster" in the sense of Vayda and Cook (1964:800)
to mean a nonexogamous socal unit that: (a) consists of two or more
clans, (b) is the largest named group in the Maring structural hierarchy,

just to the west of the Ndwimba Basin, the home of the Bomagai-Angoiang clan cluster, the people who are the subject of
this study. While the initial patrol was at Gunts, or Ngunts, the
Fungai center of settlement which is situated about half a mile
from the western rim of the Ndwimba Basin, some of the
Bomagai-Angoiang came there for their first look at the tall
strangers about whom they had heard stories for many years.

Two years later, in 1960, another patrol, this time from the
newly established Simbai Patrol Post, came to Ngunts; and the
patrol officer saw many of the Bomagai-Angoiang when he
made a brief sally through the basin. Since then the region of
Ngunts and the Ndwimba Basin has been officially adminis-
tered from the Simbai Patrol Post; but because the region is
relatively thinly populated and on the outer limits of his juris-
diction, the patrol officer visits only once a year, spending a day
or two to hold court and to take the annual census. By the mid-
1960s somewhat less than a score of other Westerners—mis-
sionaries, labor recruiters, geologists, anthropologists, geographers, entomologists, government agricultural officers, doctors—
have been there at least briefly, but the substance of the lives
of the Bomagai-Angoiang and their neighbors has been less
changed by the actual presence of the white men than by the
harbingers of their coming: bush knives, steel axe blades, some
new crops, and a dysentery epidemic, all of which arrived
along native trade routes a decade or more before 1958. Although the epidemic and the steel tools and new crops that
preceded the white men did alter the people's lives, the aggregate landscape of their basin home has changed but slightly
since the end of their Stone Age, only a few decades ago.

Neither this landscape nor the inhabitants of the Ndwimba
Basin differ greatly from the scenes and people to be observed
in the rest of the lower and middle Simbai Valley and the
adjacent Jimi Valley. Everywhere in the environs of the basin
the topography is rugged; local relief is 4,000 to 5,000 feet; the

---

(c) is the largest unit with recognized territorial boundaries, and (d) is
the largest unit whose members ever act as a single unit in fighting or in
ceremonies.

Nakemba, an Angoiang man, looking out over the lower floor of the basin. He is standing in one of the few patches of grassland in the basin.

mountains' crests and higher slopes, which are frequently under cloud, are covered with an evergreen, primary forest of the humid tropics; the lower slopes, except for the forested, steep inner gorges, are covered by an inconstant mosaic of gardens, grassland, and secondary forest in various stages of regrowth. Bare ground is rarely seen, and accelerated erosion appears to be slight; all the abundant smaller streams run clear except during and for a short time after heavy rains.

The peoples belonging to the clans and clan clusters of this general region look much alike—Melanesian, and near-pygmy in height—and their social organization and symbolic and material cultures vary only slightly from local group to local group. All clans are entangled in the pan-New Guinean network of feuds, alliances, and wife exchange with nearby enemies and allies. As is true throughout the Central Highlands and adjacent ranges to the west of Goroka (Read, 1954:13–17), houses tend to be scattered over each clan's territory rather than being concentered in a village. The clans are patrilocal and patrilineal. Men and women usually, but not always, live in separate houses. Though there are differences in the techniques used in shifting cultivation and some variation in the relative proportions of different crops, the important crops are everywhere the same: sweet potatoes, taro (*Colocasia*), *Xanthosoma*, sugar cane, *Saccharum edule*, bananas, yams, *Pandanus conoideus*, and a wide variety of vegetables.[5] Gathering of wild foods, especially leaves, is significant. Animal protein is obtained by hunting and fishing and by raising tame cassowaries and the ubiquitous domestic pig.

With regard to language, the Bomagai-Angoiang belong to the group of about seven-thousand Maring-speakers who live in the middle and lower Simbai Valley and the adjacent Jimi Valley. The Maring tongue[6] belongs to the Hagen-Wahgi-Jimi-Chimbu Family, which in turn belongs to the East New Guinea Highlands Stock, which comprises about 96 percent of the population of the highlands of Australian New Guinea and occupies all of the main valleys of the Central Highlands together with some fringe areas, such as the Jimi and Simbai valleys (Wurm, 1964: p. 77 and Map 2). Maring is the northernmost of the "Hagen-Wahgi-Jimi-Chimbu Family," which includes all of the Central Highlands in the vicinity of Mount Hagen and extends from there eastward through the Central Highlands to within twenty miles of Goroka.

---

5. See Appendixes B and C for an annotated listing of the plants mentioned in the text.

6. In the highlands of Australian New Guinea linguistic groupings have no political or tribal significance. Both enmity and alliance cross linguistic boundaries as easily as they divide and unite people who speak a common language.

Aside from this clear linguistic affiliation with the densely populated Central Highlands, there are many other indications that the Bomagai-Angoiang and the rest of the Maring-speakers are connected with the cultures of the Central Highlands and probably migrated into the Jimi and Simbai valleys from the south. Strathern (1965:186) details the indigenous trade that was carried on across the Wahgi-Sepik divide between the Jimi Valley and the Central Highlands proper, to the south. In their turn, all the Maring inhabitants of the Simbai Valley have trade and marital connections with peoples of the Jimi Valley, and the Bomagai and many other clans of the Simbai Valley say that they originally lived in the Jimi Valley. Beyond such memories and the trade and social relations that connect people locally, there is unmistakably throughout highland New Guinea, as Pouwer (1961:1) says, "a certain homogeneity and distinctiveness"; and he adds that any traveler there is continually struck by a sensation of "re-encounter"—a sensation I experience even on reading accounts of native life in many other parts of highland New Guinea or on viewing photographs of the people and their material cultures. Over and over one meets the same facial expressions, similar details of house and fence construction, the same significant crops, almost identical ways of dressing and decorating the body, the same doctrine of patrilineal descent, the same style of arrow, the ever-present net carrying bags, the same fond attachment to live pigs, and the same way of cooking slaughtered pigs.

Within this regional similarity—both throughout highland New Guinea and within the more limited area of the middle and lower Simbai Valley and the adjacent Jimi Valley—there is, of course, local diversity; and it was certain singular aspects of the Ndwimba Basin that decided me to choose it and its inhabitants as subjects for study. Some of these attractive characteristics I have already mentioned: the late arrival of government patrols, the basin's continued isolation from direct influence by Western ways, and, within the indigenous realm, the easy availability of unsettled land and the rustic reputation of the Bomagai-Angoiang and their immediate neighbors. Spatially

I found the basin home of the Bomagai-Angoiang appealing because of the distinct topographic definition of that part of the clan cluster's territory which is now in common use. Although all the Maring know the precise limits of their clan's and clan cluster's territories, few of the boundaries are marked by notable natural features: most Maring territories simply occupy a strip of land that runs from somewhere near the mountain crest to somewhere near the valley bottom. Thus, the slopes of the ranges are divided into a series of roughly parallel segments, each the territory of a particular group. In contrast, the Ndwimba Basin, which is set off from the main slopes of the Simbai Valley and its larger tributaries, is something like an island—always seductive to geographers—that is in large part

The upper basin a few hours after sunrise, when the morning mists have been burned off and the midday towering cumulus have not yet formed along the high southern crest of the basin.

encircled by the high divide that separates the upper drainage
area of Ndwimba Creek from that of other streams.

An aesthetic attraction of the basin was the extraordinary
steepness of the slopes that form the highest part of its rim; in
places these rise almost vertically, so that the streams become
waterfalls and the forested mountain crest with its dramatic
massings of cloud seems to tower close above the homes and
gardens of the basin's lower slopes and floor.

To me, then, the Ndwimba Basin gave an initial impression of ruggedness and isolation—a habitat on the edge of human settlement, a place where unimposing works of man merge
compliantly with overbearing elements of the natural landscape.
On a slighter scale certain other features attracted my early
notice; these I will sketch briefly in order to direct attention
to some of what I took to be important elements of the basin's
landscape.

I first approached the basin from the west, along the then
newly established government walking trail that leads from the
Simbai Patrol Post. Not far beyond Ngunts, at the place where
the trail runs from the territory of the Fungai clan into Bomagai-Angoiang land, there is a "mark"—a skeletal archway of
poles bedecked with ferns and other foliage set in a corridor of
painted sticks, *Cordyline fruticosa*, and other ritually important
plants. "Marks" and the boundaries that they make manifest
are of great importance throughout New Guinea. Where the
population density is high, the greatest significance of a group's
territorial boundary may be that it delimits the arable land
accessible to that group. The boundary stands as a barrier to
agricultural expansion; further territory can only be acquired by
encroachment across the boundary, an act that may either follow or cause warfare among neighboring groups. Such struggles
for land take place, for example, among the Chimbu to the
west of Goroka in the Central Highlands (Brookfield and
Brown, 1963) and among the Mae-Enga near Wabag to the
west of Mount Hagen (Meggitt, 1965). In both these areas
population densities reach more than 250 persons per square
mile, and land is in short supply. Because in the Ndwimba

Typical midday cloud conditions—the basin floor has scattered sun-shine, and the higher slopes and crest are shaded beneath towering cumulus.

Basin population density is far lower (80 to 90 persons per square mile of currently used land) and the basin's inhabitants have access to large areas of unused land, the precise demarcation of boundaries would not seem to have critical economic meaning for the Bomagai-Angoiang.

But boundaries and their "marks" also have psychic and social meanings. They enclose a province that is at least partially protected from the inimical world that lies beyond a man's own place. The "marks" along the trail prevent the entry of disease-causing spirits, who are frightened or repelled by the power resident in the passageway; similarly, human enemies from other clans are likely to fall sick if they pass through the ritual archways. Even when invited as a friend to another

clan's land, a man in pre-European times usually took food
with him because the food of an alien place might cause sickness or death. This belief is fading, but still, when a man speaks
of his clan's or clan cluster's territory as "my place," he seems
to refer to a microcosm where he feels safe and where he belongs, in large part because he and his clansmen have secured,
do secure, and will secure nourishment from the land of that
territory. Because of the strong sentiment toward territory and
the association between territory, sustenance, and continued life,
I became convinced that in the Ndwimba Basin—and seemingly throughout highland New Guinea, as well—territory defines the group. Though patrilineal descent is the ideological
basis of a clan community, a more trustworthy standard is residence within one territory. Watson (1964:14) comments on
the Central Highlands in general that "the cultural realization
of residence is the great theme of community," and Langness
(1964:172), in speaking of a specific group near Goroka, says,
"People do not necessarily reside where they do *because* they
are kinsmen; rather, they become kinsmen because they reside
there."

From the "mark" that separates Fungai and Bomagai-
Angoiang land the trail continues upward to the crest of the
basin's western rim. Scattered in the secondary forest along the
way are occasional graceful *Casuarina* trees, which in dense
groves are so much a sign of man in parts of New Guinea that
their sparseness here excites curiosity. From the narrow crest of
the western rim most of the basin can be seen. The general form
is that of a ragged amphitheater with a crenate rim, highest on
the south side and sloping downward on the east and west sides
toward the opening on the north. From the rim irregular spurs
and ridges slope steeply to the arenalike floor, which tilts gently
downward toward the north. In the narrow valleys between the
spurs and on the basin's floor, flow many streams that one by
one converge into Ndwimba Creek, the master stream that
flows northward through the basin's single low-level opening.

During my first days in the basin I was impressed by the
ever-changing clouds that usually covered the higher edges of

the basin and that at some time during the daylight hours brought shade even to the relatively sunny center of the basin. Rainfall was obviously adequate everywhere for the growth of tropical forest, but it was equally clear that the moist, cool habitat of the high southern rim had a forest different from that of the lower elevations. It was plain too that in much of the lower part of the basin the dark green leaves of the rain forest had been replaced by the lighter greens of the secondary vegetation and the people's gardens and orchards. The secondary forest appeared continuously variable but, at the same time, contained certain frequently recurring groupings, such as the complex that included the slender tree *Alphitonia incana* and the tree fern *Cyathea angiensis* or the community dominated by the white-barked *Albizia falcataria*, a large tree with the

The view across the basin floor. The floor and lower slopes are a mosaic of gardens, orchards, and secondary growth. Primary forest begins a little below the cloud line on the higher slopes.

A sugarcane-*Saccharum edule* garden cleared in high forest.

horizontal planes of foliage characteristic of many trees of the legume family.

Set off from the secondary growth by strong fences of poles and logs were the luxuriant Bomagai-Angoiang gardens. Because the people carry on some clearing and planting throughout the year, gardens in all stages of development can be seen at any time. In the initial stage, always on plots of land newly cleared from forest, the ground is covered by a jumble of felled tree trunks, shattered branches, and foliage, as though some forest-dwelling behemoths had done battle there. At a later stage the crops planted amid the forest's remnants come to dominate the aspect of the cleared plot and to cover the whole surface of the organic layer of the soil. Then, as the garden approaches abandonment, weed vegetation becomes predominant.[7] Mixed with the gardens and secondary communities are the Bomagai-Angoiang orchards, which are unfenced stands of breadfruit trees, a type of large-fruited *Pandanus*, and *Gnetum gnemon*, which bears edible leaves and seeds.

The Bomagai-Angoiangs' low, narrow houses are made of grass, leaves, and poles. Scattered either singly or in small neighborhood clusters, most are built on ridge tops; but, despite their often prominent locations, the houses remain hidden from afar because they and the small clearings that surround them are concealed and overtopped by household plantings of garden crops, shrubs, and trees. Only in the late afternoon and twilight hours are the sites of most dwellings visible, for then above the screen of vegetation rise pillars of smoke from the household fires used to prepare the day's major meal.

The people's houses and gardens are connected by a network of twisting trails, in places so steep that they become narrow, deformed ladders with steps of exposed roots. Never level, the trails lead always up or down and frequently across streams that become dangerous or impassable during heavy rain. Although the Bomagai-Angoiang take account of the effort of movement, they walk about widely both within and beyond the basin. And if the trails are thought of as links in a circuit network, the traffic that passes along them embodies the acts of communication that tie person to person and all the people to place. For example, on any day a single trail might be used in the following ways: a man armed with his bow and arrows, with an axe stuck under his waistband, paces along to help a friend clear a plot of forest for a garden; a woman leading a piglet by a leash of vine heads for her garden with her digging stick and two net bags, one to be filled with the day's harvest, the other suspended from her forehead over her back as a portable cradle for her baby; two adolescent girls gossip as they

---

7. Spencer (1966:10), I think correctly, objects to the word "abandon" when applied to the shift of cropping from one plot to another if there is any chance of reuse of the first plot at a later time. However, it does not seem inaccurate to me to speak of "abandoned gardens," because the gardens are truly abandoned. It is not the garden, but the land that once supported the garden, that is used again.

carry taro and sweet potato cuttings to plant in the part of a
new clearing granted to them by their dead father's brother;
amid shouting back and forth, a young man runs to cut off the
escape of a wild pig that a clan brother has already wounded
and now pursues through the forest; small boys bear leaf-
wrapped packages of food from one household to another; a
man and his son set out for the uninhabited forest to the east
to hunt birds for their plumage; another man takes home a
bundle of firewood; and still another simply goes to visit his
relatives and friends.

The impressions of life and habitat that I received during
the early weeks of my stay with the Bomagai-Angoiang raised
many questions in my mind. I wondered about the apparently
casual simplicity of their agriculture, compared with the tidier
and much more elaborate methods employed by many of the
gardeners of highland New Guinea (v. Brookfield, 1962). The
coincidence of deliberately dispersed houses together with strong
feelings for social coherence, shared territory, and the benefits
of reciprocity had puzzling aspects. Because each man had
access to far more land than he used, I wondered how large
an area he would choose to cultivate and what characteristics
of site he would consider conducive to a good garden. The
variety of spheres of organic resources for materials and food—
cultivated plants, stream life, wild animals, insects, spontaneously growing plants, domestic and tame animals—raised my
interest in the sources of the people's material culture and in
their diet and the relative importance of each of the several
sources of nourishment. How, too, did their diet compare in
amount and quantity with that of people in more crowded
regions?

What seemed to me to be a general condition of good health
posed questions about the causes of disease and disability and
about the ways of living that might increase or impede the
people's well-being. That gardens were not planted at higher
elevations for what clearly appeared to be climatic limitations
made me wonder about possible variations in productivity
within the altitudinal zone that was used agriculturally. The
impermanence of the gardens brought up questions about the

cycle of reuse of land and about the local reasons for practicing a form of shifting cultivation. What, too, were the extended effects of the people's occupation of the basin? Were their actions deteriorating their environment, perhaps by causing a retrogressive succession of the vegetation from forest to grassland as has been common in much of New Guinea? What would be the effect of the entry of the white men? These and many other questions relevant to the relations of place and people in the Ndwimba Basin guided my field studies there.

Tsenboi Ridge. The features indicated by numbers are: (1) a newly cleared plot, (2) a garden close to being abandoned, (3) an *Alphitonia-Cyathea-Geunsia* woodland, and (4) a grove of *Albizia falcataria*. The men said that Areas 3 and 4 had both been part of a single large garden which had been abandoned about 13 years earlier. The difference in the vegetation on them at the time the photograph was taken could be the result of a difference in microenvironments. Area 3 is on a ridge facing north; Area 4, in a draw facing more to the west.

CHAPTER TWO

Components of the Ecosystem

Closely related to this assumption that nature exists in separate masses is the idea that any one mass can be "factored." That is, that a mass can be cut up into parts, or broken down into separate components. Sometimes we appear to factor some environment as though it were a mixture of seeds of rice, wheat, and corn. Although such an action may be necessary and desirable, we should not forget that it may also be doing a gross injustice to nature.
—Frank Egler (1958:52)

The term *ecosystem* designates the total sum of organisms in a biotic community, the nonliving elements of their environment, and all the interactions that occur among these components of the system. Even if the particular system under consideration occupies as small a place as the Ndwimba Basin, the number of parts and the complexity of their interactions make fallible an attempt at a full description. Deliberately, then, my confined focus is on the basin's human inhabitants and only by extension on the other living and nonliving components that appeared to me to be directly effective parts of the human population's habitat. My description and analysis of the basin's ecosystem is organized around the concepts of structure and function. *Structure* relates both to the actual spatial arrangement of organisms and environmental elements and to the more abstract connective organization by means of which interactions take place. *Function* means the way that the parts of the system operate together and affect each other—that is, what is happening in the ecosystem. So far as it is possible, I will separate my discussions of structure and function. This chapter will be mostly limited to a description of the ecosystem's components and their structure. Chapter 3 will bear upon their functions.

The People

Population Structure and Potential. There are 154 persons (77 males and 77 females) living in the Bomagai-Angoiang territory in the Ndwimba Basin.[1] It is impossible to know the exact ages of individuals,[2] but I believe that the general form of the population pyramid shown in Figure 1 is fairly accurate. Because the population represented is so small, the pyramid's form itself can hardly be used to interpret past or predict future population in the basin. But the pyramid does record what I know about the population from other sources. The irregularly parallel alignment of the sides of the pyramid from age fifteen upwards is probably the result of an indeterminately but severely lethal dysentery epidemic that occurred sometime in the 1940s. The older Bomagai-Angoiang men all agree that the population of the basin is smaller now than it was before the epidemic;

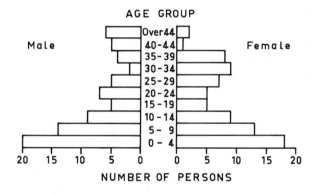
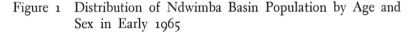

Figure 1   Distribution of Ndwimba Basin Population by Age and Sex in Early 1965

---

1. Unless otherwise stated, I use the present tense to refer to early 1965.

2. I estimated the people's ages by judging from their physical appearance and by asking individuals their state (a nursing infant, still a child of the same age as some present-day child, marriageable but not married, and so forth) at the time of certain datable or roughly datable events.

and because they want the population to grow, the men now
hospitably support what they feel to be an unusually large
percentage of widows and their children. Of the thirty-seven
women over fourteen years of age, nine are widows who, if the
Bomagai-Angoiang men were less inclined toward increasing
the population, would most likely have returned to their natal
homes, taking their younger children with them. That the
men's desire for a larger population will be fulfilled is indicated
by several lines of evidence: (1) the three lowest tiers of the
pyramid have the expansive pattern typical of a rapidly growing
population. (2) Fecundity is high. There is only one woman
in the basin who has been married more than a few years who
has not been pregnant at least once. As nearly as I can judge,
each married woman has an average of four children who
survive their first year. At present, of twenty-eight married
women, five are young brides who have not yet borne children
and two are young women, each still nursing her first child.
(3) There are five young Bomagai-Angoiang bachelors who will,
if possible, soon be married, most to girls from outside the basin.

In Figure 2 I try to show the population's economic structure by dividing the population into four age-groups. The
youngest group includes the wholly dependent—nursing infants
and children through the age of five. The members of the next
group, children from six through fourteen, are in the process of
becoming productive. The next group, ages fifteen through
forty-four, includes the most productive members of the population. The members of the last group, adults over forty-four, are
now all still active, but their productivity is diminishing. It is

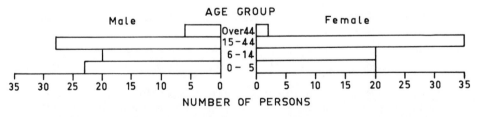

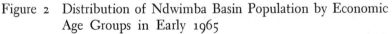

Figure 2   Distribution of Ndwimba Basin Population by Economic
Age Groups in Early 1965

clear that at present the productive members are not straining under a heavy load of nonproducers—a condition that has probably benefited the widows, who, though productive, cannot garden without male help with the jobs of clearing forest and fencing gardens.

Physical Anthropology. The Bomagai-Angoiang fall into the Melanesian or, more broadly, the Oceanic Negroid division of mankind. Within the category of Melanesian, the subgroups relevant to the Bomagai-Angoiang are Papuan and pygmy, but because of the ambiguity of the distinction between the shorter Papuans and the pygmies, I will not class the Bomagai-Angoiang as either one or the other but will simply include them with the mountain peoples of New Guinea of whom Cranstone (1961: 13) writes: "Many . . . are of short stature and may be of mixed Papuan and pygmy stock. . . ."

With regard to anthropometry, Table 1 summarizes the measurements that I took of the height and weight of nineteen adult males (68 percent of all adult males) and eight adult females (25 percent of all adult females).

Table 1. *Bomagai-Angoiang Height and Weight*

	Average Height	*Range*	*Average Weight*	*Range*
Males	61.5 in.	58–66 in.	109 lbs.	87–127 lbs.
Females	57.4 in.	55–62 in.	91 lbs.	76–110 lbs.

In body build the Bomagai-Angoiang are delicate to quite sturdy but always slender, although the children and some of the adults have protruding abdomens. The considerable variation in skin color ranges from light yellow-brown to dark brown, but it never reaches the bluish black hue seen in parts of Melanesia, such as the Solomon Islands. Their hair is wooly, or occasionally kinky, and dark brown to black in color. Many of the mature men can grow full beards and have considerable body hair. Their noses, which do not have the "Semitic" quality of some of the people of the Central Highlands, are wide, but the bridge is not markedly low. Some Bomagai-Angoiang have rather thin lips; others have partly, but never fully, everted lips.

Health and Disease. Based on my observations that they lead active lives, that they have what I consider great physical endurance, and that the majority of them are alert and usually cheerful, I would say that the Bomagai-Angoiang are a healthy population. But, of course, they are not free from disease. I have little quantitative information on the prevalence of their various ailments; but because of my close association with them and because—like any white visitor—I was looked upon as a "dokta," I became familiar with their physical complaints. During the sick calls held at the door of my hut, the most common request was for medicine for what was called *ndukma*, which in most cases seemed to correspond to a malarial ague and which usually disappeared rapidly after the sufferers took malarial suppressives. There is no doubt that malaria, which is endemic in lowland and midmontane New Guinea, is present, though not universal, in the vicinity of the Ndwimba Basin. In 1963 the Malaria Service of the Department of Public Health of the Territory of Papua and New Guinea carried out a survey among the Maring-speaking population. Of a total of 6,239 persons tested, 736 (11.8 percent) were found to have plasmodia[3] in their blood (Territory of Papua and New Guinea, 1963). Of the Bomagai-Angoiang and the neighboring Fungai-Korama, the percentage whose tests were positive for malaria was reported as 19.5 percent, although this figure indicates only the lower limit of incidence of the disease because plasmodia are not always detected in small blood samples. In the Ndwimba Basin, as in most malarial regions, the disease seldom seems to be a direct cause of death among adults, but it may be an important contributory cause because of its debilitating effects, which lessen resistance to other diseases. Among children malaria itself may be more frequently deadly; Black (1955:21) cites studies that indicate than an immunity develops with

---

3. *Plasmodium falciparum*, *P. vivax*, and *P. malariae* were all present. The only vector found was *Anopheles punctulatus punctulatus*, which is considered (Black, 1955:15) to be the most important vector in the Australasian area.

age, whereas deaths from malaria are common in infancy and childhood. Other studies also cited by Black (1955:22) suggest that in New Guinea death from malaria may not be especially limited to children because many people may reach adulthood before contracting the disease and because, with a move from one area to another, the adult is likely to meet a variety of plasmodium to which he is unaccustomed. Even if malaria is not often fatal to children, the disease does result in anaemia and may, because of enlargement of the spleen, give rise to some of the potbellies common among Bomagai-Angoiang children.

On the basis of my own observations of the Bomagai-Angoiang and the experiences with other Maring groups of a nurse at the Anglican mission at the Simbai Patrol Post, I believe that the commonest direct causes of death in the Ndwimba Basin are diseases of the respiratory tract such as pneumonia and bronchitis, which are probably promoted by the smoky atmosphere of the low-roofed houses. I do not know whether tuberculosis is present; it is common in parts of the island of New Guinea (Bierdrager and De Rook, 1954:142–143), but it is said to be rare in the Central Highlands (Bailey, 1966:15) and absent in the Chimbu area (Oomen and Malcolm, 1958:18), which is only seventy or eighty miles from the Ndwimba Basin. Other ailments include something like the common cold or a mild influenza, which, although not too serious of themselves, frequently develop into pneumonia and bronchitis. Intermittently, epidemics of more serious and sometimes lethal kinds of influenza sicken much of the population here and over much of New Guinea (Bierdrager and De Rook, 1954:145–146). Unpleasant but not serious afflictions are tinea and scabies, which often become infected. The people say that they do have parasitic worms, but not too commonly. According to the anthropologist C. Vayda, the whipworm *Trichuris trichiura* is present among the Fungai-Korama; it is therefore probably also present among the Bomagai-Angoiang. Infections of insect and leech bites, scratches, and burns are common, but septicemia and tropical ulcers seem rare. Eye infections occur, but there are no blind among the Bomagai-Angoiang.

Neither venereal disease nor yaws is now evident. Yaws may
have occurred before prophylactic penicillin injections were
given to all the people present at the 1961 census, but the patrol
officer who visited in that year reported (Village Register,
1961) that even before the injections no cases of yaws had been
seen. Leprosy and filariasis occasionally occur in the Maring-
speaking area, but neither disease is now visible in any of the
people of the Ndwimba Basin.

The Bomagai-Angoiang diet will be described in another
section, but I will note here concerning its effect on their
health that I do not believe that any of the Bomagai-Angoiang
suffer from undernourishment in the sense of receiving insufficient calories; however, some may suffer from malnutrition,
particularly from a short supply of protein. One adult, an
immigrant wife of a Bomagai man, had symptoms—listlessness
and reddish, soft, and sparse hair—indicative of protein deficiency. A few children had hair of a similar character and slight
oedema—another symptom of protein deficiency—but at the
same time were active and cheerful, which is not to be expected
in children suffering from protein malnutrition.[4] The anthropologist Roy Rappaport, who lived among a Maring group a day's
walk up the Simbai Valley from the Ndwimba Basin, also
noted symptoms of protein deficiency in a few children and
suggested that the group he studied had only a marginal intake
of protein, by which he meant that their usual protein consumption and consequent nitrogen balance was just sufficient
under ordinary conditions, but was too low for maintenance
or recovery of health under conditions of stress, such as disease,
rage, fear, mourning, or being wounded (Rappaport, 1967a:20,
22). For the Chimbu area of the highlands, where I believe the
protein supply is more limited than in the Ndwimba Basin,
Ivinskis reports that protein malnutrition is the main cause of
death among patients admitted to hospital. He adds further
(Ivinskis et al., 1956:147) that, "Pregnant women, nursing

4. See Bailey (1966) for a full description of the symptoms of
protein malnutrition and calorie undernutrition among infants of the
Chimbu population of the Central Highlands.

Gewan is wife to a Bomagai man. Her reddish hair, listlessness, and emaciation suggest a protein deficiency.

mothers, and babies are mainly affected, but the condition is
sometimes seen in both male and female adults."

Perhaps also related to faulty diet is the occurrence of
cretinism and dental disorders among the Maring-speaking
population. Toothache, loss of teeth, and the scaling off of
tooth enamel—progressing from the gum to the crown—are
common among Maring of all ages. There were no obvious
cases of goiter or cretinism in the Ndwimba Basin, but a mild
form of the latter malady is reportedly (C. Vayda, 1966: personal communication) frequent among Maring-speakers in the
nearby Jimi Valley. Butterfield (1967:18) believes that in areas

of montane New Guinea, such as the Maring area, where a
severe iodine deficiency has made goiter endemic, as much as
3 percent of the population suffers from cretinism.

   Social and Economic Organization. I have already suggested that the coherence and continuity of the Bomagai-
Angoiang as a social group rests more on common residence
within a bounded territory than on actual kinship. In this
section I will extend my geographic bias and propose other
relations between place and the organization of what might be
thought of as the Bomagai-Angoiang corporation that controls
and manipulates the resources of the Ndwimba Basin. In any
such corporate group, economic and social organization are inti-
mately connected. Questions arise only as to which is primary.
Not surprisingly, the Bomagai-Angoiang creed is somewhat different from my outsider's view. They feel, for instance, that
kinship is a condition from which flows the right to use corpo-
rately owned land, their instrument of sustenance. I believe,
inversely, that their way of reckoning kinship is a method of
distributing resources and describing who owns clan land.
Leach (1961:305), on the basis of his study of land tenure and
kinship in a Ceylonese village, goes further and asserts as a
general principle that "kinship systems have no 'reality' at all
except in relation to land and property. What the social anthropologist calls kinship structure is just a way of talking about
property relations which can also be talked about in other
ways."

   Certainly in the Ndwimba Basin, clan members are those
who use and own or come to own land within the clan territory.
Both the Angoiang and the Bomagai clans have recruited non-
agnatic males who, once their right of access to clan land has
been accepted, become, if not clan members themselves, the
fathers of clan members.[5] That is, ownership of clan land can

---

   5. There are several reasons for a man to move from the territory
of his natal clan: He may hope to avoid sickness and sorcery; he may
quarrel with a clan brother and leave his home territory in anger; or
he may flee for fear of retaliation for some misdeed such as a killing.
Whatever his reason, he frequently takes refuge in his wife's natal
territory under the sponsorship of one of her clan brothers. In this way

create kinship. And despite their patrilineal ideology, the Bomagai-Angoiang will sometimes acknowledge this possibility, saying that it is acceptable because their group needs more men. If there came to be a denser population in the Ndwimba Basin and a consequent competition for land, a man's adoption into an alien clan might become more difficult. Such is said (Meggitt, 1965:263–264) to be the case in the Central Highlands among the land-hungry Mae-Enga, who with regard to land tenure usually adhere firmly to the principles of agnation and patrilocality.

With regard to formal social organization, Maring-speakers are, as already outlined, divided into twenty-three politically autonomous units which have been called clan clusters (Vayda and Cook, 1964). The Bomagai-Angoiang clan cluster is composed of the Bomagai and the Angoiang patrilineal clans, which are not reputed to have a common ancestor. Instead, their close alliance is based on their members' view that they occupy a shared, although subdivided, territory, that they have a joint "fight ground," and that they act as a unit in fighting and certain ceremonies. The clan cluster is agamous: Bomagai and Angoiang men may marry women of the other clan of the cluster or of clans outside the cluster. The clans—by definition exogamous and reputedly descended from a common ancestor —are composed of the agnatic core plus wives and attached relatives and associates.[6] As a subdivision within the clan-cluster corporation, each clan claims a clearly delimited part of the clan-cluster territory and has its own sacred groves and private rights of hunting and gathering in particular pieces of forest land. The clans themselves are subdivided into subclans, as shown in Table 2.

I believe that the Bomagai-Angoiang men attach less mean-

---

several non-Bomagai-Angoiang men have moved into the basin, just as several Bomagai-Angoiang men have moved out.

6. Actually, Maring clans do not always fit the strict definition of clan. The men of the Bomagai subclan of Gindjin sometimes claim common ancestry with Angoiang, and the other Bomagai men say that they share ancestry with the men of another clan, also called Bomagai, who live across the crest of the Bismarck Range in the Jimi Valley.

ing to membership in subclans, or "little lines," than to membership in their clan. Some men say that the subclans hold rights to particular parts of the clan territory; but because I could not discover in the mosaic of individual holdings any clear subdivisions that related to subclan membership, I decided that the men referred only to plots owned by individuals who happened to belong to particular subclans. It is true, however, that when an individual dies without heirs, rights to his land pass to the living members of his subclan, as in the case of the Angoiang subclan of Ngigai whose single adult member holds and can apportion rights to all the land that once belonged to heirless Ngigai men now dead or permanently gone from the

Table 2.   Clan and Subclan Membership
Among the Bomagai-Angoiang

Clan	Men 16 or older	Boys under 16	Subclan	Men 16 or older	Boys under 16
			Ngigai	12 [c]	15
Bomagai	17 [a]	27 [b]	Mbaigai	2	3
			Gindjin	3	5
			Yangəgai	—	4
			Mbaigai	9	8
Angoiang	14 [d]	16	I-Begai	4	2
			Ngigai	1	3
			(Uncertain affiliation)	—	3

a. Nineteen men are now associated with the Bomagai clan, but two of them are immigrants not yet considered true clan members.

b. One 12-year-old boy is excluded from this count. He now spends much of his time in the Ndwimba Basin where his widowed mother lives, but when mature he will probably establish gardens outside the basin on the land of his father, who was not a Bomagai-Angoiang.

c. One of the men listed is an equivocal member of Ngigai and Bomagai. Originally a member of the nearby Korama clan, he immigrated into the basin to the place of his Bomagai wife about twenty years ago because he had killed a man in his own place. His son, now a mature married man, is considered a firm Ngigai.

d. Fifteen men are now associated with the Angoiang clan, but one of them is an immigrant not yet considered a true member.

basin. Some of the subclans have their own *komung* (sacred groves) and *tak'o* (ritual sites where pigs are slaughtered, dressed, and cooked), and there is a weak correlation between subclan membership and coresidence. Subclan members often act together in making bride and death payments, but members of other subclans may also participate. There is a tendency for men of the same subclan to help each other clear forest and build fences, but men of different subclans or of the other clan also frequently cooperate. The ambiguity of what it means to belong to a particular subclan arises at least in part from the ease with which the subclans fuse and divide. Some Bomagai men say that the Gindjin subclan will soon fuse with Mbaigai and that the four fatherless Yangɔgai boys, who along with their mothers are "looked out for" by Ngigai men, will become Ngigai. If the single adult member of the Angoiang subclan of Ngigai were not such a dominant and aloof man, he would probably already have merged with one of the other Angoiang subclans—an action that his three sons may take when they are adults and their father is dead. That the several subdivisions within the clans are maintained suggest that, among the Bomagai-Angoiang and the other New Guinean groups divided into subclans, some form of segmentation is advantageous, perhaps as a way of allocating resources and ensuring cooperative labor at a level of social organization above that of the family. From talking with Bomagai-Angoiang men, I also gained the impression of a certain enjoyment of "team spirit" in belonging to a subclan, but then this too may have adaptive advantage.

Bomagai-Angoiang married couples and their children form economic units, but only occasionally does the whole family live together under a single roof. Of the thirty-four men of marriageable age, twenty-four are married, five are young bachelors, and five are widowers. Because four of the married men have two wives each, there are in a sense twenty-eight married couples, only four of which live together; the remaining twenty-four couples reside in separate men's and women's houses. Every widow and woman married for a year or so, whether a co-wife or not, has her own house; [7] a bride usually lives in the house of her husband's mother or another older woman during the first year with her husband's clan. Sons up to about the age of five and unmarried daughters live together with their mothers and the domesticated pigs in the women's houses. Boys over five sleep in the men's houses, which, unlike those in many parts of highland and lowland New Guinea, are small and shelter at the most three or four adult males. Unless they are traveling outside the basin, girls and women almost always sleep in their own homes; the men and boys are less stable and often move about night by night from men's house to men's house. Women do not enter the men's houses, but husbands make conjugal visits to the wives' houses.

The married pair or, among unmarried adults, some male-female combination is the basic productive unit among the Bomagai-Angoiang. The male is responsible for clearing forest and building fences around the garden plots. Men also plant some of the crops, do at least a little of the weeding, and work in the gardens at specifically masculine chores. The expectation is, however, that women will do the steady work of planting, maintaining the garden, and providing a daily supply of vegetable food for their male partners, children, and the domestic pigs. Though hunting and fishing with weapons and traps are principally left to the men, women sometimes catch small animals and river life by hand. Both sexes do some selective collecting of edible leaves and other plant materials within the in-

---

7. Bomagai-Angoiang co-wives are not expected to be especially cooperative, but neither do they show as a general state the mutual antagonism of co-wives in the Central Highlands, as described by Read (1954:23), who writes: "Co-wives are almost invariably hostile to one another, and a suspected slight or insult is sufficient to start a fight which may end with one woman urinating in the mouth of her defeated opponent." Of the five pairs of Bomagai-Angoiang co-wives (each of four of which pairs presently has a husband and one of which is widowed) the members of each of three of the pairs live in the same hamlets and associate daily. The wives of the other two pairs do live in separate hamlets, but only one set of co-wives maintains a feud—and that only because one of the wives is an exceptionally "strong" (aggressive, domineering) woman, who is frequently asserting her primacy by attacking her co-wife.

habited part of the basin, but usually only the men go on gathering (and hunting) expeditions to the montane forest and the uninhabited lands to the east of the basin. The men build all the houses, but the women collect the grass that is often used for roofing material.

The men of the Bomagai and Angoiang clans often speak of themselves as a unit and refer to "our land," or "our ground," as if the clan territory were a communal possession, which it is in the sense that any man who gardens there must—with the exception mentioned below—belong to or be somehow temporarily or permanently attached to the clan. However, this sense of corporate ownership applies literally only to the territory as an abstract whole or to certain ungardened forest tracts. The right to reuse a particular plot belongs to the man who last gardened it, and the decision of when to regarden is made by

A family, with characteristic implements—the man with an axe and bow and arrows, the woman and her daughter with dibbles.

that owner or, as he perhaps should be called, manager. The
initial rights to land are gained by clearing previously unused
land, by patrilineal inheritance, or by receiving a grant from
the manager. Women, who of course do not hold land rights in
this patrilineal and patrilocal society, garden in the plots assigned to them by their husbands, fathers, or other male garden-
partners. Occasionally permission to use individually held land
is granted across clan boundaries to men who are firm members
of a different clan, as in the case of a Bomagai man who allowed
a *Pandanus* orchard to be planted on his land by an Angoiang
cousin. It may have been out of such arrangements that there
developed the tradition of *yingomongo* territory, which is a zone
of land held jointly by both clans where members of both
clans own land in an intermixed pattern.

Politically and with regard to social status, the Bomagai-
Angoiang share the equalitarian ideology that is common in
montane New Guinea. (See Salisbury, 1964.) The opinions
of all clansmen are to be equally respected, and decisions related
to group activities are to be made only when, after a full discussion, "the talk becomes one." To a considerable degree this
ideal is reality among the Bomagai-Angoiang, but they too
have something like the "big men" described in almost all
accounts of native life in New Guinea. According to the
Bomagai-Angoiang, "a big man has many gardens, pigs, and
axes; and people listen to him when he talks." He often has two
wives also, for wives both require wealth for their purchase and
contribute wealth through their care of gardens and pigs. In
the Ndwimba Basin there are four or five men who are, or
approach being, "big men," none of whom is outstandingly
primal. The other men do listen when they talk, but the limited
authority that they wield issues not from any official rank in a
hierarchy of power, but only from their personal influence, the
strength of their rhetoric, and the sense of reciprocal obligation
that they can inspire in their clansmen. Futhermore, the "big
men" would attempt to sway opinion or incite action only in
such momentous matters as community ritual or immorality;
the power of decision in daily life and in routine economic

matters belongs entirely to individuals. Such independence naturally does not mean that the Bomagai-Angoiang do not cooperate, but only that they do not need a community coordination of economic effort like that presided over by the Trobriander chiefs and garden magicians as described by Malinowski (1921).[8]

The population resident in the Ndwimba Basin has not only an internal network of reciprocity, which will be described later in detail, but also has many ties with peoples beyond the basin. Before warfare was prohibited by the patrol officers, these might mutually obligate whole clans or clan clusters and might be based on either enmity or alliance. Now, ties that extend beyond the basin are only between individuals or small intraclan groups and are usually based on one of several possible kin relations. Because brides must come from outside the clan, all women married to Bomagai or Angoiang men have extraclan familial relations, which are maintained by the women's visits to their natal clans and by visits to the basin by guests from their natal clans. Similarly, girls born into the Bomagai and Angoiang clans move out of the basin and provide further links with other clans. This emigration does not expand contact between clans as much as might be expected, however, because when possible a man pays for his bride by sending a sister to his bride's clan so that the sister marries one of the bride's clan brothers. If a bride is not paid for by this means, the husband and his subclan associates form permanent affinal relations with the girl's clansmen through the bride payments, which are scattered from the time of the girl's marriage to her death. My information on affinal ties is incomplete, but, in order to show in a partial way the character of the network of relations that is one result of the immigration of wives, I represent in Map 2 the places of origin of twenty-three Angoiang and Bomagai wives.[9]

---

8. A slightly different and much more detailed discussion of Maring "big men," especially in traditional settings, is presented by C. Lowman-Vayda (1968).

9. As already stated, there are in the Ndwimba Basin twenty-eight married women and nine widows. Of these, seven are natal Bomagai-Angoiang, of which six now live with their natal clans for one reason

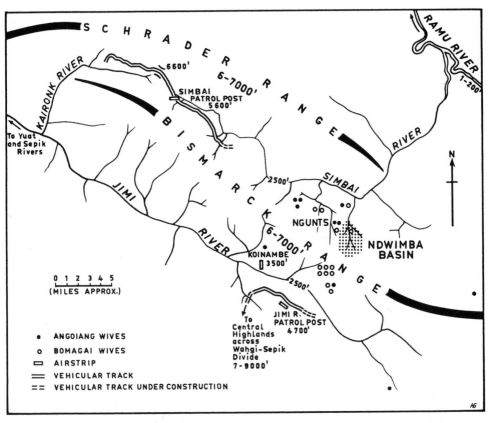

Map 2   Place of Origin of Bomagai-Angoiang Wives

Beyond the relations that revolve around the wife, there are other interclan connections, such as those of cross-cousin, parallel cousin, and maternal uncle (including both the mother's biologic and clan brothers) that are significant enough to be designated by special terms. For example, there is the relation termed *ngwiche*, or "one-talk," which implies a sense of mutual friendship and obligation. All Angoiang men are *ngwiche* with Bomagai men, and vice versa; and men whose mothers are sisters are also *ngwiche*. Because when sisters marry they often

---

or another and one is an Angoiang woman who has gone in marriage to a Bomagai man. Therefore, the twenty-three women shown on the map represent 74 percent of the women now in the basin who are not living with their natal clans.

go to separate clans, the *ngwiche* relation can create interclan ties beyond that of the wife's or mother's clan. When a man travels, he is free to sleep in his *ngwiche*'s house, and often there are trading connections in feathers, pigs, or other goods between men who are *ngwiche*.

The Physical Character of Their Habitat

Topographic Elements. It is obvious from my description of the Bomagai-Angoiang's affinal and other ties with alien clans that the topographic limits of the Ndwimba Basin do not totally enclose the people's activities. However, the basin—especially its northern, lower part—is the heartland of Bomagai-Angoiang life and consequently will be the focus of my description of the physical character of their territory. Map 3 shows the form of the basin, the approximate elevations ($\pm$ 500 feet) of various features, and most of the important local place names. An aerial photograph of the basin and vicinity appears on page xiv.

The general form of the basin is that of a ragged, elongated amphitheater with a crenate rim. Except from the narrow opening to the north, the amphitheater's sides rise steeply from the slightly tilted, arena-like floor. The most impressive rise is that of some 4,000 feet from the basin floor to the southern and southeastern rim, a high, forested, and little-used rampart dissected by the headwater tributaries of Ndwimba Creek. From the basin's lower western and northeastern rim the amphitheater's sides descend to the floor as a half dozen fingerlike spurs, each named by the Bomagai-Angoiang and each a node of settlement. Figure 3 shows the irregularly stepped profiles of the narrow crests of two of these spurs. Sites that the Bomagai-Angoiang particularly favor for houses are the narrow treads, sometimes artificially widened, of these sporadically stepped spurs.

Easily seen in the rugged topography of the basin and the surrounding area are manifestations of the tectonic activity that has raised the whole of the great highland backbone that extends along the longitudinal axis of New Guinea from the island's eastern tip to Geelvink Bay near the western end of

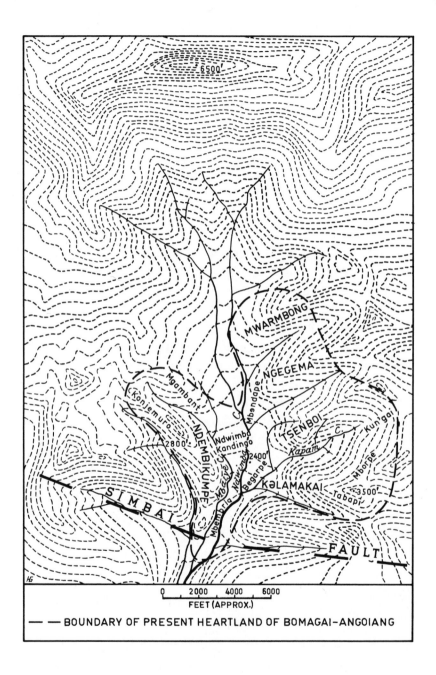

Map 3   Form-line Map of the Ndwimba Basin

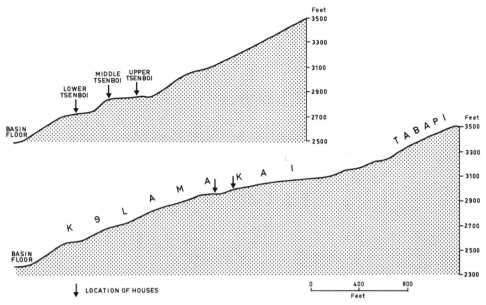

Figure 3   Slope Profiles of Tsenboi and Tabapi-Kəlamakai Ridges

West Irian. The Bismarck Range, that segment of the highland backbone in which lies the Ndwimba Basin, is a complex horst that follows the general northwest-southeast structural trend of the island. Along the Bismarck Range's northern side extends the Bundi Fault Zone, which occupies a poorly defined trench that marks the presence of a set of faults that run from near the head of the Simbai Valley through the Ndwimba Basin to the vicinity of Bundi (Dow and Decker, 1964: pp. 6–7 and Plate 10.) Many morphological indications, such as rejuvenated streams, point to continued fault activity in this region. Even more immediate evidence comes from the several pronounced earthquakes that I felt during my year in the Maring area. These jolts, which were strong enough to cause considerable swaying of the houses, were accepted by the Bomagai-Angoiang as rather commonplace happenings.

The Simbai Fault, which is the largest fault of the Bundi Fault Zone, crosses the northern edge of the Ndwimba Basin. The geologists Dow and Dekker (1964:7), who surveyed this region, believe that movement along the Simbai Fault once

dammed the outlet of what is now the Ndwimba Basin and
caused the deposition of the Quaternary alluvium whose surface
now forms the floor of the basin. This explanation does account
well for the gentle slope (about 5°) of the basin's lower,
northern floor, a gentleness that is unusual for this mostly
precipitous country, where alluvial deposits are rare. Toward
the south the slope of the floor becomes steeper as it starts to
rise toward the high escarpment that forms the southern side of
the basin. The streams, flowing in their upper reaches in steep-
sided valleys between the ridges that descend from near the
basin's rim, proceed generally northward across the floor, where
they have now cut into the alluvium to depths of from five to
twenty-five feet. The water in the larger streams quickly rises
several feet with hard rains of any duration; but because the
watershed is small, the streams soon return to their lower levels
when the rain has passed. Because of the frequency of rains,
only the smallest springs and rivulets in minor tributory gullies
ever go dry. In the stream channels and banks as well as on
the interfluvial surfaces of the basin floor, many angular and
semi-angular boulders are exposed, some of them at least twenty
feet and many of them six or seven feet in length. Even toward
the center of the basin floor, the boulders are in places so
closely jumbled together that it is possible to walk many yards
by stepping from one to another. The boulders' angularity suggests an origin in rock falls or landslides. Their presence in the
center of the basin indicates either that they were moved there
by some sort of stream action from the talus accumulations at
the foot of the basin's steep slopes or that in the not-too-distant
geologic past there have been mass movements of a scale sufficient to carry a great amount of debris from the slopes onto
the present floor of the basin. But now, despite the many slopes
that exceed 20°, the heavy rainfall, and the deep mantle of
weathered material that covers hard bedrock, the individual
Bomagai-Angoiang sees little degradation in his lifetime. The
streams contain a visible suspended load only during and just
after heavy rains; otherwise they appear completely clear. Masses
of soil and regolith do sometimes slip several yards, especially

over the areas of shale bedrock, but the loosened mass is seldom jumbled enough to bury its cover of vegetation, and the landslide scars are quickly covered by the pioneering plants that also invade garden clearings.

Climatic Elements. In terms of generalized surface-wind systems, the Ndwimba Basin at a latitude of a little above 5° south lies in a zone where it might be expected that the intertropical convergence would dominate, but where trade winds might have influence during part of the year. Or, in more specifically regional terms, all of New Guinea might be expected to experience monsoon-wind reversals because of the island's location between the continental masses of Australia in the southern hemisphere and mainland Asia in the northern hemisphere. Actually, the air circulation of New Guinea and the islands of Indonesia to the west cannot be fully explained either by the general model of world wind systems or by the traditional concept of the Asiatic monsoon (Palmer, 1951), But it is well recognized that over New Guinea there does exist a seasonal variation in air movement and stability and a consequent variation in rainfall. Curry and Armstrong (1959:253) write that the area is characterized by:

. . . surface southerlies and easterlies in July and variable winds in January with a marked westerly component in the south and a northerly component in the north. Rain occurs in both months, the areal distribution of values depending on exposure, but with a tendency to more rain in January.

Brookfield and Hart (1966:8) elaborate on the seasonality of rainfall in the tropical southwest Pacific:

Over most of the region there is only a single maximum of mean rainfall, shown . . . to lie between late-December and late-March—and most commonly in February—over most of the region. . . . Over most of the area with a tendency to a rainfall maximum in the weeks between the end of December and the end of March, the driest week, under mean conditions falls between early May and August. . . . There is generally a very rapid transition between the rainfall conditions of the January-March type and those of the May-

August type, occurring between mid-April and mid-May, during which time the southeasterlies seem to advance very rapidly northward at the expense of the perturbation belt. The withdrawal of the effective incidence of the southeasterlies after August is far more gradual.

That such is the approximate pattern of rainfall in the general vicinity of the Ndwimba Basin is substantiated both by the six-year records of rainfall kept at the Simbai and Jimi River patrol posts [10] and by the descriptions given by the Boma-gai-Angoiang and their neighbors, who speak of what are to them the two most important seasons: the "time belong rain" that occurs during the southern hemisphere's summer and "time belong sun" of the southern hemisphere's winter. Because my measurements of rainfall in the Ndwimba Basin are fragmentary, covering only all or parts of six of the months from September 1964 to July 1965, I must estimate both actual monthly rainfall and average annual rainfall. Table 3, which gives my estimate of these average conditions, is based on my measurements, a similarly broken set of measurements kept at Ngunts in 1962–1963 by the anthropologists C. and A. P. Vayda, and on my extension of a comparison of these measurements with the records kept at the Jimi and Simbai patrol posts.[11]

Table 3.   *Estimated Average Rainfall in the Ndwimba Basin*
(*In Inches, at 3,500 Feet*)

J	F	M	A	M	J	J	A	S	O	N	D	Annual
20	20	20	18	12	6	7	9	14	15	16	18	175

Because the record is so short, there can be no statistical validation to a description of rainfall intensity, variability of rainfall from year to year, or the incidence of dry and wet spells.

---

10. Mean monthly rainfall calculated from five-year records of the Simbai and Jimi River patrol posts are published in Brookfield and Hart (1966).

11. John Street in a personal communication (1969) estimates that the Ndwimba Basin's average annual rainfall is between 170 and 200 inches.

On the other hand, I have no reason to believe that unusual conditions prevailed during the period of my observations in the Ndwimba Basin or the period during which data was collected at the two nearby patrol posts. As noted for all of New Guinea by Brookfield and Hart (1966:18), variations in rainfall intensity—that is, average rainfall per rain day (defined as a day having at least 0.01 inch of rain)—are closely related to seasonal variations in amount of rainfall: low intensities accompany the drier season, high intensities, the wetter season. For the Ndwimba Basin in 1965 I have data from which to calculate intensities of 0.84 inch during the two wet months of February and March and an intensity of 0.37 inch in June, which I believe to be the driest month, on the average. These figures mask a wide variation in day by day rainfall; for instance, during the wet month of February six rain days received less than 0.20 inch apiece, whereas eleven rain days each had over an inch and the rainiest day had 2.24 inches. Much of the rain falls from cumulonimbus clouds in short-lived tropical showers, which may occur as early as ten o'clock in the morning but are commoner after two or three in the afternoon and most common between six and eleven at night. Though they may be intense, the showers are small in extent, frequently drenching only one part of the basin, while the rest remains dry. In expected contrast, the regional disturbances that do sometimes occur bring longer-lasting rainfall over wider areas. I measured rainfall only at Tabapi, which is at an elevation of 3,500 feet on the western rim of the basin; but I believe that aggregate rainfall is about equal everywhere in the basin below 4,500—that is, in all the inhabited and cultivated part. Above 4,500 feet on the higher slopes and summit of the southern wall, rainfall is doubtless higher.

The rainiest day during my stay in the basin was 16 May 1965, when four inches fell in a steady downpour during the night. The current-flattened grasses on stream banks and the washed-away bridges gave evidence that the basin's larger streams rose four to five feet during this storm, but by the following morning the streams had receded to normal levels and were flowing clear. Even the bare slopes of newly cleared plots showed almost no evidence of erosion. Only on the paths, where the cushioning layer of organic matter had been worn away by passing feet, did the effects of the heavy rain leave clearly visible traces in the form of minor gullying and deposition. In other words, the basin and vicinity seem well adjusted to heavy rains, at least under present conditions of use.

Based on their regional investigation of the tropical southwest Pacific, Brookfield and Hart (1966: p. 13, Map 10) state that the central cordillera of New Guinea has a comparatively low variability of rainfall about the mean. The short rainfall record (1959–1964) at the Simbai and Jimi River patrol posts supports this view. For that six-year period Simbai had an average annual rainfall of 120 inches, a high year of 133 inches, and a low year of 110 inches; during the same period the Jimi post had an average of 123 inches, a high year of 140 inches, and a low year of 112 inches. Percentage variations in the same month in different years are greater, as shown in Table 4.

Table 4. Variation in Amount of
Monthly Rainfall, 1959–1964
(In Inches)

	Simbai Patrol Post			Jimi River Patrol Post		
	Aver.	Max.	Min.	Aver.	Max.	Min.
J	14.7	24.13	3.88	13.4	21.7	5.5
F	13.9	20.19	4.13	14.4	20.0	3.7
M	13.3	23.84	7.89	17.0	18.2	12.5
A	13.0	16.49	8.34	12.8	20.4	5.7
M	7.1	9.14	4.57	8.0	14.1	3.9
J	4.1	6.81	1.33	4.4	7.8	2.0
J	4.9	12.97	2.51	5.4	12.1	2.6
A	7.8	13.55	4.88	7.0	8.7	3.4
S	9.9	17.13	6.05	8.3	14.0	6.1
O	9.0	14.21	5.66	10.2	17.7	6.8
N	8.7	13.24	8.15	11.4	13.1	9.4
D	11.2	19.87	6.38	12.6	16.2	6.6

The greatest impact of the monthly variations in rainfall is felt by the local people when the drier and wetter seasons are partially reversed, as happened in 1963. In that year, which was noted as a year with prolonged dry spells over much of Australian New Guinea (Brookfield, 1966:55), the Jimi River Patrol Post received 75 percent more rainfall than average in June, while in January, in February, and in April it received less rainfall than in June and less than half the average rainfall for those usually wet months. If the people's agricultural calendar were more rigid, such a shift of the wetter and drier seasons would be disruptive; but, given their methods of planting, such a shift leads only to some inconveniences and confusion,[12] rather than to actual hardship.

When asked for their complaints about the basin's climate and weather, some Bomagai-Angoiang commented that there was sometimes more rain than to their liking during the "time belong sun," but none, on the other hand, appeared to know the meaning of drought. Nor do I believe that their crop plants suffer, except perhaps very infrequently, from a deficit of soil moisture. During my stay in the Ndwimba Basin, the longest period with no measurable rainfall was three days; most series of days with rain were separated from each other by only one rainless day. Table 5 shows the nine dry spells of five or more consecutive days with no rainfall that occurred during a continuous period of 258 weeks at the Jimi River Patrol Post, which I estimate receives an average of 50 inches less rain per year than the Ndwimba Basin and which—because of its position with respect to local topography—is less subject than the Ndwimba Basin to frequent orographic showers. In expectable

---

12. Although the Bomagai-Angoiang do not keep any real account of the passage of years, they do know how to reckon the expected coming of the wetter or drier seasons by noting the position where the sun rises along the eastern rim of the basin. Fittingly, as they explain it, when the position of sunrise moves toward the southern sector where there is a foggy, wet forest on the higher part of the rim, it is "time belong rain"; when the sun rises far to the north toward the lowland Ramu Valley, which the Bomagai-Angoiang associate with heat, it is "time belong sun."

accordance with the annual pattern of precipitation, as well as with what the people say, this short record from the patrol post shows that the dry spells are concentrated in midyear, thus augmenting the drier season; but, even so, "dry months" or "drought days" are not common at the patrol post and must be rare or absent in the moister Ndwimba Basin. "Dry months" (months whose aridity has a determinative effect on vegetation) and "drought days" (days on which the water balance falls to zero and plants suffer a consequent water shortage) can be calculated in several ways. Because the climatic data available cover such a short length of time, my estimates of the presence or absence of drought conditions in the Ndwimba Basin are presented only as likely possibilities. But all the methods of calculation that I apply to what data I have indicate that the Ndwimba Basin has a perhumid climate; such also seems clear from the vegetation. Following Lauer's use of the De Martonne "index of aridity," I calculate (12×154 mm. $\div 21.1°$ C. $+ 10$) for the average driest month of the Ndwimba Basin, an index of 59, which is well on the humid side of Lauer's *Trockengrenze*. Brookfield (1966:57–59) applies to New Guinea the Schmidt and Ferguson (1952) system of describing climate in terms of the occurrence of wet and dry months; on the basis of this system the Ndwimba Basin falls into a category defined as having no dry season. Van Steenis (1958:27) defines six tropical "phytoclimates" on the basis of the number of rainy days in the

Table 5. *Length of Dry Spells of Five or More Days*
at the Jimi River Patrol Post
(In Consecutive Days Without Rain)

	J	F	M	A	M	J	J	A	S	O	N	D
1959					9	5				6	5	
1960						5 *	6					
1961										9		
1962	7				5							
1963												

* June 27–July 1

four driest consecutive months of the year. The wettest phyto-
climate, which he calls "everwet," has more than forty rainy
days. According to the five-year record of rainfall available to
me, the four driest consecutive months (May, June, July,
August) at the Jimi River Patrol Post had an average of eighty-
five rainy days and a range of from seventy-one to ninety-nine.

By all these criteria, the Ndwimba Basin and its vicinity
have a permanently humid climate. But if the actual monthly
figures, rather than the averages, are considered, there are
occasional "dry months." Following either the Schmidt and
Ferguson system or the three-inch minimum for a "humid
month" set by B. J. Garnier (Fosberg, Garnier, and Küchler,
1961:343), there were two "dry months" (June 1962 and July
1960) in a five-year period at the Jimi River Patrol Post. However, even if the Ndwimba Basin does occasionally have a
month with as little as 2 inches of rain (which is unlikely), the
effect of the month's low total amount is allayed by the
scattered distribution of showers throughout the month. As
van Steenis (1958:27) notes, "generally a shower of 5–10 mm. will
saturate the upper soil layer and all that is in excess of it does
not influence the 'wetness' of that particular day."

If the water-budget approach is applied to data from and
suppositions about the Ndwimba Basin, there is still no water
deficiency calculated for the month of June. That is, if potential
evapotranspiration is estimated (using the Penman equation)
to be 4 inches (John Street, 1969, personal communication),
available moisture at field capacity in the top 20 inches is
estimated to be 4 inches (a not very generous estimate for the
humus-rich, clay soils of the basin), and rainfall is estimated
to be 6 inches, there remains a sizeable moisture surplus. If the
further assumptions are made that the roots of most crop plants
do not reach to 20 inches and that the soil is not at field capacity
at the beginning of the month, June can be brought close to a
calculated water deficiency. But I doubt that, even with these
conditions, the soil's moisture reserve is exhausted; and, contrary to the assumption of a low reserve at the beginning of
June, it appears that at that time the reserve is actually main-

tained near its maximum by the gardening practices that will
be described in Chapter 3.

Undeleterious though they probably are to the productivity
of crop plants, the drier season and its accompanying dry spells
have relevance to the Bomagai-Angoiang agriculture: burning of
felled debris is easier; there is less leaching of ash and of the
nutrients accumulated in the soil that is exposed by cutting
away the forest; and garden work is less frequently interrupted
by rain than at other times of year.

If rainfall and cloud conditions were constant throughout
the year, there might be a range of about 3 degree F. in the
annual march of average monthly temperatures in the Ndwimba
Basin. But with the especially cloudy conditions during the
summer and the clearer conditions during the winter, the
normally slight equatorial range of temperature is still further
muted, so that at my recording site at 3,500 feet the months of
January and June 1965 had the same average temperature of
70.1 degrees F., which is very close to the average for each of the
months of the year. Daily maximums range from the low 80s on
especially sunny days to an occasional 71 degrees on continuously cloudy and rainy days; daily minimums range from 63 to
66 degrees. That the nights are often cloudy and the dew point
is usually almost the same as the average minimum temperature,
prevent further chilling at night. On the basin's northern floor,
which is about a thousand feet lower than my principal recording site (3,500 feet), the temperatures measured were the
expectable 2½ to 3 degrees warmer during the day, but only
1 degree warmer at night, an indication either that cool air
drains onto the basin's floor at night or that there is a relatively
higher radiation loss than from the surrounding slopes because
the floor tends to have less nocturnal cloud cover. Elevations
above 4,500 feet are of course cooler on the average than the
lower elevations and, because cloud prevails, have less variation
in daily range of temperature and never reach the maximum
temperatures of comparable elevations in the less clouded, open
valleys of the Central Highlands. Frost never occurs in the
cultivated and inhabited part of the basin and probably never

occurs even on the highest rim, where there are no hollows in which cold air could accumulate. The minimum temperatures in the low 60s for the inhabited area are cool enough to discomfort the nearly naked Bomagai-Angoiang. They build nightly fires in their houses and, when outside at night or early in the morning, make the pan-highland, self-hugging and warming gesture of grasping each shoulder with the opposite hand. That altitudinal differences in temperature have meaning to the basin's inhabitants and to all other Maring-speakers is clear from their division of their environment into *kamunga* and *wora*. *Kamunga* refers to high-elevation, "cold" land; *wora* is low elevation, "warm" land. Frequently the people also speak of the transition zone between the two as *kamunga-wora amang*, *amang* meaning "center" or "between." In the Ndwimba Basin, *kamunga* lies above and *wora* below about 3,000 feet; *kamunga-wora amang* occupies a floating transition zone from about 2,800 to 3,200 feet.

Relative humidity is usually high. In the early morning, when temperatures are in the 60s the relative humidity is over 90 percent. If the day is rainless and sunny, with temperatures reaching the high 70s or into the 80s, relative humidity falls to between 60 and 70 percent; on overcast or rainy days, relative humidity remains over 70 or 80 percent.

Because of the interaction of the moisture-rich air and the mountain slopes, clouds are an almost continuously visible component of the Ndwimba Basin weather and climate. They seem to belong not to a separate realm of sky, but to the immediate landscape. Close at hand, they are constant in their inconstancy. During the daylight hours the clearest time is early morning, but, on the average, only one morning in six is clear or almost clear, and during my stay in the basin, clouds never remained absent throughout a whole day.[13] Frequently in the early

---

13. I gathered some numerical data on the basin's cloud cover, based on observations of percentage of cover at 8:00 A.M., noon, and 4:00 P.M. Averaged, these data show the daytime sky to be hidden by cloud by the following percentages: September, 62; January, 87; February, 84; March, 90; May, 65; June, 75. Because the June record is for only the first half of the month, which was a wetter and cloudier

morning there is a stratus deck or light cirrus cover, under
which the air can be clear or can contain some fog or mist near
the basin floor or tiny cumulus along the higher crests. The
high clouds, fog, and mists are usually gone by 0800 or 0900,
when the scattered cumulus along the crests have begun to
coalesce and develop into a connected line of towering cumulus
that indicates the highest parts of all the nearby mountain
ranges. By midday the summits of the towering cumulus have
usually risen far above the mountains, and their bases have
extended downward one or two thousand feet below the crest,
so that the higher slopes are obscured but the center of the
Simbai Valley and the lower northern part of the basin remain
fairly clear of cloud. Sometimes the rank of clouds may extend
outward over all or part of the basin, bringing shade and often
showers. Commonly after such midday showers, the cloud over
the basin partially breaks up, and there is intermittent sun in
the early afternoon. Usually by late afternoon the cloud cover
is again complete or almost complete, and the base of the
clouds may have descended still lower down the slopes. If rain
comes, as it often does, with this expanding cloud the basin's
valleys and ridges become veiled by mists of cumulus fractus,
which shift about under the influence of an upvalley wind that
blows from the east and north almost every late afternoon and
early evening. On rainy days which have high cloud from
morning to night because of the passage of some general perturbation, similar low mists and fog drift all day through the
basin air.

There is a close inverse relation between cloudiness and the
radiation received at the ground. The lessening of radiation
that accompanies cloudiness has both direct and indirect effects
on plant growth: directly, the photosynthetic process diminishes
as light intensity falls; indirectly, the lessened radiation leads
to lower daytime temperatures of soil and air, which also
diminish photosynthesis and slow the growth process. (See

---

period than expected by the Bomagai-Angoiang, the June figure given
is probably higher than average. See Note 14 for further details on
cloud cover.

Chang, 1968b.) Thus, although the amounts of moisture and the theoretical receipt of radiation at this latitude are favorable for plant growth all year, cloudiness may at times hinder growth. Certainly, the composition and structure of the montane forest on the basin's southern rim are strongly affected by the persistent cover of cloud, which also prevents cultivation and settlement there and down to an elevation of about 4,000 feet. Elsewhere in montane New Guinea where the semipermanent cloud base is higher, cultivation and settlement both ascend farther up the slopes. At lower elevations in the inhabited zone of the basin, the effect of the complex interactions of light intensity, temperature, and the characteristics of different species of plants is uncertain. On days of dense cloudiness, light is greatly reduced; Phillips (1960:51) gives a reduction of from five- to tenfold for the humid-forest region of Africa. But on days when the lower basin is clear while towering cumulus rise along the high southern wall, radiation on the lower floor of the basin must be intensified because of reflection from the clouds. On the other hand, by their action in reducing nighttime cooling, the clouds are the cause, once removed, of increased plant respiration at night and a consequent decrease in net photosynthesis and crop production. Without further measurements, the most that can be said of the ecologic effect of cloudiness is that it must affect plant growth throughout the basin and it almost certainly acts to lower crop yields and lengthen maturing times on the higher edges of the cultivated zone.[14] However, under present condi-

---

14. Chang (1968a:142–144) makes relevant comments on cloudiness in Melanesia and on agricultural productivity in cloudy regions: "Recent Tiros meteorological observations, analyzed by James C. Sadler, University of Hawaii, show that the mean monthly cloudiness in the tropical southwest Pacific exceeds five-tenths throughout the year. This remarkable consistency is not matched in any other extensive area of the tropics, not even the Congo or the Amazon. The cloudy area in the southwest Pacific, with an annual rainfall of more than 80 inches in most places, extends from Papua-New Guinea southeast to Fiji and coincides roughly with Melanesia. . . . The greatly attenuated solar radiation, the persistently high nighttime temperature, and the excessive rainfall all combine to depress the agricultural productivity of the humid tropics to a level below that of most temperate regions during their growing season."

tions of agriculture, cloudiness is not the only factor limiting yields; for example, the experiments that John Street and I (Clarke and Street, 1967) carried out in the basin showed that under existing light conditions an increase in the soil's nutrient supply would raise yields. For the sunniest part of the basin, Went's (1959:232) opinion regarding the photosynthetic process in general is probably right: ". . . it is all the secondary processes which are required for optimal plant growth which prevent the full potential utilization of the sun's energy by plants."

On the other hand, the relation between aspect of slope and the sun's annual progression of inclination points again to the significance of variations in the amounts of radiation received at the ground. Cloudiness occurs all year, but—as the name "time belong sun" indicates—the drier midyear season is sunnier than the rest of the year. Because of the basin's latitudinal location at 5° 25′ south, the slopes which face north receive somewhat more insolation annually than those which face south. That the sunniest season falls during the northern-hemisphere summer means that this inequality in receipt of insolation is increased. The effects of this inequality of radiation received by slopes facing north and those facing south are only dimly apparent in the perhumid and forested Ndwimba Basin, but they are clearly visible on east-west ridges in the nearby Jimi Valley. There the northern slopes are grass and the southern slopes are forest—not naturally, but because the agriculturally more desirable northern slopes have been subject to more felling of the original forest in order to make garden clearings. Over a long time, the clearing process has resulted in the replacement of forest by grass. The succession of the anthropogenic grassland back to forest is prevented by the fires that the people set, mainly for entertainment, whenever they pass through the grasslands. The Bomagai-Angoiang also believe that gardens on the slopes facing north yield a little better, other things being equal, than gardens on slopes facing south. However, a garden planted on poor soil on a slope facing north yields less than a garden on good soil on a slope facing south.

Their Spheres of Resources

The basin's topography and regional climate are not directly used or much controlled by the Bomagai-Angoiang. They are, rather, conditions of the spatial medium in which the people act. Less independent components of the ecosystem and ones that the people use in a more immediate way include spontaneous vegetation, soil, cultivated plants, wild and feral animals, and domestic and tame animals. These components can be thought of as the set of spheres of resources on which the Bomagai-Angoiang depend for materials and sustenance. The heartland of this supportive realm lies in the northern part of the basin where all of the Bomagai-Angoiang men now live, except those who have permanently emigrated, and where all of their gardens are planted, except one "bush garden," far to the east. The extent of this currently inhabited and cultivated heartland is shown on Map 3 and is clearly evident in the aerial photograph of the Ndwimba Basin on page xiv. The heartland is embedded in the larger and less intensely used total territory of the Bomagai-Angoiang. On the west this territory extends beyond the rim of the basin downslope for several hundred yards toward the houses and gardens of the Fungai clan. On the north the lands of Fungai and Kono (a clan whose center of settlement lies a few miles to the north of the basin) extend a small distance into the basin, but this area is not now much used by these groups. On the east the Bomagai-Angoiang territory merges into uninhabited forest land where clan boundaries are not strictly delimited, although the Bomagai, the Angoiang, the Fungai, and the Kono all claim certain parts on the basis of having "bush gardens" and planted *Pandanus* trees there. To the south the uncultivable forest land that caps the basin's high southern rim separates Bomagai-Angoiang land from the territories of the Jimi Valley peoples. Even though much of their total clan-cluster territory is uninhabited and uncultivated, it all provides resources to the Bomagai-Angoiang. The conterminous cultivated heartland itself is valuable for hunting, fishing, and gathering, as well as for gardening. That land outside the heartland but still within the clan cluster's boundaries is used more sporadically for gathering special materials, for hunting, and for planting the occasional outlying garden. There is also, as mentioned in my discussion of social and economic organization, some exchange with nearby groups across group boundaries; these extra-basin spheres of resources will be described at the end of this section.

Spontaneous Vegetation. The difference between the climates of the highest and lowest parts of the basin makes expectable an associated difference in the vegetation of the altitudinal extremes. If the basin were undisturbed by man, one would expect a continuum of vegetation between the extremes, even though the plant communities at the ends of the continuum would be clearly distinct from each other. Such a gentle gradation does occur on the higher slopes; at lower elevations human activity has caused a sharp boundary below which grow planted gardens and orchards, as well as the variety of types of secondary vegetation that has sprung spontaneously from once-cleared land, and above which grows forest on land that has never been cleared. It would be misleading, however, to imply either that this boundary is wholly artificial or that the forest above it is unaffected by man. In the basin, as in much of montane New Guinea, clearing ceases near the elevation above which low temperature or the presence of semipermanent cloud makes gardening unproductive. Thus, the location of the boundary between secondary and primary forest is induced more by climatic conditions than by human choice. In prehuman times there must also have been some differences in the primary vegetation across this break in the gradients of cloud cover and radiation receipt, but certainly not as pronounced a boundary as exists now. Now too, though the forest above the zone of cleared land is never cut en masse, neither is it truly natural in the sense of being undisturbed by man. For such a vegetation Fosberg (1962:257) has suggested the useful term "altered primary forest"—that is, forest that has never been completely cleared but that has been altered by less extreme human activities. Some alteration extends through all the area traversed by the

Bomagai-Angoiang; here, as in most of the tropical world, there is no truly natural vegetation—hence, my use of the substitute term "spontaneous vegetation" to mean all forms of vegetation not planted by man.

As with almost any description of the vegetation of the humid tropics where forest abounds, my categorization of plant communities is impressionistic, and my descriptions are far from complete. Further sampling and longer observation might have changed my picture of the outstanding types of vegetation in the basin; but, on the basis of the work I did, I divide the basin's spontaneous vegetation into three major types: montane-crest forest, lower montane rain forest, and secondary vegetation. The first two are subdivisions of altered primary forest; the last type, which includes several subdivisions, comes in its most advanced stage of succession to resemble the lower montane rain forest. Within the floristic frame of New Guinea, both my montane-crest forest and midelevation rain forest fit fairly closely into Robbins (1959:179–184) "lower montane rain forest formation" and Van Royen's (1963:12, 14, 21–23) equivalent "mid-mountain vegetation." Both these authorities say that in New Guinea the lowland vegetation meets the montane forms at elevations near 3,000 feet; however, in the local area of the Ndwimba Basin, I saw no significant difference between the forest at 2,200 feet (about the lowest elevation in the basin) and that at 3,500 or 4,000—though, of course, any potentially natural differences are masked by human disturbance. For the stake of brevity and of readability by nontaxonomists, I will concentrate on physiognomy rather than floristics in the following descriptions of types of vegetation. Further information on floristics is presented in Appendix B.

Montane-Crest Forest. The montane-crest forest [15]

---

15. Although "mossy forest" or "cloud forest" might seem fitting names for this community, I avoid them because they have been used by Brass (1964) and Robbins (1959) for other communities in New Guinea and because there are objections to both terms (Brass, 1964:210; Robbins, 1959:194–195). "Montane-crest forest" applies only to the vicinity of the Ndwimba Basin. Elsewhere in New Guinea, mountaintops at different elevations and with different climatic conditions have a

covers that part of the basin that lies above 5,000 to 5,500 feet—
that is, the most humid, cool, and cloudy zone. Trees of the
genus *Pandanus* are the most striking plants of this forest, where
at least three *Pandanus* species grow at elevations above 5,500
feet. All share the grotesquely spreading prop roots near the
base of the tree and the widely spreading "hands" of giant,
bladelike leaves that make up the crown of the tree. Two of the
Pandanus species are the tallest trees of the montane-crest forest;
rising above the smaller and darker-foliaged understory, they are
easily visible from a distance. Where abundant the tall *Pandanus*
provide a coverage of about 50 percent of the ground surface.
Occasionally one palm or hardwood tree almost reaches the
height of the high *Pandanus,* but these trees never dominate the
Pandanus as a component of the vegetation. Below the 80- to
100-foot-high discontinuous canopy of *Pandanus* is a tenuous 20-
to 50-foot-high stratum composed of younger plants of the tall
Pandanus species, the shorter *Pandanus* species, small palms
such as *Orania,* and a variety of dicotyledonous trees. A giant
member of the banana family—probably *Musa ingens,* the
largest herb known (Simmonds, 1962:15)—is also at home here.
Trees of the genus *Nothofagus* (the southern hemisphere
beech), which often dominate the mountain forests of New
Guinea, are not found on the high crest of the Ndwimba Basin,
for it is probably at slightly too low an elevation. *Nothofagus*
are present not far away on slightly higher crests where the
vegetation beneath the lofty beeches is very like that of the
crest forest of the Ndwimba Basin.

There is variation in the density of plants in the lower
stratum of trees in the montane-crest forest: in some places
they are eight to ten feet apart; in other places they form a
dense thicket. Only a few tree trunks in this stratum attain
diameters at breast height of more than a foot. The large
epiphytic ferns and orchids common in the lower montane rain
forest are replaced here by moss, which covers the trunks and
branches of the trees with a wet, spongy growth, often several

different vegetation from that described here.

inches thick. The generally sparse shrub layer includes young plants of the higher layers, as well as ferns, a ginger (probably *Alpinia*, which may reach above a proper shrub layer to heights of fifteen or twenty feet), and a member of the arrowroot family, perhaps *Phrynium*. Beneath the scattered shrubs are a few transgressives and some forbs such as *Begonia*. Moss and lycopods cover the ground in places, but the ground is mostly bare of green growth. The wet soil lies hidden beneath a layer of sodden litter. A few dicotyledonous lianas, as well as species of *Freycinetia* (a climbing member of the *Pandanus* family) ascend the trees; here and there other half-climbing, half-sprawling plants such as bamboos, rattan palms, and some large ferns occupy much of the lower space of the forest.

Sound and color seem muffled in the montane-crest forest. Fragments of cloud often veil the trees. Daylight is usually dim. The air feels chill and damp. Without the streams which always flow at lower elevations, the crest forest is mostly silent except for the intermittent falling drops of water and the occasional cry of a bird. The scattered bright red and orange fruits that have fallen from two of the *Pandanus* species only accent the dullness of the mossy tree trunks, the dark leaves, and the brown litter on the ground. Were it not for the many and omnipresent leeches that hump searchingly over the wet surface, animal life would seem almost absent. But this silent and inhospitable forest does hold resources valuable to the Bomagai-Angoiang. The seeds of two of the *Pandanus* species [16] bear edible kernels, which the Bomagai-Angoiang like but collect only casually while in the crest forest for other reasons: the elongate leaf blades (some more than ten feet long) of all the high-elevation *Pandanus* species are used for the construction of hunting shelters; the leaves of one of the *Pandanus* species are collected, tied into bundles, and carried down to

16. These were identified as *Pandanus julianettii* and *P. foveolatus*. In parts of New Guinea inhabited to higher elevations than the Ndwimba Basin, the seeds of *P. julianettii* can be an important food resource, and the tree is, or comes close to being, cultivated. See, for instance: Barrau, 1958:53; Meggitt, 1962:89; and Brookfield and Brown, 1963:48.

the inhabited zone, where they are woven into mats and used as roofing material. The wood of the *Orania* palm is used for arrow foreshafts and points. Long segments of wild bamboo serve the Bomagai-Angoiang as string for their bows; one of the taller palms (not identified) is used to make the bow itself and, before war was prohibited, for the shafts of the fighting spears. The wood of another palm, *Gronophyllum chaunostachys*, is also used for arrow foreshafts, and its sheathing leaf bases are used as wrapping and as containers for making sauce from the seeds of the lower-elevation, cultivated *Pandanus*. Also, this palm's slightly astringent "cabbage" is collected and eaten, raw or cooked. The large sprawling fern *Gleichenia brassii*, which is the object of special collecting trips into the forest, is esteemed as a heavy lashing for binding fence posts and poles together. Birds, including some of the birds of paradise, live in the trees of the crest forest, where men search them out for their decorative feathers. The cassowary, valued for its flesh, quills, and eggs, lives on the floor of the forest. Several small marsupials, hunted for both fur and flesh, also inhabit the montane-crest forest.

Lower Montane Rain Forest. Many of the components of the flora of the montane-crest forest are also present in the lower montane rain forest, but the physiognomy of the two types differs noticeably, and there is some floristic loss and gain with change in elevation. Below 5,000 to 5,500 feet the high-elevation *Pandanus* species and some of the palms disappear. The thick coating of moss on the tree trunks of the crest forest thins and is partly replaced by epiphytic orchids and ferns. Dicotyledonous lianas become more common than at the highest elevations but do not completely replace the climbing *Freycinetia* and the sprawling rattan palm. The forest comes to be dominated by dicotyledonous trees, often slightly buttressed and sometimes a hundred feet or more in height. Most trees are less than two feet in diameter at breast height; the largest reach three feet and occasionally more. There is no constant stratification in this forest: in places there seems to be only a single layer of trees forming a canopy at a height of about 80 feet, with a few trees emerging higher; elsewhere a lower stratum of trees,

reaching from 30 to 50 feet, is overshadowed by a canopy-form-
ing stratum that stretches to between 80 and 100 feet. Under
the mature trees there is often a dense subcanopy, varying in
height from 10 to 25 feet and made up of low trees, transgres-
sive saplings, and tree ferns. The shrub layer is sparse, if only
the nontransgressive plants are considered, but there are some
four-to-five-foot ferns, some taller gingers, and a few shrubs. The
herbaceous layer varies: in spots there is an almost solid, knee-
high growth of soft ferns, *Selaginella*, and of such forb species
as *Begonia* and *Elatostema*; in other places the herbaceous layer
is absent, and the ground surface is bare of green vegetation.
Passage through the lower montane rain forest is usually easy
except across young landslide scars or other disturbed places,
where the way is blocked by thickets of sprawling bamboo,
ferns, and herbaceous weeds. Visibility at eye level is everywhere
quite limited.

Although not as varied as lowland tropical rain forest, the
basin's lower montane rain forest contains a large number of
species of trees and nothing approaching a pure stand of a
single species. Members of the oak family, specifically *Castanopsis acuminatissima* and the acorn-bearing *Lithocarpus* sp., are
common as in much New Guinean forest. Particularly striking
trees are the red-barked *Dillenia* sp. and several species of *Ficus*,
which are often exuberantly cauliflorous. Palms are present but
less numerous than in the crest forest. A single sago palm
(*Metroxylon* sp.) was noted on the basin floor beside Ndwimba
Creek, but sago is not known as a food to the Bomagai-Angoiang
or any of their neighbors. Several wild *Pandanus* species different from those of the crest forest appear in the lower montane
rain forest; of these only one, *P. papuanus*, approaches the
height of the high-elevation *Pandanus* species, but, unlike them,
it is not congregated in groves and consequently never dominates
the vegetation as *Pandanus* trees often do in the crest forest.
The shorter *Pandanus* of the lower montane rain forest also
grow dispersed through the forest rather than clumped together.

In the lower montane rain forest, the Bomagai-Angoiang

hunt a variety of animals and gather a miscellanea of materials. For this, they make special trips into the forest, during the course of which they may incidentally collect such wild plant foods as the tender leaves from *Phrynium* sp., tree ferns, and some of the species of *Ficus*, like the riparian *F. iodotricha*. *Castanopsis acuminatissima* bears large numbers of small nuts, which are eaten either raw or cooked. Mushrooms gathered in the forest are singed over an open fire and eaten as snacks. Fruits like that of *Spondias dulcis*, the berry from *Rubus moluccanus*, and a wild mango are available in the forest, but they are of little interest to the Bomagai-Angoiang, who eat them in passing only when especially hungry. Materials collected in the forest include: a *Dendrobium* orchid sought for its yellow stem that is used on decorative headbands to hold the bodies of bright green beetles (*Cetoniidae*); leaves and wood of the *Pandanus* trees, whose multiple uses are listed by species in Appendix B; cordage from all the lianas and light vines; abrasive leaves from a *Ficus* sp. for sandpapering arrow shafts; leaves from *Phrynium* sp. and *Alpinia* spp. for lining earth ovens, wrapping food, and for roofing; the underbark of *Ficus iodotricha* used, as are many other plant fibers, for making string for net bags and aprons; bands of flexible bark stripped from a *Lauraceae* known to the Bomagai-Angoiang as *ap krm* and used to make eel traps, above-ground ovens, and men's waistbands; wood from a palm of the genus *Licuala* used for bow shafts and arrow points; and wood for fuel and for the construction of houses and fences from a variety of trees. A forest tree known to me only by the native name of *ap paiem* has an aromatic wood, a piece of which is carried by some men and smelled for the reviving effect it has on them when they feel ill. Another tree, possibly a *Litsea*, bears seeds that are ground into a paste that is reputed to heal sores. The types of animals hunted in the lower montane rain forest will be described in a later section. The forest also serves the Bomagai-Angoiang as a reservoir of space and as an accumulator of soil-enriching organic matter. When the forest is cut, as it is occasionally, the land

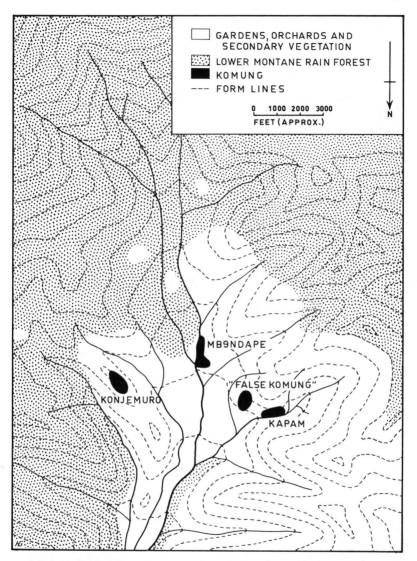

GARDENS, ORCHARDS AND
SECONDARY VEGETATION
LOWER MONTANE RAIN FOREST
KOMUNG
FORM LINES

0   1000 2000 3000
FEET (APPROX.)

N

MB9NDAPE

"FALSE KOMUNG"

KONJEMURO

KAPAM

Map 4   Generalized Vegetation of the Lower Ndwimba Basin

beneath it becomes available for new gardens and for the expansion of secondary vegetation.

   Secondary Vegetation. Where the basin has been cleared of lower montane rain forest, there now grow planted gardens and orchards interspersed in a complex mosaic of spontaneous secondary communities. The constant variation that is encountered in walking through the secondary vegetation is the result not only of differences in the length of time since clearing, but also of variations in physical conditions from site to site and of differences in the kinds of seed available and the season of the year when the secondary plants were taking hold in the garden or orchard that preceded the secondary community. As an example of this variation, I indicate on Plate 6 two distinct secondary communities, reputedly of the same age, that are growing side by side. Both came up, say the people, on a single large garden plot that was cleared about fifteen years ago. But, as described under Plate 6, a difference of micro-environmental conditions within the plot is presumed to have led to the distinction in the secondary communities. Because there is at least some variation in the season of maturation of seeds of different pioneer species and because gardens fall out of use in all seasons of the year, sites with identical micro-environments may also have different types of secondary growth. Another cause of the variety is the long fallow period, which allows the secondary regrowth on any plot to pass through several changes before being cut. And when it is cut, the boundaries of the fresh plot seldom coincide with those of previous clearings in that vicinity, so that the new regrowth further adds to the multiplicity of the surrounding types. Finally, because during clearing, when enough ground has been opened and enough timber is available for fences, the men often simply pollard and leave standing the remaining large trees. If these sprout, there come to be in a few years full-sized trees in the midst of young spontaneous woodland, which further adds to the complexity of the secondary vegetation.

   As a resource for the Bomagai-Angoiang, the secondary

communities are used more than the two types of altered primary forest. The whole secondary zone serves as a foraging ground for domestic pigs and as a hunting ground for the men, who pass through it daily on their rounds. Except for the small areas of grassland, all types of second growth serve to reinvigorate the soil after gardening. The secondary communities also serve as sources of plant food and materials. I will outline in the following pages the particular resources contributed by each of what I recognized to be distinct and recurrent communities of secondary vegetation in the Basin.

    1. INCIPIENT LOWER MONTANE RAIN FOREST. When a garden falls into disuse, the host of small ferns, forbs, and grasses that spring up from the unweeded ground are soon overshadowed by a variety of taller plants that include the fast-growing seedlings of pioneer trees. Within a decade these trees have formed a young forest, 20 to 60 feet high, in whose understory grow trees typical of the lower montane rain forest. If the young forest is not cut, the sun-loving short-lived pioneer species are gradually replaced by true rainforest species. Within thirty years after clearing, the forest is taking on the aspect of the lower montane rain forest, lacking only the larger trees and fuller development of epiphytes and lianas of the latter forest. From then on, floristically and with regard to resources, the secondary forest becomes increasingly indistinguishable from the altered primary forest, except that for several more decades the absence of forest giants makes the younger forest easier to clear. Within that part of the basin now subject to clearing, 5 to 10 percent of the total secondary vegetation falls into this class of incipient lower montane rain forest. For the land under secondary forest of such an age, the Bomagai-Angoiang's feeling for private rights to management begins to fade away, and rights to the whole zone of old forest revert to a clan or subclan, whose members may then assert individual rights by cutting where they will. Often this procedure is legitimized by the authority of some old man who says either that he cleared the plot in question himself when young or that a now dead clans-

man once gave rights to the plot to him. On this basis he grants permission—gives sanction—for the plot's reuse by a younger clansman.

2. ALPHITONIA-CYATHEA-GEUNSIA WOODLAND. In Chapter 1 I mentioned the frequent presence in the secondary vegetation of the white-barked tree *Alphitonia incana* and the tree fern *Cyathea angiensis*. Another tree, probably *Geunsia farinosa*, which is less striking in appearance, is co-dominant with the fern and the *Alphitonia*. Together these three species form a woodland that is the basin's commonest recurrent type of regrowth. This woodland assumes its distinctive character within five or six years after the garden it displaces has fallen into disuse. The young *Geunsia* and *Alphitonia* trees and the *Cyathea*, all fifteen to twenty feet high, form a thin thicket with an almost continuous but shallow canopy, through which can pass many flecks of sunlight to the dense understory of grasses, forbs, and low ferns. The expectable growing dominance of true forest trees beneath the woodland cover is slowed by the men, who unintentionally maintain the light-tolerant pioneer species by thinning the woodland by felling some of the regrowth trees and *Cyathea*. On the other hand, there may also be mature forest trees rising above young woodland communities. In one place, for example, when the land was cleared in about 1958 for a garden, a seventy-foot *Lithocarpus* was pollarded but not felled; when I saw the site in 1965 the *Alphitonia-Cyathea-Geunsia* woodland that had grown up was dwarfed by the vigorously resprouted *Lithocarpus*.

In the woodland the trees, the tree ferns, and the understory plants all provide the people with food and materials. From all the plants of the tree stratum, but especially from *Alphitonia*, comes wood for fuel and fences. *Cyathea* in addition provides edible leaves. The understory plants provide cordage, edible leaves, and medicine.

3. GROVES OF ALBIZIA FALCATARIA. Less common than the stands of *Alphitonia-Cyathea-Geunsia* woodland are groves of *Albizia falcataria*. The spreading, distinctively horizontal clouds of foliage make these groves of large, white-barked

trees a prominently visible community. Fast-growing, *Albizia falcataria* may reach heights of sixty feet or more within ten years; [17] their canopy is fairly continuous, but the thin foliage lets through considerable light. The undergrowth varies: in a young grove the *Albizia* rise above a jungle of sprawling ferns and other low plants; in a longer-established grove the *Albizia* have beneath them a scattered lower story of trees—of genera such as *Geunsia*, *Saurauia*, and *Ficus*—fifteen to twenty feet high, beneath which grow the ginger *Alpinia*, ferns, and a field layer of soft forbs such as *Elatostema*. Despite the undergrowth, the size of the *Albizia* and their broadly spreading branches lend the interiors of the groves the same atmosphere of spaciousness that characterizes the primary rain forest.

As a resource the leguminous *Albizia* is most valuable for increasing soil fertility. According to the people, who spare its seedlings during garden weeding, *Albizia* is the most restorative of all the trees. Where it has grown, the ground is said to be "soft" and to have "grease." "Taro planted there will come up big." Presumably the ameliorative effect of a fallow of *Albizia falcataria* comes at least in part from the nodules containing nitrogen-fixing bacteria that have been found on its roots (Burkill, 1935:85). The wood of A. *falcataria* was esteemed for shields, now no longer made.[18] It is still used to make the bodies of drums.

4. JUNGLE. Every old garden or garden site not long in disuse supports what might be called jungle—a growth of weedy plants five to ten feet high so close together and intertwined that passage is difficult. But compared with more densely populated territories farther up the Simbai Valley, little jungle persists in the Ndwimba Basin. Here and there, however,

---

17. The people say that *Albizia* grows faster than any other tree, even the *Casuarina* spp. Richards (1962:71), citing G. Haberlandt (*Eine botanische Tropenreise*, Leipzig, 1926), says that in Java A. *falcata* (now designated A. *falcataria*) reaches a height of 25 m. in six years and 35 m. in ten years.

18. Burkill (1935:84–85), citing Rumpf's *Herbarium Amboinense*, records that the Malay of Amboina also used *Albizia falcata* for shields because of its combination of lightness with resistance to penetration by weapons.

on relatively dry or degraded sites where saplings of woodland
or forest species cannot gain quick dominance, the jungle remains for several years before being shaded out by taller growth.
The thick canopy of jungle vegetation prevents the growth of
most of the heliophilous herbs that crowd over the sunny
ground of unweeded gardens, so that the commonest plant
less than five feet high is the shade-tolerant grass *Paspalum
conjugatum*, which in places forms a dense, low thicket. One
stand of two-year-old jungle that I sampled contained the following plants in its dominant story: remnants of the abandoned
garden in the form of banana plants, spindly shrubs of manioc,
and clusters of canes of *Saccharum edule*, all intertwined with
the vines of cultivated yams: small *Cyathea angiensis*; several
species of smaller ferns; six- to eight-foot saplings of a variety
of regrowth trees; one fifteen-foot *Geunsia*, resprouting from its
pollarded trunk; many specimens of a weedy wild banana (*Musa*
sp.); a low, spreading *Piper* tree; a tall sedge; *Alpinia* spp.; some
soft vines; and the tall grasses *Miscanthus floridulus* and *Poly-
toca macrophylla*.

A jungle such as this provides the Bomagai-Angoiang with
edible leaves from the *Cyathea angiensis* and some of the
smaller ferns, as well as other forms of food from the old garden
plants, whose products become available for gathering—unless
the garden's owner objects—by all the owner's clansmen or
subclansmen. Like the leaves of the cultivated banana, those
of the wild *Musa* serve the people as natural umbrellas, wrapping material, plates, and clean surfaces on which to prepare
foods. The sprawling ferns and vines provide cordage. The strong
stems of the *Miscanthus* grass are used to make arrow shafts.

5. GRASSLAND. Grassland, the rarest type of regrowth in the basin, covers less than 5 percent of the total area
occupied by secondary vegetation. It occurs only on the driest
sites on the tops of spurs, and its small presence there does not
point to the permanent conversion of forest to grass that has
happened in much of New Guinea; instead, the basin's grasslands are but a transient stage in the succession back to wood-

land and forest.[19] The Bomagai-Angoiang divide the basin grasslands into two types. One, *korndo* (the Maring name for *Imperata cylindrica*) grows in the driest sites; the other, which grows on somewhat moister sites and is designated by the linked name *mbombak-tamo*, is a variable mixture of two *Ischaemum* species (both *mbombak*) and *Paspalum conjugatum* (*tamo*). Shrubby ferns are mixed with all the grasses.

The grasslands are a less valuable resource than any of the other communities of secondary vegetation. They are not cleared for gardens because of the reputed infertility of the soil beneath them and because of the difficulty of initial clearing and subsequent weeding, especially of the *Imperata* culms that sprout persistently from rhizomes. Feral and domestic pigs do bed in the grasslands and forage there for insects and worms. For the people, *Imperata* and some of the ferns provide light cordage, the *Imperata*'s white flower plumes are used for hair adornment, and *mbor* (the local name for one of the weedy ferns found in grasslands, possibly a *Thelypteris*) is draped on the ritual gateways, where it is believed to help prevent the passage of sickness from one place to another.

6. MISCELLANEOUS TYPES AND PLANTS. For the sake of brevity I have omitted mentioning many plants in my descriptions of secondary vegetation in the basin. Among them are garden and trailside weeds, members of the understories of distinct communities, minor components in the dominant stratum of distinct communities, or part of a vegetation cover that lacks as clear a personality as each of the communities already described. From this pool of plants the Bomagai-Angoiang draw a wide range of items including food, medicine, cordage, decoration, construction materials, wrapping material, fiber for

19. As evidence of their impermanence, all the Ndwimba Basin grasslands contain tree species but have none of the grasses (such as species of *Themeda, Eulalia, Arundinella,* and *Ophiuros*) that grow in the extensive grasslands of the more heavily settled parts of the Simbai and Jimi valleys which indicate a permanently established grassland of the type described by Robbins (1963:52–53) as a stabilized disclimax community.

bark cloth, and glue. In Appendix B I give as full a listing as is
possible of these plants and their uses.

 Komung. There remains one further type of vegetation that, although initially spontaneous, is now deliberately
maintained by the people as a permanent part of their habitat.
The territories of all Maring clans contain these *komung*,
which are spirit-inhabited, sacred groves—some associated with
an entire clan, some only with a subclan. According to local
belief, everyone in a clan or subclan would sicken and die if the
large trees or tree ferns of their *komung* were cut; however, it is
not dangerous to take small vines for tying sugar cane or to collect for food the leaves of a forest-understory tree fern. In
essence, then, the *komung* are zones of altered primary forest,
mostly surrounded by land that has at some time been cleared.
In the *komung* of the Ndwimba Basin the dominant 80- to 100-
foot rain forest trees provide an almost complete cover over the
fairly open understories. The shrub layer of ferns and other low
growth is easy to walk through. The field and ground layers are
usually sparser than in ordinary lower-montane rain forest because of the heavier human traffic through the *komung*. Many
Maring *komung* are on sites unfavorable to agriculture, often
on stony ridge tops. The Angoiang *komung* of Konjemuro follows this pattern. (See Map 4 for locations of the basin
komung.) The Bomagai *komung* of Mbəndape and Kapam,
although not ridge tops, are also in spots not too good for
gardens: Mbəndape's soil is a sandy, easily eroded igneous
debris; Kapam *komung* lies where basin-floor boulders are especially common.

 The *komung* serve as sources of seed for the recolonization
of rainforest trees within the zone of clearing, although in the
basin—unlike other parts of the Maring area—all the gardens
are close to ordinary rain forest in any case. The Mbəndape
komung is especially unimportant in this regard because it
adjoins lower-montane rain forest. Because the *komung* are
remnants of a habitat something like the primary rain forest,
they also serve as places where rain forest birds and animals can
be hunted close at hand. In the basin this function is expanded

by the presence of a "false *komung*," which is a plot of rain forest not charged with spiritual danger but left uncut as a kind of private hunting preserve for its claimant, Wun, a Bomagai "big man" who has built a tree house there wherein he waits for birds with bow and arrows.

Soil. Everywhere in the basin the soils have the characteristics typical of oxysols of the humid tropics. A contrast might be anticipated between the soils on the sloping sides of the basin and the alluvial-colluvial soils on the basin floor; but in their profiles and, according to my measurements and the estimation of the Bomagai-Angoiang, they do not significantly differ in their fertility. Presumably, the deposits on the floor have been long enough in place (although post-Pleistocene in origin according to Dow and Dekker, 1964:23) to have acquired the zonal qualities of the in situ soils on the slopes. Lying over deeply weathered parent materials,[20] the profiles of the basin soils typically grade downward from a friable, porous, brown layer a few inches thick and rich in organic matter, into sticky clays, which are predominantly yellow and orange. Lateritic layers are absent, as would be expected, because the intermittent dehydration believed (Sherman *et al.*, 1953) to be important in their development is minimized by the continuous cover of vegetation and the infrequency of dry spells. I tested the pH, the nutrient content, and the soil bulk density of basin soils under all types of vegetation. I also sent samples to the Department of Soil Science at the University of Hawaii for testing for pH and nutrient content.[21]

---

20. I had samples of the basin bedrock identified and could roughly outline the geology of the basin, but such data seem irrelevant to my discussion because there is little indication that the original variations in the now deeply weathered parent material affect the fertility of the soils used for gardens. In some places, such as Tsenboi Ridge, the igneous substratum has weathered into a soil with a coarser texture than that of a soil overlying mudstone, but the people feel that there is no difference between the productiveness of the two types. As I mentioned, there has accumulated at Mbəndape *komung*, which lies at the base of an igneous ridge, a soil with a particularly coarse and easily eroded texture and perhaps a low nutrient reserve—but being under *komung* (perhaps because of the poor soil) it is never cultivated, anyway.

21. My tests for pH and nutrient content were done in the field

The median pH of the top four inches of the soils tested was 5.5, with a range from 4.7 to 6.5. The least acid soils were found in gardens and in one set of samples collected under a ten-year-old *Albizia* grove; the most acid soils were under grassland, where aeration is poor, and under primary forest. The higher pH of soils under gardens, compared with soils under forest before clearing, results from the addition to garden soils of bases in the ash derived from burning the felled forest cover. In one new garden I collected sets of soil samples both from places where there had been burning and from places where no burning had occurred—Bomagai-Angoiang burning being quite spotty. The aggregate pH of the soil under the burns was 5.6; that from unburned places was 5.1. These findings agree in essence with the opinion of Nye and Greenland (1960:70) and the results recorded by Popenoe (1959) of his attempt to measure the influence of shifting cultivation on soil properties in lowland eastern Guatemala where (Popenoe, 1959: Table 1, p. 74) the 0–2 inch layer of forest soil had a pH of 5.75 compared with a pH of 6.37 in soil of cleared land and a pH of 5.85 in soil under two-year-old second growth. That the pH of young second-growth soil is lower than that of the cleared land reflects the gradual loss of bases by leaching and crop removal (Popenoe, 1959:74). According to the chemical analyses, burning did not increase the soil's available content of phosphorous, potassium, or magnesium; calcium increased by 50 percent. The Bomagai-Angoiang, who burn mainly simply to dispose of felled debris, consider burning beneficial to the soil but not essential for good yields. Generally they burn only the trash of a sloping garden's center and top; at the bottom and sides they throw the trash over the fence. If a long wet spell follows cutting, so that burning is difficult, they consolidate the trash of the garden's center into large heaps and plant in the unburned clear-

---

with the Hellige-Truog Combination Soil Tester, F48–697. Soil bulk density was determined by finding the ratio between the weight of an amount of soil and the volume of water required to fill the hole (lined with a plastic bag) formed by the soil's removal. The tests in Hawaii were done by Wade W. McCall, Associate Specialist in Soil Management, University of Hawaii.

ings. They do believe that the lack of burning may somewhat lessen yields of tobacco, yams, and *Colocasia*, which are usually planted in ashy spots, but not that it affects yields of other crops, which are often not planted beneath ash, anyway.[22]

With few exceptions, my soil analyses and those done in Hawaii showed the soils of the Ndwimba Basin to be generally low in available plant nutrients. Table 6 shows for the collected soil samples the average, median, and range of the nutrient content.

Table 6. *Available Nutrients in Ndwimba Basin Soils*
(Pounds per Acre, 0–7 Inch Layer)

	P	K	Ca	Mg	NO_3	NH_3
Average:	48	107	2,588	210	56	119
Median:	25	80	1,000	250	31	125
Range:	trace–200	40–320	trace–6,000	trace–500	31–93	25–500

In order to supplement the chemical analyses, which can serve only in a limited way as an index of soil fertility (Nye and Greenland, 1960:98), I also carried out fertilizer-response trials and plant-tissue tests. Because there was an aggregate increase in yield with application of fertilizer, the fertilizer trials, detailed in Clarke and Street (1967), showed that the soils possessed a deficiency of nutrients. The plant-tissue tests, which I carried out on the leaves of sweet potatoes from several gardens of various ages, were designed to measure the nutrients present in the plant tissues and hence also in the soil. These tests, too, showed that nutrients are not abundant in the soils of the Ndwimba Basin.

The plant-tissue tests did not show a decline in the nutrient level of the soil over the Bomagai-Angoiang cropping period, but some of the chemical analyses did point to a slight decline. The measurements of yields from gardens of various ages car-

---

22. Baldanzi's (1961) report of experiments on the effects of burning at Curitiba in Brazil indicates that burning does improve crop production (wheat was the test crop) without damaging long-term soil fertility.

ried out in connection with the fertilizer-response trials indicated
a lessened productivity from the soils of older or abandoned
gardens, compared with the soils of new gardens, and suggested
that a decline in nutrient content could be one of the causes.

Table 7.   Nutrients in Ndwimba Basin
Plant Tissues
(Leaves of Ipomoea batatas)

Nutrient Content
(On Hellige-Truog Scale)

P	low to medium
K	low
Mg	very low
NO₃	low
NH₃	very low to low

The literature and the possibility for discussion of the reciprocal relations of soil and vegetation under a system of shifting cultivation seem almost endless. Because exact knowledge
is lacking as to what happens in the cycle of alternation of
forest fallow and garden, I shall make only a few general remarks on the subject. The Bomagai-Angoiang and Nye and
Greenland, who have written (Nye and Greenland, 1960) the
most comprehensive work on the relations of soil and shifting
cultivation, explain the necessity for forest fallow in similar
ways. The Bomagai-Angoiang say that if they replanted a plot
immediately after having harvested crops from it, at least some
of the crops [23] in the new garden would not yield at the initial
level, partly because the "grease" imparted to the soil by the

23. *Colocasia* and the yams are singled out as being particularly
susceptible to falling yields; sweet potatoes, cassava, sugar cane, and
Saccharum edule would, the people believe, continue to yield well if
replanted in the same plot without an interval of fallow. In the
relatively densely populated Kaironk Valley thirty miles west of the
basin, the same plot is often used twice in immediate succession. The
first crop is *Colocasia*; after it is harvested, sweet potatoes are planted as
the second crop. It is probable that between the first and second
plantings the moisture-holding capacity of the soil has declined, along
with the nutrient content.

forest fallow would have been used up during the first cropping. Their belief in the benefits of the forest fallow is nicely expressed by the name, *nduk mi*, that they give to the secondary arboreal communities that come up in disused gardens. *Nduk mi* means "garden mother." In differing language the western scientists say:

Low organic matter levels are probably the commonest factor associated with the low fertility of tropical soils. At present most of the exploitable soils in the tropics are cultivated by shifting cultivation, and here organic matter levels are sustained by additions from the vegetation which develops during the fallow period. Provided the fallow is sufficiently long these additions will maintain a satisfactory equilibrium level (Greenland and Nye, 1961:478).

The length of time necessary for secondary cover to restore soil fertility to pregarden levels is a moot matter dependent on many varying conditions. For what they call the "super-humid forest regions of south-east Asia and Central Africa," Nye and Greenland (1960:127–128) believe that an alternation of ten to twenty years of fallow with one or two years of cropping will maintain soil fertility through many cycles of gardening. Reynders (1961:38) believes that in the Vogelkop region of West Irian the soil re-attains its original condition after a rotation period of fifteen to twenty years, initiated by eight months of cropping sweet potatoes and *Colocasia*. Carneiro (1960:231) in describing the slash-and-burn agriculture of an Indian group of tropical South American gives as a stable cycle twenty-five years of fallow, alternating with three years of cropping manioc. The Bomagai-Angoiang gardens have an eighteen- to twenty-two-month cropping period, which alternates, according to my estimate, with an average fallow that may be as long as forty years. I cannot know whether this cycle is stable or not. I doubt that any human ecosystem is permanently balanced; but I believe that, if maintained in its present form, the Bomagai-Angoiang's fallow-garden cycle would keep fertility at almost constant levels and make quite slow a successional retrogression of vegetation in the basin.

The Bomagai-Angoiang believe that all types of trees restore soil fertility but that certain species are especially valuable. Some men say that *ap kobanum* (*Ficus* ? *pungens*) is one of these trees.[24] All the men agree that the basin's two *Casuarina* species and *Albizia falcataria* are especially valuable; but for the basin the *Casuarina* are irrelevant because they are only rarely part of the fallow. As already noted in the prior description of *Albizia*, they may be associated with nitrogen fixation. One set of soil samples that I collected under an *Albizia* grove registered (according to the Hellige-Truog verbal scale) "high" for ammonia but "very low" for nitrate. The other set of samples of *Albizia*-fallowed soil, which I collected under another grove about the same age as the first, registered "very low" for nitrate and "low" for ammonia, but aberrantly high in pH (6.5) and phosphorous ("very high"). Without further study I can only say that I have faith in the Bomagai-Angoiang assessment of the high restorative capacity of the *Albizia*, but cannot explain the action.

Another source of enrichment of some basin soils is the bodily wastes of the Bomagai-Angoiang. Near each settlement are what might be called feces fields, one for each sex, where the settlement's inhabitants discharge fecal matter and urine. After an area has been thus used for a while, it is given up in favor of a fresh place. Later, when the feces have decomposed, the field, which is regarded as a good garden site, is cleared for crops.

Although plots fallowed under the especially restorative secondary communities or once used as feces fields are doubtless more productive as gardens than areas with other histories, they are not considered so much better that the Bomagai-Angoiang make special efforts to obtain them for gardens. I believe that, with the exception of pronounced differences in elevation, the people pay more attention to microvariations within a single plot than to variations in aggregate fertility from

24. Interestingly, the Maenge people of the area around Jacquinot bay on New Britain also list *F. pungens* Reinw. as a tree that has nutritive effects on the soil (Panoff, 1970:74).

plot to plot. Within several square yards in any individual garden, there are sudden changes in soil quality. For instance, in one place a large log rotted, while close by the roots of an upturned tree exposed the lower clay layers of the soil; here an *Albizia* grew; there a stunted jungle covered the narrow crest of a spur; here the slope was exceptionally steep; there the soil accumulated on a natural terrace; here garden trash was burned; there the ground was free of ash. The Bomagai-Angoiang, as they plant seeds and cuttings singly with a dibble, note such microvariations in soil characteristics and plant accordingly— certain crops in soil that is *ank* ("hard," relatively infertile), other crops in soil that is *nak* ("soft," friable) and *ndi* ("good" —that is, dark in color and judged to be fertile). All soils fallowed under grasslands are considered to be infertile and are not used in the forested Ndwimba Basin. Chemical analyses of grasslands soil support the people's opinions: the most acid soil I measured (pH 4.7) was under an *Imperata-fern* community. All nutrients tested for, except nitrogen in the ammoniacal form, were present only in very small amounts ("very low" on the Hellige-Truog scale) or absent, in the case of calcium. Ammoniacal nitrogen was found in a "medium" amount. Yield trials substantiate the people's belief in the infertility of unturned grassland soil; when such soil is turned before planting, the yield more than doubles (Clarke and Street, 1967:10), but the Bomagai-Angoiang, some of whom are aware of the benefits of tillage to grassland soils, see no reason to expend the time and effort, when satisfactory yields can be had from unturned, forest-fallowed soil.

The few measurements that I made of soil bulk density (nineteen samples in all) suggested that the soils of old gardens are denser (an average density of 1.35) than soils of primary forest and secondary forest over five years of age (an average of 1.16). In some old gardens the topsoil was sticky and had lost the soft, friable feel of forest soils. Popenoe (1959:74) in his Guatemala experiments also found greater soil densities under cleared land than under forest. Such increases in density reduce permeability, but, as Popenoe (1959:74) and Nye and

Greenland (1960:85) note, there is no evidence that an increase in density is a cause of declining yields.

Cultivated Plants. The Bomagai-Angoiang maintain their cultivated plants in fenced gardens, in a few unfenced plantings, in orchards, around their houses, and in some cases in a semi-cultivated state both near their settlements and in the bush. From their cultivated plants the people get food, materials, and a psychic satisfaction that derives both from an appreciation of the decorative plants and from a feeling that by planting they secure a continuity of sustenance and tenure for themselves and their kin.

In Appendix C is an annotated list of all the Bomagai-Angoiang cultivated and semicultivated plants of which I have a record. In the following sections I will describe the look and general location of the several ways that the people have of arranging and aggregating their cultivated plants. In Chapter 3 I will deal with the methods of planting, the planting cycle, and the yields of the cultivated plants.

Gardens. The gardens of the Bomagai-Angoiang are planted on land fallowed under secondary growth, or occasionally on plots newly cleared of lower montane rain forest. Specifically, in 1965 about 10 percent of the gardens in use were newly cleared (and the land claimed) from what the people considered virgin forest; another 5 percent were on land cleared of virgin forest by the present operator one fallow period ago. All but a very few "greens gardens" are fenced to keep out domestic and feral pigs. Because a single fenced enclosure may contain either one man's garden or several men's gardens, the size of the enclosures varies from less than an acre to more than five acres. At any time of year there are gardens that are new or only a few months old as well as maturing and mature gardens, five to fourteen months old, and incipiently disused gardens, fourteen to twenty months old. To the Bomagai-Angoiang the most important division of the gardens into types is a separation of the *ndang-wan nduk* ("taro-yam garden") from all other types; the latter receive the general name of *nduk auwari*, which might be translated as "garden nothing" or "unimportant garden."

The people look on the *ndang-wan nduk* as their most significant sources of food, as their true gardens. Ideally, in the "garden heart" near the center of the *ndang-wan nduk*, the men plant *Cordyline fruticosa*, pile the taro and yam cuttings before planting, and work spells to ensure the garden's good health and harvest. Actually, not all men perform these rituals, but they still rank the *ndang-wan nduk* as more important than the other types of gardens, which lack recognized "garden hearts" and never have ritual associated with planting. The *ndang-wan nduk* are relatively rich, especially in the "garden hearts," in the ritually significant crops of taro and yams. Some men say that the important food crops—sweet potatoes, manioc, and *Xanthosoma*—are never planted in the "garden heart"; others say—and this is nearer to the usual case—that only a few of these plants are put there. The gardeners tend to concentrate manioc and *Xanthosoma* near the garden's edge, but these crops may be planted anywhere in the garden. Sweet potatoes are usually spread throughout the garden.

Somewhat depending on the spirit of the moment, the Bomagai-Angoiang further subdivide the *nduk auwari*, or "unimportant gardens," into a number of types. Some common names for these types are:

a. *kem-kong nduk* (*Hibiscus manihot-Xanthosoma* garden)
b. *koia nduk* (sweet potato garden)
c. *kong-koia nduk* (*Xanthosoma*-sweet potato garden)
d. *koia-mbaundi nduk* (sweet potato-manioc garden)
e. *mbep nduk* (greens garden)

These kinds of gardens usually contain taro and may contain yams. Another name, *mbo-mungap nduk* (*Saccharum officinarum-S. edule* garden), usually refers to an *ndang-wan nduk* in its old age, when the taro and yams have been harvested but the garden remains productive of *mbo, mungap, Hibiscus manihot*, and bananas. Or, the combination *mbo-mungap* may be linked with *koia-mbaundi* (as *mbo-mungap-koia-mbaundi nduk*) to indicate a new garden where the *Saccharum* species, sweet potatoes, and manioc are planted in abundance, but yams and taro are scarce. Whatever their type, the Bomagai-Angoiang gardens share the characteristics of an apparent disorder of crop placement, a complete lack of water control or tillage in the sense of turning or working the soil, an incomplete removal of the fallow vegetation, and a vertical organization of crops into several tiers.[25]

To convey the nature of a Bomagai-Angoiang garden, I will summarize an actual traverse run in a five-month-old *ndang-wan nduk*. A garden of this age is productive of pumpkin, the bean *Psophocarpus tetragonolobus*, *Hibiscus manihot*, *Rungia klossii*, and a few old cucumbers, most of which have already been harvested. Bananas, the *Saccharum* species, and the root crops have not yet begun or are just beginning to produce. From the fence at the edge of the garden the ground is invisible beneath a continuous cover of crop vegetation in which only a few weedy forbs and ferns are noticeable. To enter the garden is to wade into a green sea. To walk is to push through irregular waves of taro and *Xanthosoma* and to step calf-deep in the cover of sweet potato vines. Overhead, manioc, bananas, sugar cane, and *Saccharum edule* provide scattered shade. Rising above the flood of crops are remnants of the forest which was there before clearing—two *Pandanus papuanus*, preserved for their useful leaves, and the pollarded trunk of an *Elmerrillia papuana*, now sprouting a ball of foliage from its lopped-off top. On the traverse through the garden, the ground of the first three-foot segment is covered with the *tukaya* variety of sweet potato. Rising out of the mass of vines are a weedy forb and a taro plant. In the next segment the *tukaya* sweet potato is mixed with the *alepun* variety. Together they cover the ground

25. In their appearance, then, the Bomagai-Angoiang gardens resemble the shifting gardens of lowland New Guinea, which are briefly described by Robbins (1962:318, 322), or what Watson (1965a:297) calls "plantings," which occur in the Central Highlands along with the more common orderly, tilled, clean-cleared, and often drained gardens.

solidly and are partly shaded by two *Xanthosoma* with twenty-two-inch leaves. Beneath one *Xanthosoma* is an edible wild fern. By pushing aside the sweet potato vines, one can see a weed form of the edible-leafed, cultivated *komeruk* (*Commelina* sp.). In the next segment the continuing mixture of sweet potato varieties is almost completely shaded by a *Xanthosoma*, a weedy fern, and the edible wild form of the cultivated *Setaria*. Next a five-foot *wunum* variety of banana dominates the ground cover of *daier* sweet potato. In the following segment the *daier* vines are mixed with the *airpo* variety, and a small *Colocasia* stands next to a seedling of the secondary tree *Geunsia farinosa*—a presage of the future vegetation on this site.

Now fifteen feet into the garden, one encounters a seven-foot *wunum* banana plant around whose base there spreads the cover of sweet potato vines that extends continuously from the fence. In the next segment is still more sweet potato, as well as a not-before-encountered variety of taro, another kind of weedy fern, a *Xanthosoma*, and the sprouting stump of a *Ficus* species, seven inches in diameter. Then comes a *nunong* banana plant, followed by the stumps of two trees felled to clear the plot. Beyond the stumps a spreading, vaselike cluster of *amp'san* sugar cane has yet to be tied together. Next, *airpo* sweet potato vines climb over a jumble of decaying logs and continue beyond, where two five-foot *Maoutia* saplings have been left until they are large enough to harvest for their underbark—an important source of fiber for string-making. In the following segment a vigorous cluster of taro plants stands above the sweet potatoes that continue unshaded through the next segment. Beyond is another tree stump and a three-foot weedy fern with a cultivated yam (*Dioscorea alata*) twining about it and trailing off into the sweet potatoes. In the next segment wild *Setaria* and sweet potatoes abut a throng of taro plants that continue several feet to a weedy fern and a rank pumpkin vine bearing a nine-inch, yellow fruit—which, upon being noted, was harvested by the Angoiang garden-owner who accompanied me on the traverse.

Beyond the pumpkin were several waist-high taro, which

continued a few yards to an *ngun* variety of *Saccharum edule*—
around whose six-foot-tall stem twined a yam vine (*Dioscorea
pentaphylla*). Nearby was a bush of the edible-leafed *Hibiscus
manihot* and beyond it, tied to a pole, a *Psophocarpus tetragonolobus* bearing greenish-black seed pods the length of a man's
forearm. On the far side of the *Psophocarpus* began a twenty-
foot-long thicket of manioc planted here because the ground,
being "hard," was judged unsuitable for taro. Beneath the light
canopy of the manioc were a few weeds, tree seedlings, and a
drying cucumber vine from which all the fruits had been
harvested. On the far side of the manioc thicket was another
zone of taro, then a patch of ground covered with sweet potatoes dominated by the two *Saccharum* species. And so the
garden continued with successive variation to its farthest edge.
The heterogeneity of species and varieties within such a garden
extends to individuals of the same variety of a single species.
Of two taros of the same variety side-by-side, one may be waist
high and luxuriant, the other knee high and stunted—the difference being caused by variation in the richness of the soil, in the
vitality of the planting stock, and in the length of time since
planting, which may vary by weeks.

Some quantitative data on Bomagai-Angoiang gardens are
presented in Figure 4, in which I show the frequency with
which the major crops occur in 383 three-foot-square samples
observed in gardens of all types and ages. This information is
provided only as an aid in giving a quantitative impression of
what the gardens look like; frequency of occurrence need not
reflect the proportion of a crop in the garden's total yield or
the importance of that crop as food. For instance, the areal
preponderance of sweet potatoes over *Xanthosoma* is misleading because *Xanthosoma*'s production of tubers is spatially more
concentrated than that of sweet potatoes, and, I believe, the
yield per unit of area is higher for *Xanthosoma* than for sweet
potatoes.[26] My garden traverses verified my impression that

---

26. Barrau (1958: 43, 48) estimates the average yield of *Xanthosoma* in Melanesia to be eight tons per acre and that of sweet potatoes
to be three to six tons per acre.

nearly the entire Bomagai-Angoiang inventory of garden crops (about thirty-five species) occurs in all types of gardens except small, unfenced "greens gardens," which are a kind of incidental planting. One "greens garden" examined was 50 by 50 feet and contained *Hibiscus manihot* pumpkin, taro, and *Rungia klossii*, all crops not much susceptible to damage from pigs. The woman to whom the garden belonged had, after seeing a plot of what looked to her like good soil on a small section of a steep bank, planted the little unfenced garden there as a supplement to her other gardens, all of which lay within her husband's larger enclosures.

Weediness of gardens varies with their age and the industry of their managers. Some people do not weed a new

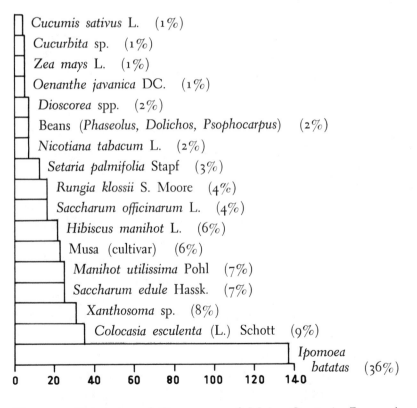

Cucumis sativus L.   (1%)

Cucurbita sp.   (1%)

Zea mays L.   (1%)

Oenanthe javanica DC.   (1%)

Dioscorea spp.   (2%)

Beans (*Phaseolus, Dolichos, Psophocarpus*)   (2%)

Nicotiana tabacum L.   (2%)

Setaria palmifolia Stapf   (3%)

Rungia klossii S. Moore   (4%)

Saccharum officinarum L.   (4%)

Hibiscus manihot L.   (6%)

Musa (cultivar)   (6%)

Manihot utilissima Pohl   (7%)

Saccharum edule Hassk.   (7%)

Xanthosoma sp.   (8%)

Colocasia esculenta (L.) Schott   (9%)

Ipomoea batatas   (36%)

0   20   40   60   80   100   120   140

Figure 4   Frequency of Occurrence of Major Crops in Bomagai-Angoiang Gardens

garden until it is two or three months old; others work more steadily. If left unweeded, a two-month-old garden may have between the crop plants an almost continuous cover of *Ageratum* and *Crassocephalum*, the two commonest weedy forbs of young gardens. Less noticeable in young gardens, but even more numerous, is the grass *Paspalum conjugatum*. Next in order of decreasing frequency the weed species are *ndiki* (a wild *Musa*), *Coleus* sp., seedlings of the tree *Homalanthus*, the ferns *Cyclosorus truncatus* and *Cyathea angiensis*, and the host of other pioneer plants listed in part in Appendix B. Gardens in their productive period of medium age are usually kept well weeded; gardens more than twelve months old become increasingly weedy until, by the time they are eighteen months old, they look more like jungle than garden.

Gardens are established everywhere within the zone indicated on Map 4, except in the *komung* and on slopes steeper than 40 to 45 degrees. As already noted, a few gardens are placed in what is considered virgin forest. Now, within the basin these are either on the basin floor at both the high southern end and the low northern exit or toward the pass that leads from the basin to the uninhabited country to the east. In altitude, 80 to 90 percent of the gardens are below 3,700 feet and 60 to 70 percent are in the *wora*, that is, in what the Bomagai-Angoiang class as the warmer and more productive part of their habitat.

Orchards. In contrast to an individual garden, which lasts only a year and a half to two years, an orchard that a man plants lasts through the rest of his life and passes on to his sons. The people's name for what I call orchards is *komba-naenk nduk*, which means *Pandanus conoideus-Gnetum gnemon* garden, indicating the orchards' two most important cultivated trees. Breadfruit (*Artocarpus altilis*) and *Ficus wassa* are minor components. The *komba-naenk nduk* are scattered everywhere on the inhabited and cultivated part of the basin floor but are especially concentrated around the base of Tsenboi Ridge between Mbɔndape and Kapam *komung* and just to the southwest of Ndembikumpf Ridge. (See Maps 3 and 4.) Orchards are also planted on the basin's lower slopes above the floor, usually in depressions or gullies where the soil is especially moist and the trees are sheltered from wind. In size, continuous stands of orchard trees vary from less than an acre to several acres. Most of the smaller stands and all of the larger stands belong to more than one owner, each man having one definite portion of the entire stand. There are no obvious boundaries separating different individuals' stands; the men simply remember which trees are theirs, often by reference to unobtrusive markers, such as a *Cordyline fruticosa* or a clump of bamboo. Because *komba-naenk nduk* need not be fenced against pigs, the boundaries between orchards and neighboring secondary growth are also unobtrusive.

The average proportion of species in the orchards is about 60 percent *komba* (*Pandanus conoideus*), 20 percent *naenk* (*Gnetum gnemon*), and 20 percent breadfruit and *Ficus wassa*. Some bamboo also is often planted in the *komba-naenk nduk*. Because the trees are spaced only ten to fifteen feet apart, there is a fairly continuous canopy, fifteen to twenty-five feet high, of the long, blade-shaped *Pandanus* leaves. Above that rise the more widely scattered, spreading breadfruit and *Ficus* and the taller, more slender *Gnetum*. The understory, which is thinned occasionally with a bush knife, consists largely of ginger, ferns, and the shade-tolerant grass *Paspalum conjugatum*. As with the gardens and secondary growth that surround them, the orchards are of all possible ages, from newly established to over-mature stages transmuting into other kinds of vegetation. All the orchard trees also appear singly here and there in gardens and secondary bush.

The resources obtained from the *komba-naenk nduk* are detailed in Appendix C and will be described further in Chapter 3. Here it is sufficient to say that the *Pandanus* fruits provide an important vegetable oil and the *Pandanus* leaves are used for roofing; the *Gnetum* gives fiber for string, and its leaves, fruits, and inflorescences are eaten; the breadfruit has edible seeds; and the *Ficus*, edible leaves. There are also edible leaves on some of the ferns that come up spontaneously in the *komba-naenk nduk*.

Dooryard Plantings. The Bomagai-Angoiang maintain many plants around their houses, as well as in their regular gardens and orchards. Examples of actual dooryard plantings will be given in the section on habitations. Here I will mention only the general categories of resources obtained from such homestead plants. Because any of the crops of the regular gardens may also be put in small dooryard gardens, emergency sustenance is available at the houses in times of sustained bad weather and when the planters feel too sick to go far from home to their larger gardens. Plants such as *Celosia argentea* and the *Coleus scutellarioides* are planted as "house adornment" about the settlement, as well as for "garden adornment" in the regular gardens. Other dooryard plants meet both ritual and decorative needs— *Cordyline* is everywhere, and an *Acalypha* species, *Codiaeum variegatum*, and *Homalomena* are common. *Bixa orellana* and *andonk* (?*Curcuma longa*), which are sometimes planted near the houses, serve both as "house adornment" and as a source of dye. Banana plants, scattered throughout the settlements, provide food as well as leaves for lining earth ovens, wrapping food, and emergency thatching; decorative fences of *Heliconia* supplement the supply of large, useful leaves. Many people put out a little tobacco as a dooryard plant and pluck the leaves for smoking material when mature. And every settlement is graced by at least one clump of bamboo, a plant of many uses.

Semicultivated Plants. Several of the plants useful to the Bomagai-Angoiang exist on both sides of the line that often in the primitive world only nebulously separates cultivated from wild vegetation. In the basin these plants grow in gardens and orchards, about the settlements, and in the secondary and altered primary communities. Their sprouting or seeding may be encouraged or only tolerated; but, once spontaneously present, they are allowed to remain until they fulfill a human need.

In the montane-crest forest the aggregation of *Pandanus*

species into groves may be totally nonanthropogenic, but I suspect that the chopping and gathering associated with collecting the products of the high-elevation *Pandanus* (especially *P. julianettii*) somehow encourage the maintenance and perhaps the expansion of *Pandanus*-dominated stands of forest. That *P. julianettii* is considered a cultivated plant elsewhere in New Guinea lends weight to this suspicion. Downslope in the lower montane rain forest there are indications that the growth of the more useful trees such as the species of *Ficus* may be encouraged by a casual slashing down of competitors. However, it is in the secondary and cultivated communities where the people move about daily that the semicultivated plants most readily originate. While, for instance, a man is clearing forest for a new

Bomagai women at ease in the fenced enclosure around a house. The woman at the right is making string from the fibers of the underbark of *Gnetum gnemon*.

homestead or orchard, he will leave uncut a *Ficus trachypison*, valuable for its abrasive leaves, and will only trim a clump of bamboo that may have sprung from a fence post put in place years ago. Spontaneous *Casuarina* are encouraged or tolerated near settlements and ritual places. In clearing for gardens, any valuable tree is apt to be only pollarded or topped, rather than felled—or, if felled, with the knowledge that the plant will sprout again from the stump. During weeding, many spontaneously occurring plants are spared; examples already mentioned are *Albizia falcataria*, the fiber-bearing *Maoutia*, and the weed forms of *Coleus* and *Setaria*. Other planted species that also grow wild or have weed forms are *Commelina cyanea*, breadfruit, *Codiaeum variegatum*, *Ficus wassa*, and *Phaleria* sp. In sum, many spontaneous plants, even those that come up in gardens and orchards, are to the Bomagai-Angoiang not pests but boons—unplanned but welcome assets that the people maintain without domesticating.

Domesticated and Tame Animals. Of the three domesticated animals—the pig, the dog, and the fowl—the pig is the most important. Almost all of the pigs now in the basin appear to be of the aboriginal type, long-snouted, slab-sided creatures classed as *Sus scrofa papuensis* by Laurie and Hill (1954), but some European varieties have been introduced into the Simbai Valley by agricultural officers and will be interbred more and more with the aboriginal type. Of the domesticated animals, the pig is the only one that contributes significantly to the people's food supply. It is always part of bride payments and—as is common in all Melanesia—is the animal that is accumulated in large numbers for recurrent ceremonial slaughters (see Vayda, forthcoming). The people feel affection for their pigs, and each animal that lives past infancy is given a personal name and becomes in a sense a member of the family.

At present there are 78 household pigs in the basin, of which 26 are adult females, 18 are adult males, and 34 are juveniles. Because most of the males are castrated before they mature, pregnancies of female domesticated pigs most frequently result from unions with the abundant feral boars. I was told, but could not confirm, that an occasional domestic male is allowed to reach sexual maturity and to mate once or a few times before being castrated. The domesticated pigs are distributed fairly evenly among the people, so that the average figure of about two pigs in the care of each woman is close to actuality, with a few exceptions. This ratio of animals to women, who do most of the work of caring for the pigs, indicates a herd of moderate size. The people say that now they have "few pigs"—a judgment that I think is doctrine until they are close to having "many pigs"—that is, enough for a mass slaughter and too many to care for conveniently. At present, the women do not complain about the work necessary to feed pigs;[27] such complaints do arise when the pig population becomes denser, as Rappaport (1967b) describes for the Maring clan cluster of Tsembaga, who live a day's walk up the Simbai Valley from the basin. Estimating from the pig-human ratio present among the Tsembaga when they had a ritual slaughter, I believe that if the Bomagai-Angoiang had forty to fifty more pigs, pig husbandry would become an unwelcome burden to the women, who would then have, on the average, between three and four pigs each. Furthermore, as pigs become more numerous, so do porcine invasions of gardens, which are a threat both to the human food supply and to amity and cohesion within the clans and the clan cluster because fights often break out when one man's pig damages another man's gardens.

Besides being killed in great numbers at the occasional mass slaughters that traditionally bore on interclan rituals of alliance and enmity,[28] pigs are also killed and eaten at times of death or illness within the clan. For example, when four women died during a short period in 1963, about twenty pigs are said to have been killed as part of the mourning ceremony. Thus, the

---

27. Pigs are allowed to forage around the outskirts of settlements and in the secondary bush during the day. In the evening they are called home and given supplementary food of manioc, small sweet potatoes, and Xanthosoma tubers that the women have harvested for them in addition to their harvesting for human needs.

28. See Rappaport (1967b) for a full description of the traditional Maring ritual cycle that leads to mass pig slaughters.

size of the pig herd depends in part on the health and survival of the people. A place is said to be "bad" if its inhabitants are often sick and consequently must kill pigs a few at a time, slowing the accumulation of animals for the mass ceremonial slaughter. A place is "good" if the number of pigs increases rapidly.

Pigs are the property of the men, but almost all pigs have their homes in compartments within the women's houses. Occasionally a man may care for and keep a piglet with him at night, but as the animal grows older he gives charge of it to his wife or a female relative, saying something similar to what one man told me: "I don't like pigs when they are alive—only when they are dead. Let the pigs stay with the women." [29]

Dogs, on the other hand, are associated with the men. They sleep in the men's houses and are named by the men, and the men talk to them in a special, high-pitched tone, joking about the dogs' sexual activities and desires. There are only thirteen dogs in the basin so that many men do not have any, but a dog's owner is usually willing to lend his dog for a hunting expedition. Too small to attack adult feral pigs effectively, the dogs do rouse pigs and serve as guides once the chase has begun. They also aid in smelling out and treeing some of the wild marsupial game. Doubtless, without the dogs hunting would be somewhat less productive or would take more of the men's time and energy; but my impression is that the dogs' help in hunting is not very significant and that dogs are more esteemed as pets and companions than as economic assets. On the other

---

29. Bulmer (1967:20) writes that the Karam of the nearby Kaironk Valley feel that "women are always potentially dangerous because of their childbearing capacities and menstrual activities, but you have to live with them. Pigs are also filthy creatures, but you have to live with them, too."

The Bomagai-Angoiang attitude is similar, although my feeling is that in the basin the men's aversion to women is not as extreme as that of the Karam men or that reported for the Central Highlands (see, for instance, Meggitt, 1964). In contrast with the reported reticence of the Enga in the Highlands (Meggitt, 1964:209–210), the Bomagai-Angoiang men often joke about sexual matters among themselves and quite casually described sexual behavior to me.

Ngirapo sharpens the blade of his axe while his dog waits nearby.

hand, unlike pigs, the few dogs are in no way a burden on the people. They are fed only small scraps of meat and bits of cooked tubers and pumpkin, which they gulp down eagerly. Unlike some New Guinean peoples, including Maring groups who live where the take from hunting wild animals is less than in the basin, the Bomagai-Angoiang never eat dogs.

The New Guinean domesticated dog is tentatively classed by Bulmer (1968:307) as *Canis familiaris hallstromi*, which is the same scientific name often applied to the feral or "wild" dog present in parts of New Guinea. Certainly the Bomagai-Angoiang dogs strongly resemble, at least superficially, the New Guinea "wild dogs" that I saw on display in the Sydney zoo. There are no feral dogs in the basin, but some Maring report that they are present in parts of the high forest. The basin dog is tan and white or black and white, prick-eared, and short-haired. They howl but rarely bark.

I did not take a census of the people's few fowl, but estimate that there are not more than thirty in the basin. Fowl are the least important of the domesticated animals and are said to be only recently introduced, which appears to be the case in some other parts of New Guinea, too (S. and R. Bulmer, 1964: 48). Little attempt is made to increase the number of fowl. The eggs when found are usually eaten, no matter what the stage of their development, so that chicks hatch only fortuitously. Occasionally a fully grown bird is killed and eaten. Fowl are casually fed some scraps and peelings; otherwise they forage for themselves about the settlements.

Morning in Ndembikumpf hamlet. The women sit in the sun and gossip before leaving for their separated gardens. There is a cassowary chick in the foreground. Behind the women are household plantings.

Much more highly valued than the domesticated fowl are the tame cassowaries, which number two adults and about seven younger birds.[30] When hunters find a cassowary's nest in the forest, they watch it off and on until the eggs hatch; then they capture the chicks, which soon become quite tame. Young birds are kept in small shelters of leaves at night; by day they are carried about by their master or follow closely after him as if they had imprinted on the human being. The birds are carefully provided with water and fed sweet potatoes, papaya, bananas, pumpkin, and perhaps other garden crops. Because as they approach maturity they begin to be dangerous, especially to children, the cassowaries are confined to a pole stockade by the time they are about three feet tall. Eventually they are either killed—by strangulation with a vine—and eaten on a special occasion by their owner and his associates or they are used in a ceremonial exchange, where a single adult cassowary has a value equal to several pigs. The people savor cassowary flesh, especially delighting in the rich orange fat or oil. The birds' long wing quills are used as decorations by inserting them through the pierced nasal septum, and the plumes are used in headdresses. The cassowary, like the dog, is a "male" animal; the pig, as already indicated, is "female." This dichotomy is common, perhaps universal, in montane New Guinea. See, for instance, Meggitt (1964:208), who describes the same conceptual division among the Enga of the Wabag area.

Feral and Wild Animals. Within the basin the wild cas-

---

30. This cassowary is probably correctly classed as *Casuarius bennetti*, which Bulmer (1967:10) lists as present in the nearby Kaironk Valley. What Bulmer writes about the cassowary there is wholly applicable to the basin's bird: "The cassowary is very much larger than any other bird, or bat, in the Karam domain. Although the local mountan species (*Casuarius bennetti*) is a pigmy cassowary, much smaller than the species in lowland New Guinea and northern Australia, adults probably weigh fifty pounds or more, at least six times as much as the harpy eagle (*Harpyopsis novaeguineae*), the largest flying bird in the region. It is in fact the largest creature in the New Guinea mountains other than man and the pig. With size goes strength. While the wild cassowary is in no sense ferocious, being timid and avoiding man as far as possible, it has powerful legs and extremely sharp claws and can inflict serious wounds if cornered."

sowaries have retreated from the zone of clearing and are found only in the remote higher parts of the lower montane rain forest and in the crest forest. Beyond the basin in the uninhabited forest to the east, the birds descend to lower elevations. The men sometimes try to creep close enough to a known cassowary nest to shoot the unsuspecting occupant. When they encounter a cassowary walking in the forest, they give chase; but few birds are taken. I estimate that only four or five are killed each year. Much more important as game are the feral pigs that roam throughout the zone of secondary vegetation, as well as in the lower reaches of the primary forest. The already large feral population of pigs is augmented by domesticated pigs that stray from home and keeper. After three or four months the owner loses claim to such strays, who then become fair game for any hunter. Countering this loss from the stock of household animals, is the gain made when feral piglets are captured alive and tamed. I estimate that three to four feral pigs are shot each month by the Bomagai-Angoiang. These animals' average weight is about fifty pounds, which means that there is somewhat over a pound of undressed pig per person per month—not an insignificant amount, considering the usual protein intake in many parts of highland New Guinea. As a further if indirect benefit to the people's diet, the more feral pigs that are killed and eaten, the fewer the pigs that are left to ravage gardens whenever they find a way through the fences. In fact, a hunt often begins because a feral pig has called adverse attention to itself by getting into a garden.

Within the basin's many environmental niches, lives a wide variety of wild animal life useful to the Bomagai-Angoiang. In Appendix D I give an incomplete inventory of this resource. Here I mention only the broad categories.

Scores of flying bird species add enlivening accents to the sights and sounds of the basin—the white gleam of cockatoos glitters against dark green valley slopes; the living notes of hidden birds chime in the somber damp of the crest forest. Sharing the basin with the birds and valuing them for feathers and food, the people know and name them all. Most birds are taken with the three-pronged arrow and are eaten after being lightly cooked in embers. If their feathers are colorful, they are worked into a headdress. Certain birds are especially sought after for plumage; most valued is an orange-plumed bird of paradise which, after being cleaned, is used whole as a headdress and is an important item of trade. The total amount of bird flesh eaten in a year is not large, but birds do provide an irregularly continuous protein supplement, especially to the good hunters, who usually eat the birds they shoot rather than sharing them, as is done with larger game. The large eggs of the flightless bush turkeys, such as *Megapodius* sp., are occasionally found and eaten.

A number of small marsupials and rodents live in the basin. As with the birds, the people name the varieties and know their

An Angoiang man dressed for a dance. Phalanger fur, bird-of-paradise plumes, and recently introduced trade beads are included in his headdress.

habits and habitats. All are hunted with arrows and traps or, in the case of garden and house rodents, caught by hand. Before being eaten, they are cooked either directly in the fire or in the earth oven. The fur of several phalangers is valued for armbands and headdresses. As with the birds, the total amount of flesh from rodents and marsupials is not large but is sporadically continuous, amounting perhaps to ten ounces monthly per person. Because men do not consider rodents a proper food, there is a channeling of wild protein to women and children. On the detrimental side, rats become a pest in older gardens, and some of the phalangers also take garden crops, especially bananas. The large, fruit-eating bats, which are also hunted and eaten, may attack bananas, too.

The basin's cold-blooded life is not neglected by the people in their search for food. Eels, taken by spear, trap, and now by hook from the many streams, are the most important resource in this class. Sometimes three feet long, the eels may weigh as much as four pounds. In certain seasons seven or eight are taken every day. Also in or near the streams are found catfish, a shrimplike crustacean, and frogs.

Away from the water the people capture and eat snakes (the largest being the green python *Chondropython viridis*), lizards, a land crab, snails, insects, and spiders. The men eat the python, larger lizards, and a much-relished grub called *kima;* small snakes they usually give to the women or children. The snails, insects other than *kima,* and spiders are generally eaten only by the children—mostly, I think, by boys—who scorch them briefly in the fire before eating.

Extra-basin Spheres of Resources and Trade. On the west the Bomagai-Angoiang territory extends over the basin's rim a short distance downslope toward the Fungai settlement of Ngunts. (See Maps 1 and 5.) At present the people have a few *Pandanus* orchards here and use the rest of the area lightly for hunting and collecting, but not for gardening. To the east on the other side of the basin, a day-and-a-half's walk away through uninhabited forest, is a place called Kumoints, where several Angoiang men have a jointly fenced sweet potato garden and both Angoiang and Bomagai men have small stands of the cultivated *Pandanus* and little unfenced "greens gardens" dominated by *Hibiscus manihot*. Setting out cultivated plants in Kumoints is not new to the Bomagai-Angoiang, but both the size and number of the unfenced plantings is greater now than it was a decade or two ago, and fenced gardens of tubers are a recent innovation. The men go to Kumoints either to hunt phalangers and birds of paradise or because the area lies about halfway on the trail between the basin and an outlying settlement of the upper Jimi River people with whom the Bomagai-Angoiang have marital connections. Decades ago fathers of men now living planted small numbers of *Pandanus conoideus* and *Hibiscus manihot* in likely places in Kumoints, such as where a windfall had opened a small spot in the rain forest. It is said that they did not fell trees themselves because the biggest trees of the primary forest were too large to cut easily with stone axes and—more to point, I think—because their enemies the Kono and Fungai also had hunting grounds in the vicinity of Kumoints and would have heard the sound of axes and come to shoot the Bomagai-Angoiang men, who were far from home. Now that the government has forbidden killing and all the men have steel axes, some men have begun to clear the forest in Kumoints.

The Angoiang sweet potato garden in Kumoints was collectively fenced and cleared in 1964 by eight Angoiang men and boys under the leadership or impetus of Ngunt, an Angoiang widower and "big man," who says that he felt the Angoiang should have more food available in Kumoints. The eight males and their female gardening partners all walked together from the basin carrying planting material. At Kumoints they built bush shelters and, after felling the trees, set out their individual garden plots within the single, collectively built fence. Now, except for the few women who pass by on visits to the upper Jimi peoples, only the males visit and care for these gardens—especially Ngunt, who is for some reason strongly drawn to Kumoints, where he spends more time than in the basin. Bomagai men tell of a similarly fenced garden of tubers that they had in Kumoints a few years ago but abandoned when it was broken into by feral pigs. Now they have only the *Pandanus* and *Hibiscus*, which are not bothered by pigs. But they will probably soon establish another bush garden.

Compared with the cultivated plants within the basin, the gardens and plantings in Kumoints provide the Bomagai-Angoiang with little food, but they do facilitate the use of the uninhabited forest as a hunting ground, from which wealth in the form of fur and feathers (later to be exchanged for wives, pigs, and other goods) can be accumulated. Also obtained from Kumoints are *kima*, the grubs greatly savored for food. The men girdle an *ap ambrap* (an unidentified tree not present within the basin) and fell it a few years later, when its decaying wood is rich with these grubs.

Before the Europeans came to the Simbai Valley, the Bomagai-Angoiang and their neighbors each formed units that were nearly self-contained economically. But, as in most of the world, considerable trade was carried on in what might be called luxury goods. Individual Bomagai and Angoiang men had trading connections with men of other groups in the Simbai Valley and with men of the Jimi Valley to the south and the Jimi Valley outposts to the east of the basin. Except for salt springs and quarries for stone axes, each of the group territories of the whole realm within which the people traveled and had trading associates contained close to the same range of necessary resources. But goods not available locally did enter this realm and move about within it; further, within the realm there had developed habits of trade that appeared to be nonessential for subsistence, with functions that were not immediately economic. The only direction in which there apparently was not a flow of trade goods to and from the basin is the north, beyond the adjacent group's territory on the northern side of which the mountains become lower toward the lowlands of the Ramu River Valley. This is the only direction in which the environment is markedly different from the mountains and may therefore have been expected to produce different and valued goods. But the lowlands held no attractions for the people of higher

Ndwimba, an Angoiang man. His outer necklace of seeds of the *Planchonella* tree is pre-European in type. The inner necklace is made of recently introduced trade beads.

ground. One man, looking out at the Ramu Valley from the basin's western rim, expressed what has probably long been the general, and accurate, view of the lowlands: "It is a bad place, hot, filled with poisonous snakes. We would fall sick if we went there."

In pre-European times the Bomagai-Angoiang could give pigs, women, plumage, fur, and forest products such as *Dendrobium* orchid stems in exchange for their imports. These same exchange items are still used, but now added to the inventory are a miscellany of accumulated European goods, as well as coins acquired as bridewealth or as payment for carrying cargo or doing other labor for the patrol officer and other outsiders. The range of desired imports has, of course, also increased; of particular interest when I was in the basin were steel tools, matches, beads, commercial salt, fishhooks, and containers. But now, as in the past, the exchange of goods across the basin's boundaries results in little net loss of materials and energy from the basin. Pigs and women move in and out in about equal numbers. The exchange expense of steel and stone tools is and was offset by the gain in efficiency of labor that comes with the use of the tools. The other items imported now or in the past necessitate only a minor outflow of products, largely renewable in any case.

Many European goods flowed through native trading links into the basin before the actual coming of the Europeans. Steel axes, followed by bush knives, appeared in the 1940s and then came in increasing numbers, while imports of stone axes died out completely. The previously vital stone work axes, as well as the thinner, more finely made ceremonial axes, came mostly from the Ganz River and the Tsenga quarries, which are located south of the Jimi River not far from the Jimi River Patrol Post. (See Map 1.) From these quarries, which were among the major quarries of highland New Guinea (Chappell, 1966), the stone blades moved outward in all directions until some became accessible to the Bomagai-Angoiang, after reaching a people such as the Jimi River Bomagai, with whom some of the basin's inhabitants had connections. The stone work axes were essential for gardening; the ceremonial axes were valued for use in ritual and war, for display, and for bridewealth. With the coming of steel, stone work axes were abandoned almost immediately in favor of the superior tools. The stone ceremonial axes may have remained of value a little longer, but now, with the end of wars and the associated ritual, they too are considered nearly worthless antiques. But axes, now of steel, remain an important part of the bridewealth.

The Bomagai-Angoiang also had pre-European trade contacts through which there moved shells (valued for adornment) and salt. The salt was relatively local in origin, coming from salt springs up the Simbai Valley. To judge from the slight information I have on this matter, it appears that at times the

Bomagai-Angoiang men could go to the springs, even though they lay well beyond their territory. I have intimations that there was a kind of *pax salina* that made possible the work of evaporating the salty water without fear of ambush. The salt from the springs was also obtained through trading links. Ropes of *Nassa* shells were probably imported long before the coming of the Europeans. The probable direction of their passage toward the basin from the place of their origin on the north coast was via the Sepik and Yuat rivers into the Kaironk Valley and thence to the upper Simbai Valley. But *Nassa* shells also at some time flowed back toward the north from the Central Highlands, for a basin man showed me what he said was an imported headband of a style characteristic of the upper Wahgi Valley. I do not know whether such movement was pre-European. Golden-lip pearl shell (*Pinctada maxima*) is also present in the basin and is still esteemed and included in bridewealth. Almost certainly the golden-lip shell that is now widespread in inland New Guinea comes from the south coast of the island and is a recent introduction into the Simbai Valley, arriving via the Jimi Valley after the Europeans had penetrated the Central Highlands in the early 1930s and began to introduce golden-lip shell in quantity as a trade item (Hughes, 1969). Very rarely the Bomagai-Angoiang obtained one of the pots with pointed ends that are made in the coastal hills to the north of the Ramu River. The pots appear to have entered the Simbai area via Bundi and the upper Jimi Valley. In 1965 there was to my knowledge only one such pot, said to be old, in the basin. It had been obtained from the upper Jimi Valley outpost that lies beyond Kumoints. A more valuable import was and still is the black wood of an unidentified palm that is brought in from the Jimi Valley and is the best wood for making bows.

In the past the import of items such as palm wood and stone work axes provided equipment that eased the Bomagai-Angoiang quest for sustenance. But—excluding from consideration the interclan exchange of women—most of the other items coming into the basin had little utilitarian value or else were also available in the basin. Pigs and salt (which could be and was obtained locally from plant ash) appear to fall into this latter category. On the other hand, shifting inequalities in the density of pigs may have stimulated trade; and the salt from salt springs was of a different chemical composition and had a different taste from the salt of plant ash (Hughes, 1969). Rappaport (1967b:108–109), speaking of the Tsembaga of the Simbai Valley, provides one explanation for the apparently nonessential trade by suggesting that, because the demand for nonutilitarian valuables is less definitely limited than the demand for such necessities as work axes, the trade in valuables by maintaining trading connections serves to ensure that the trade in necessities continues. That is, Rappaport argues that in the New Guinean situation, where relations between groups and connections between individuals in lengthy trading chains were uncontrolled by any central authority, reciprocal needs were an undependable motivation for maintaining permanent trading connections without some further goad. The rewards of the trade in luxury goods could be interpreted to be social connections, aesthetic pleasures, and psychic gratification from bargaining and acquiring that were sufficient to keep trade links open, even though most of the goods were not strictly necessary for subsistence.

Their Material Culture

Watson has suggested that the Central Highlands changed fairly recently from an economy based primarily on hunting by wandering bands to the economy of sedentary horticulturalists which was found by the European explorers. As part of the support for his argument, Watson uses the nature of the material culture of the highland people. I do not agree with all of Watson's line of reasoning or with his conclusion,[31] but his com-

---

31. I do not believe that sweet potatoes—no matter when they were introduced to New Guinea—had the revolutionary impact on agriculture that Watson attributed to the crop. Sweet potatoes yield more than taro and yams in the lower-elevation highland gardens and on poor soil, and they are more likely to survive in the higher-elevation gardens, but taro and yams together with a variety of minor crops could have provided a substantial food supply in the highlands before the

ments on material culture apply with even greater force to the Bomagai-Angoiang than they do to the highland people of whom he (1965a: 303–304) writes:

One fairly obvious point may be made at the outset: the material culture of all the Highland peoples so far reported is either portable or expendable. They produce no monumental art, stone- or earth-works, large structures such as the "house tambaran" with carved posts, canoes, slit gongs, or the like. Their implements are simple, such as the digging stick, wooden spatula for turning the soil (in some areas), bow, arrow, shield, spear, club, and small tools and containers of bamboo, bone, chipped stone, or wood. Only the polished stone axes are of great value and not readily replaced, and these are portable. With a few exceptions, probably all at the fringes of the Highland area, such as the Markham valley, pottery is absent or imported. The most widely and frequently used cooking vessel is a section of bamboo which usually is consumed the first time it is used on a fire. With a few exceptions such as pandanus nuts, large stores of food appear to be lacking.

At present, the chief cultural commitment to stable residence is found in the extensively fenced and ditched gardens, dwellings, pig houses, and, in some areas, watchtowers and palisades. The greatest waste in fighting, apart from the loss of life, was conse-quently the abandonment or destruction of these works, especially when groups were driven from their land and were obliged to take refuge with a host group or establish a new settlement elsewhere. The lack of notable additional impedimenta is consistent with a long history of nomadism and a short one of intensive, sedentary garden-ing.

---

introduction of sweet potatoes. I believe, as I suggested earlier (Clarke, 1966), that rather than the recent revolutionary change suggested by Watson, there occurred over a long period in some places a drift from extensive to intensive gardening. I see the cause of the change to be an increasing population, not a new crop. The elaborate cultivation tech-niques now associated with sweet potatoes in parts of the highlands are necessary not because of the characteristics of the sweet potato plant, but because of the intensification of the agriculture and the consequent changes in soil and spontaneous vegetation. Brookfield and White (1968) write on the same theme and detail the archaeological evidence against a recent revolution in agriculture in the New Guinea highlands.

Lacking tilled or ditched gardens, watchtowers, or palisades, having almost no food storage, and building houses smaller and more easily replaceable than many of those in the highlands, the Bomagai-Angoiang have even less labor and substance invested in material culture than the highlanders. One could say, in fact, that their organization of land rights and their knowledge of the local environment are more valuable to them than the items of material culture that I describe here.

Houses. The Bomagai-Angoiang bent to build their houses on the crests of spurs is apparent in Map 5, which shows house distribution and clan boundaries. About 70 percent of the houses are directly on the crests of spurs, and several of the remaining houses are on a prominence of some sort. When I asked the men why they placed their houses on lofty sites, they replied with some variant of one or more of the following explanations: (1) "Our fathers' grandfathers built there, so we built there"; (2) "Low ground is the place for gardens; higher ground is the place for houses"; (3) "We like to be up high where we can look around to see our place and to know who is coming"; (4) "We like to be away from the noise of the streams so that we can call out to each other." In short, as they see it, the men have traditional as well as practical and aesthetic reasons for their choice. There is a further climatic advantage to crest sites, which none of the men mentioned to me. The crests are relatively cool during the day because they are exposed to wind, whereas at night they are as warm or warmer than the basin floor onto which there is a nocturnal flow of cold air, which often veils the floor with an early-morning pool of fog, absent from the spur crests above. By June of 1965 the spur-crest location of houses was even commoner than in February of the same year, which is the time represented on Map 5, because during that interval all of the Angoiang inhabitants of the basin floor at Ndwimba Kandingo had moved to the crest of the spur at Kɔlamakai.

Such shifts of settlement are characteristic of the Bomagai-Angoiang; almost no one stays permanently at one site. The Angoiang move from the basin floor to Kɔlamakai came about

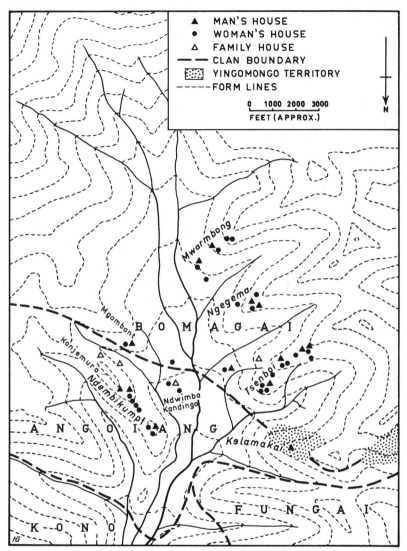

Map 5   House Distribution and Clan Boundaries, February 1965

because of the attractive force of the government rest house at nearby Tabapi, where I lived during part of my stay and where the patrol officer holds the annual census. Because the Angoiang now at Ndembikumpf are also planning to move to Kɔlamakai and some Bomagai men say they will move to Mborpe, which is Bomagai land near Tabapi, the basin population will soon become more concentrated than it has been since the 1940s. Then, after the Bomagai-Angoiang had fought the Fungai and the Kono, the Bomagai gathered at Mgambant and the Angoiang gathered at nearby Konjemuro because that part of the basin was far from their enemies and was thought to be a good place for accumulating the pigs necessary for the ritual slaughter that would resolve the consequences of the fight. Then came the dysentery epidemic, which incited the people to disperse their houses, for sickness of humans or pigs acts as a repellent force, leading the people to feel that a place is "bad" so that they want to move away from it. Sickness also raises the suspicion and fear of sorcery, which also make people want to get away from suspect neighbors.

It is naturally customary for a man to build his house on his own clan's land, either on a site that he or his father previously has occupied or on land granted by a clansman. The houses in Map 5 follow this pattern except for the two houses occupied by Angoiang that are on Bomagai land at Mgambant. Mber, the Angoiang man who built there, is also an exception to the tendency to shift house sites frequently. After helping Wun, a Bomagai "big man," clear land for houses at Mgambant while the Bomagai were aggregating there in the 1940s, Mber for some reason settled at Mgambant at Wun's invitation. When the dysentery epidemic came and all the Bomagai left Mgambant to scatter over the three Bomagai ridges (Mwarmbong, Ngegama, and Tsenboi) across the basin from Mgambant, Mber alone, with Wun's permission, remained at Mgambant. There he has lived ever since, and there he says he intends to stay, even though his wife died there and he himself was seriously ill recently. Now, at Mber's invitation, a young Angoiang man and his wife share the Mgambant site with him.

The lengthy and now expanding Angoiang occupation there suggests the possibility of a future formal annexation of Mgambant by the Angoiang. The house in *yingomongo* territory along the ridge in Kɔlamakai is occupied by Angoiang men, on a site traditionally Angoiang. It is to a place just downslope from this house that several other Angoiang men and women moved after February 1965.

All the houses look much alike—low, shaggy, brown humps —but each has individual features, some of which I show in Figure 5.

The method and materials of construction of all houses are similar. Two, three, or four large, pointed posts driven into the ground support the ridgepole. From the ridgepole, pole rafters slope down to the top of the wall and support laths of bamboo,

Housebuilding. These men are attaching prefabricated shingles of bamboo leaves to laths of *Miscanthus* grass stems and the split prop roots of *Pandanus papuanus*.

saplings, or the split prop roots of *Pandanus papuanus* to which
the roofing is attached with vines. Many plants are used for
roofing: leaves of *Pandanus* spp., bananas, the bananalike *Heliconia*, *Phrynium*, and *Alpinia*; bundles of *Imperata cylindrica*
or other grasses; or shingles prefabricated by fastening together
two large leaves of the bamboo *Bambusa forbesii*. The walls,
never more than four feet high, are made of the very long leaves
of *Pandanus papuanus* or of strips of bark, both of which
materials are fastened between a series of small posts driven
into the ground and lashed together with vines. The front of
the house is straight, the back rounded. Near the back the sides
are often farther apart than at the front, so that to crawl inside
through the low entrance—seldom more than three feet in
either direction—is like penetrating a cave with a narrow
mouth and an expanding interior. Inside the floor is packed
earth, often covered with peelings and spit-out fibers of the
sugar cane that the people eat at home as snacks and as rainy-
day food. Behind the rear ridgepole post the earth floor may
continue, or there may be a bamboo platform a few inches
high; here the people sleep, usually curled on their sides, either
on the bare bamboo or on mats woven of the leaves of *Pandanus
limbatus* or *P. danckelmannianus*. Every house has at least one
hearth, a circle of rocks around a depression. Because there is
no smoke hole and the doors are often closed with planks, smoke
from the fires, which burn all night, escapes only slowly by seep-
ing through the roof. Piles of firewood are dried on a rack
suspended above the hearth. Tucked behind the rafters, which
glisten black from the smoke, are bundles of drying tobacco
leaves and leaf-wrapped packages or bamboo tubes containing
such valuables as feathers or seeds for new gardens. In many
houses the owner has dug an earth oven near the door for use
in bad weather. In good weather outdoor earth ovens are used.

The houses are located in what could be called hamlets or
neighborhoods, each of which is in an enclosure fenced to keep
out pigs, which at night can enter the women's houses through
gateways in the fence. Most hamlets consist of a family house
or some combination of men's houses, women's houses, and

a.

a. Detail of front of house with
   front overhang of roof cut away.

FLOOR PLANS

0   5   10
|__|__|__|
    Feet

o Ridgepole posts   ╬ Wall posts
⊙ Earth oven   ⋰ Hearth
++++++ Fence

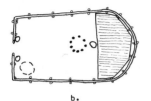

b.

b. Man's house. Two to three men
   and several boys sleep in this
   house. Bamboo platform at rear.

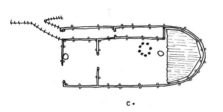

c.

c. Woman's house. A single married
   woman with no children lives in
   this house. The two compartments
   along the side are for pigs, who
   enter through their own doorway
   from a fenced passageway. The
   pigs are kept in separate compartments at night to prevent
   fighting. Like most women's
   houses, this house has an interior
   wall that secludes the woman's
   sleeping chamber from the doorway.
   Bamboo platform at rear.

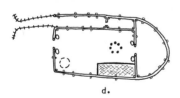

d.

d. Family house. Living in this
   house are a man and his wife,
   two small boys, and three unmarried girls. A sixth child,
   an adolescent boy, sleeps in a
   man's house at another hamlet.
   The man sleeps on the mat on the
   opposite side of the house from
   the pig compartments. The woman
   and children sleep in the rear
   chamber where there is no bamboo platform. After the children
   are asleep, the woman may go to
   the man's sleeping place. One
   pig compartment contains two
   large females, the other two
   small males. An eight-inch
   cassowary is kept inside the
   house at night.

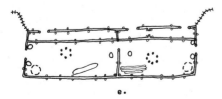

e.

e. Women's house. This is the only
   house of this type in the Basin,
   but it is said not to be an innovation—just a style seldom built.
   Each chamber is occupied by one
   woman (a mother and her daughter-
   in-law) and is essentially a separate house. Rather than mats or
   platforms, wooden planks are used
   for sleeping. The side openings
   into the pig compartments are also
   an unusual feature.

Figure 5   House Details and Floor Plans

family houses. At present the Bomagai-Angoiang have four family houses—that is, single houses in which both the husband and wife commonly sleep. Such cohabitation is usually temporary. For instance, an Angoiang husband and wife and their children, all of whom had been sick, moved from their man's and woman's houses at Ndembikumpf into a family house at Konjemuro. Now that they are settled there, the husband plans to build himself a man's house. Another family house is occupied by a childless, recently married couple who had also moved because of sickness to the newly built family house. The husband says that after his wife has a child he will build himself a separate house. In the few settlements that consist of a single house, either a man's or a woman's, the isolation is temporary, as with the solitary Bomagai woman's house in Ndwimba Kandingo. First built as a family house, this dwelling became a woman's house when the husband moved to a man's house at Tsenboi. Soon he will build a woman's house there, and his wife will abandon the house at Ndwimba Kandingo.

The plants of gardens and of spontaneous secondary communities pervade the hamlets, weaving them smoothly into the surrounding landscape. All the plants close about the houses have meaning; they all meet human needs or wants. The houses themselves, transient like the plants, take form out of local materials and then, having served, become decrepit and disappear, their materials passing to different uses. With Map 6 and its accompanying notes, I try to specify this organic character of a particular hamlet, giving an indication of the general character of all the hamlets.

Fences. Fences are made of horizontal logs or poles laid between double rows of pointed posts that are driven into the ground and fastened together with cordage of vines, strips of bark, and fern stems. On steep slopes wooden braces are added to help hold the posts upright. Where possible, large logs and slopes too steep and high for pigs to climb are incorporated into the fence line, to save labor. Before steel axes were introduced, where practicable, ditches partially excavated with dibbles and deepened by diverted streams were also used to keep

Family house in a fenced clearing.

pigs out of the gardens. Or, if pigs were especially numerous, a combination of a fence and a ditch might be used.

Tools and Weapons. The Bomagai-Angoiang received their first steel axe heads from the upper Jimi Valley in the 1940s. Initially the steel axes were hard to come by, and few men had them. For the past ten years, however, they have become increasingly available as patrol posts and airstrips have been developed in the Jimi Valley and at Simbai. All men now have one or more steel axes apiece, for wealth and for bride payments as well as for chopping. Thus, steel axes have completely replaced both the thick-bladed, stone work axe and the thin-bladed, fragile, stone ceremonial axe that was highly valued for bride payments a decade ago. The long, narrow handles attached to the steel heads are usually made from the wood of a *Garcinia* sp. and closely resemble the handles once attached

NOTES TO MAP 6

1. Abandoned woman's house built by Ndwimba, who with his wife moved from Ndembikumpf because they both were sick. The house is slowly being taken apart for firewood by the current inhabitants of the hamlet. Ndwimba and his wife, who now live in an isolated family house, often come to Ndembikumpf in the afternoon for the day's major meal and social gathering.

2. Several trimmed *Ficus wassa*. Some were planted and are privately owned; others came up spontaneously or were here before the area was cleared for houses—these belong to all.

3. Woman's house occupied by a widow and her young daughter. Her sons, one about seven, the other about ten, sleep in men's houses, sometimes in this hamlet, sometimes elsewhere. Her two pigs come home at night and are admitted to their compartments through an entrance in the fence. Five Angoiang men built her house; they also assign space to her in their garden clearings. In return she brings them food from the gardens and remains in the basin so that her sons will grow up feeling that they are Angoiang, as their father was. If she returned to her natal clan, her boys might remain there as adults.

4. Spontaneous *Ficus trachypison*, available to all. The abrasive leaves are used to polish arrow shafts.

5. Two small *Phaleria* trees belonging to Ndwimba. The underbark is used to make string; the purple-red fruits, as playthings by babies.

6. Papaya. Several papaya trees have sprung up from seeds discarded around the settlement. The papaya belong to all. Aside from being eaten, the green fruits are used by the boys, who kick them or roll them downslope as moving targets for practice with their toy bows.

7. Clump of ?*Curcuma longa* planted by one of the hamlet's women.

8. *Homalomena* sp. Several patches of this decorative and ritual plant have been set out about the hamlet.

9. Several tobacco plants. Old stalks are recurrently trimmed. Tobacco plants grown in the hamlets are fertilized with ash from the household hearths.

10. Outdoor earth oven. This public oven is the social center of the hamlet. In the midafternoon the people gather and lay banana leaves over the packed earth around it, so that they have clean surfaces on which to prepare food for cooking in the oven. After the food is cooked, the people squat about the oven and eat.

11. Public outdoor hearth where rocks are heated for cooking in the earth oven.

12. Six-and-a-half-foot-high roofed shelter that covers another public earth oven and hearth that are used on rainy days for cooking pigs.

13. Abandoned woman's house. The occupant left Ndembikumpf permanently because she was sick there.

14. Patch of tobacco plants intermixed with several spontaneous seedlings of *Ficus wassa* and *Phaleria*.

15. Sugar cane.

16. Tobacco. Many tobacco plants are scattered separately about the hamlet as well as being planted in patches (see 9 and 14).

17. Beans twining up a bamboo pole.

18. *Ap yingra məki*, the decorative and ritual *Acalypha* sp.

19. Men's house in which two adult men usually sleep—one a bachelor, the other married to the woman in House 21. Several boys often sleep here, too.

20. Currently unoccupied man's house built by the married man now

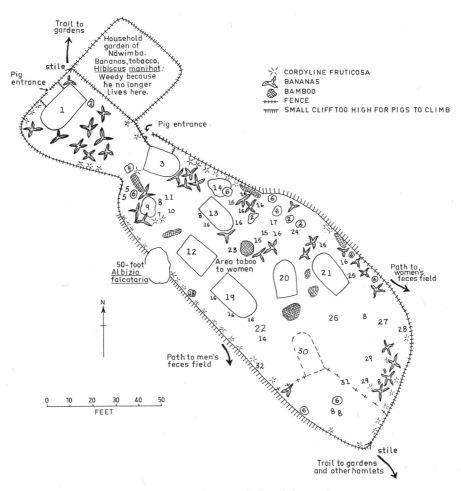

Map 6 Hamlet at Western Ndembikumpf

sleeping in House 19. He moved because the roof started to leak badly. He plans to tear down the old house and build another on the same spot.

21. Woman's house occupied by a young married woman and her nursing son. Having no pigs now, she has no need for a pig entrance. Earlier this woman lived with her husband's stepmother in the now-demolished House 30; then he built her a house of her own.

22. Stakes stacked up to dry. They will be used as wall posts in the reconstruction of House 20.

23. *Kont' mbint,* an above-ground oven for cooking the heads of male feral pigs. A ring of *Alphitonia incana* stakes bound together with vine, it is decorated with *Alphitonia* leaves whose light undersides are considered attractive. It is lined inside with banana leaves. Only the men eat the head. If male pig heads were not cooked in this fashion, the men say that their ancestors would not help them in hunting and without their help no more feral pigs would be taken. Domestic pigs are not cooked here, but in a ritual place outside the hamlet.

24. Patch of *nimp*, the *Coleus* species used as a decorative and dye plant. Planted by the woman in House 21.

25. Lima bean, *Phaseolus lunatus*, planted beside House 21, now sprawling over the roof.

26. Grassy area of hard-packed earth. Two earth-oven holes, now abandoned, remain as testimony that the area was once more used than now.

27. Young *Pandanus conoideus* planted by the man who built Houses 20 and 21.

28. Patch of wild *amami*, the *Coleus sp.* used as bedding for babies and as a breech wiper.

29. Unidentified purple-leafed forb used for decoration, which is planted by cutting.

30. Site of the demolished house of the mother of the man who built House 20. Now the site is grown with several tobacco cuttings, some tobacco seedlings, bananas, and cucumber and pumpkin vines. The cucumber and pumpkin are self-propagated from seeds that were in the house debris; ordinarily they are not planted in the hamlets. It is recognized that the ash and debris of the house make good soil.

31. Remnants of the fence that was necessary when pigs lived in House 30. Now it is mostly rotten and used for firewood. Fence built to replace it in new location shown on map.

32. Bundle of fifteen-foot bamboo poles resting against a *Cordyline fruticosa*. The poles were brought from bamboo growing on the basin floor for the reconstruction of House 20.

CORDYLINE FRUTICOSA: Omnipresent about the hamlets, especially along the fences. In places it becomes the fence or serves to support the fence. Much of the *Cordyline* belongs to all the men, who seize fresh bunches of leaves when they need them as a buttocks covering. A special red variety is owned privately and is saved to wear at ceremonies.

BANANAS: Many banana plants of all ages grow scattered through the hamlet. More valuable than the fruit are the leaves, which are used for roofing, lining the earth ovens, and wrapping food, and as clean surfaces for food preparation and eating. Each plant is privately owned by one of the men resident or once-resident in the hamlet. Once planted, the bananas are maintained permanently by encouraging the growth of suckers as the mother plant dies.

BAMBOO: Planted clumps of bamboo are privately owned, and stems may be cut only by the owner or with his permission. Bamboo that sprouts spontaneously from the fence posts belongs to all. The stems are useful as rafter poles, cooking tubes, water containers, and tubes for storing seeds, salt, and other valuables.

AREA TABOO TO WOMEN: Women passing through the hamlet must walk on the southwest side of the men's house, for the ground there is a little lower than the house. If women walked on the northeast side, which is a little higher, the men would get sick or suffer from tinea. In all hamlets the men's houses are on slightly higher ground than the women's houses.

WATER: The hamlet's inhabitants usually get water from a spring about five minute's walk to the south. When the spring dries up, during prolonged dry spells, they get water from Mbaiye Creek which is about ten minute's walk away at the base of a steep slope. Water is carried in bamboo tubes with some of the center nodes punched out.

The fenced passageway at the right admits pigs to their compartment within this woman's house. The girl wears a golden-lip pearl shell around her neck.

to the stone axe heads.[32] Bush knives, or machetes, are now common, too, but are not as highly valued as the axes, which the men keep with them almost always. Bush knives and axes are obtained as part of bride payments or by trade in exchange for pigs, feathers, or the coins accumulated by trade and by working for the patrol officer and other outsiders.

Since war was prohibited, spears and shields have not been made. Spears were made of palm wood and might be decorated with circlets of marsupial fur. The spear point was sharpened from the palmwood shaft itself or made from the beak of a bird

---

32. The stone axe heads were set between two parts of a split piece of hollowed wood, which was then tightly bound with vine, bark, or fern stems. In its turn the split piece of wood was bound to the handle.

attached with fiber to the shaft. Now valueless, few spears remain in existence. The large *Albizia*-wood shields, which were roughly incised and painted, are still used; they make good "doors" with which to close the entrances into houses when the owners are away.

Unlike the spears and shields, bows and arrows—which were also used in war—remain important today because of their use in hunting. Men walking about the basin are seldom without their bows and a handful of arrows, ready should they sight a feral pig or some wild game. The bow and three basic types of arrows are illustrated in Figure 6. The three-pronged arrow is used for birds, snakes, lizards, and small mammals, including bats. The blade-pointed arrow is used at short distances and the spear-pointed arrow at longer distances for the larger marsupials, pigs, cassowaries, and—in the past—men. The point of the spear-pointed arrow may be made of bamboo, *bəna* palm, or occasionally a hardwood dicotyledon. Some of the spear points are carved into a series of barbs designed to break up on impact, leaving many hard-to-extract pieces of wood in the body. The men say that this type of point was once made just for use against human enemies; they are still made, somewhat for nostalgic reasons, and used at times for game. The men can shoot the unfletched arrows fifty to seventy-five feet with considerable force and accuracy; beyond that distance the arrows' potency diminishes rapidly.

The dibble, so important in planting and harvesting, is the simplest of artifacts. Any stick of proper size is picked up and sharpened at one end. A man may give a sharpened dibble to his female garden-partner, or she may bring a stick to him for sharpening. As the axe and bow and arrows are to a man, so the dibble is to a woman: she scarcely ever leaves the hamlet without her dibble, using it as a staff while she walks. Unlike some people of the Central Highlands who have a wooden, paddlelike spade, neither the Bomagai-Angoiang nor any of the other Maring-speaking peoples have native digging implements other than the dibble.[33]

---

33. See, for instance, Vicedom and Tischner (1943–1948 I:185–

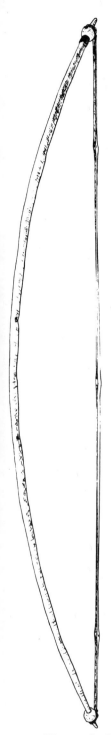

Bow: Bow of montane-crest-forest palm; string of bamboo; string brace of any available wood; binding of *Freycinetia*, *Calamus*, or *Dicranopteris linearis*.

a.

b.

c.

d.

a. Barbed point for spear-pointed arrow.

b. Spear-pointed arrow: Point of bamboo; foreshaft of palm wood; binding of *Calamus*, *Freycinetia*, and *Dicranopteris linearis*; shaft of *Miscanthus floridulus*.

c. Blade-pointed arrow: Shaft of *Miscanthus floridulus*; blade of bamboo; foreshaft of *Gulubia* palm wood; bindings of *Freycinetia*, string, and *Dicranopteris linearis*.

d. Three-pronged arrow: Shaft of *Miscanthus floridulus*; prongs of hardwood *ap kamjeka*; binding of fiber from *Gnetum gnemon*; glued with exudate of *Euroschinus papuanus*.

Figure 6   Bomagai-Angoiang Bow and Arrows

Wut with Bomagai-Angoiang bow and arrows.

Containers. Net bags are woven by the women from the tough string they make by twining together on their thighs the underbark of several trees, both cultivated and spontaneous. The string may be dyed with *andonk* (? *Curcuma longa*) or *Bixa* and decorated with strands of marsupial fur. The weaving is skillfully done with the help of *Pandanus*-leaf spacers and a needle made from the wing bone of the large bat *Dobsonia*

186) for a description of the wooden spade of the people living near Mount Hagen in the Central Highlands (Map. 1).

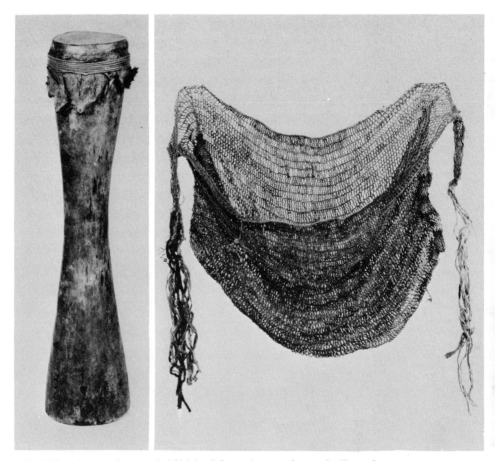

Left: This dance drum of *Albizia falcataria* wood was hollowed out with burning coals. The drumhead is of skin of wallaby *Thylogale bruijni browni*. It is 20 inches high. Right: The ubiquitous net carrying bag, which is made by the women with locally manufactured string.

moluccensis. Loosely woven, the bags are elastic but quite strong; a woman may carry home from the gardens as much as fifty pounds in a single bag. Lined with a *Pandanus*-leaf mat and soft *Coleus* leaves, the bags also serve to carry babies.

The large leaves of many types of plants are used to wrap food for cooking and goods, such as feathers, for storage. Soft leaves folded into wrapping material include those of *Heliconia*, *Phrynium*, and the wild and cultivated banana; if a sturdy pack-

age is wanted, palm sheaths or tough *Pandanus* leaves are used
as an outer wrapping. Packages are tied with vines, strips of
bark, or the stems of grasses and ferns.

Tubes of bamboo are used for cooking, storage, and carrying water. Beans, greens, small game, or *Pandanus* sauce are
stuffed into a tube, open at one end; then the open end is
plugged with leaves, and the tube is put in the fire; before the
bamboo is burned through, the food is cooked. Stopped-up
tubes are also used to hold feathers, seeds, and *Pandanus* oil.
Segments of large bamboo many feet long are the principal
water containers. With all the node partitions punched out
except the bottom one, such a tube will hold many quarts of
water. *Lagenaria* gourds and the large shells of cassowary and
bush turkey eggs are, like bamboo, used for storage, especially
of *Pandanus* oil and salt. Thin strips of bamboo fastened with
vine or fern stems are used to make cages for newly caught
cassowary chicks.

In the course of food preparation the Bomagai-Angoiang
need something like a bowl only when making the sauce of
cultivated *Pandanus* seeds. This need is met by folding up the
edges of palm sheaths or with a large wooden bowl hollowed out
with an axe. Water dishes for cassowaries are made from the
halves of gourds or carved from the soft wood of *Cyathea
angiensis*. One *Cyathea* dish was equipped with a lid of the
same material to prevent dogs from drinking the cassowaries'
water.

No pottery is made in the vicinity of the basin, but the people have received a few pots by trade. One man has a bomb-
shaped pot with a pointed bottom that he got in trade from
upper Jimi Valley people who may have gotten it from further
east or from the Ramu Valley. Aufenanger and Höltker (1949:
9, 55) report that pots that look very similar are imported from
the Ramu Valley by the Gende, who live in the Bismarck Range
about fifty miles southeast of the basin.

Bridges. Smaller streams are forded. Where busy trails cross
larger streams, log bridges are made, either of a single large log
or several smaller logs lashed together with vine.

Rain shelters. While the men are clearing forest for a garden, they often build a lean-to scaffold of poles covered with large leaves, such as those of the wild banana. Here they sit during showers or when they are hot on sunny days. After the clearing is finished, the shelters are not maintained for use by the women during garden work. When it rains while a woman is away from home, she makes an umbrella of any available large leaf.

Fire saws. Before the introduction of matches, which are a popular item of trade, a fire was started with a fire saw, consisting of a strip of bamboo that was whipped back and forth under a split stick whose halves were held apart by dry tinder. With such a device tinder can be ignited within thirty seconds.

Above-ground ovens. I have described a *kont' mbint* (Note 23, Map 6), made by lining a circle of stakes with leaves. Another, but nonritual, kind of above-ground oven is made by coiling and fastening the flexible bark of a tree known as *ap wombəna* into a cylinder. Before each use the oven is lined with leaves, usually banana.

Traps. For small game the Bomagai-Angoiang makes snares with nooses of vine, and triggers and springs of vine and sticks. Pit traps with sharpened stakes at the bottom are put along the trails of feral pigs. The most elaborate trap is for eels; it is made of a cylinder of *ap krm* (a *Lauraceae*) and connected sticks and vines that spring the cylinder's opening shut and enclose the eel when it takes the insect bait. This trap is effective, but entraps only one eel in a night. Perhaps ill-advisedly, I took into the basin as trade goods nylon line and fishhooks, which turned out to be immensely popular because they enabled one man to catch several eels in a short time. As a result, most men abandoned the eel traps shortly after my arrival. Eels are also caught by building dams of rocks lined with leaves and then rousing the eels and seizing them by hand with an abrasive leaf, such as that of *Ficus pachyrachis*, that makes it difficult for the eel to slip away.

Mats. The leaves of several of the species of wild *Pandanus* are woven into mats for sleeping surfaces or for lining net-bag

Nakemba is weaving *Dicranopteris* fern into a belt like
the one he is wearing over his bark waistband. The
"brass" on his forehead is the emblem of a *tultul*, a community official appointed by the patrol officers.

baby carriers. Before being woven, the leaves are dried, their
spines are removed, and they may be softened by being passed
through fire.

Drums: (See page 115). The Bomagai-Angoiang drums are
ceremonial; they are never used for signaling. They are made
either of wood from *Albizia falcataria* or from two other trees
for which I have no identification. The wood is carved into an
hourglass shape, hollowed out inside by blowing on hot coals
through a bamboo tube. The drumhead is made of the skin of
the wallaby *Thylogale bruijni browni* with a strip of intact fur

as decoration. The head is tied on with vine or with the locally made string and sealed with clay.

Clothing and Bodily Decoration. Women wear belts of bark or string, from which they suspend small aprons of separate strands of string over their genitals and buttocks. Carefully modest, the women are always concealed. Over their genitals the men wear—with less concern for modesty—strips of woven string. Behind they wear a bunch of *Cordyline* leaves or sometimes a spray of ferns. Their belts may be of flexible bark, vine, or woven strands of fiber. Recently the people have obtained some cloth, which the men substitute for the native coverings, and the women wear hanging from their heads.

Adorning the body is an integral part of preparing for a ceremonial dance. Women and—especially—men also casually decorate themselves in daily life. The simplest adornment is "grease," which, by making the skin shiny, is considered to enhance a man's or woman's beauty. Sources of "grease" are oil squeezed from the cultivated *Pandanus* and fat from pigs and cassowaries. Face and body paint is made from red and black earths, charcoal, *Bixa* seeds, and from a white, chalky mineral imported into the basin from the Jimi Valley and the upper Simbai Valley. Necklaces are still made of seeds and trade shells and armbands are still woven from fibers of fern (*Dicranopteris*) and palm (*Calamus*); but recently introduced glass beads will probably soon replace the native materials. Marsupial fur is made into armbands as well as headdresses. Another headdress still popular is made from the green shells of a beetle (*Cetoniidae*) set in the yellow stems of the *Dendrobium* orchid, but glass beads strung on nylon line will soon replace this, too. Feathers make the most valued headdresses. Feathers from many kinds of birds are used; the yellow and red-orange feathers from two species of bird of paradise are the most highly valued. Men and boys often pick fern leaves or flowers, such as *Celosia argentea* and the white plumes of *Imperata* grass, to stick in their hair as a decoration. The bark cloth turbans that the people once wore over their uncut hair during certain stages of their lives were painted with *Bixa* and the other coloring agents.

An Angoiang man strips a piece of flexible bark for a waistband from an *ap krm* (*Lauraceae*).

Since the coming of the patrol officers, the turbans have been abandoned and all the Bomagai-Angoiang keep their hair cut short "in the style of the kiap" (kiap: Pidgin-English for patrol officer). Some men wear cassowary quills and lengths of wood through their pierced nasal septums; some men and women have made small holes along the flare of their noses into which they stick toothpick-like pieces of wood.

Funeral platforms. Now, at the suggestion of the patrol officer, the people bury their dead. Previously, in accord with a custom widespread in New Guinea, they laid a dead person on a platform, which I gather was a simple scaffold of poles. *Cordyline* and perhaps other ritual plants were planted beside the platform. Eventually the platform rotted, along with the body, and fell down; then a little earth, leaves, or sticks might be put over the pile of rotted wood and bones. The ritual plants remained as a reminder of the dead person and the place of burial. Each subclan has a burial place, but people need not be buried there. One man, for instance, recently buried his wife under some *Cordyline* just beyond his hamlet fence, saying, "When I look at the *rumbim*, I think of my wife."

CHAPTER THREE

Place and People

A tree has roots, but men do not;
we must plant or we would die.
—NAKEMBA, *an Angoiang man*

Examples of Subsistence Behavior

Within the Bomagai and Angoiang clans the basic food-pro-
ducing unit is the individual land-owning man and his female
garden partner or partners. But this unit is far from self-contained: all persons are integrated with the rest of the clan
population—and to a lesser extent with nearby extraclan populations—through a network of social ties inseparable from economic connections. To illustrate this human integration and
to show some of the interactions between place and people, I
will use the subsistence behavior of three Angoiang men.

Example 1: Tamo. Tamo is a bachelor about twenty years
old. His mother and father are dead. His consanguineal relatives
in the basin are his brother Nek, (a bachelor about eighteen
years old), and his half-brother Ndwimba (a married man about
forty years old). Tamo lives at Ndembikumpf in the same men's
house as Kunbun (a young married man) and several boys.
Because he is young and unmarried, Tamo is not an important
man. He says of himself that he is a "little man" or a "nothing
man" who does not know about *kunda*.[1]

In June 1965 Tamo had three gardens in operation (Map
7, Figure 7). In order from youngest to oldest these were:

---

1. *Kunda* is a power and knowledge that some men have but
others lack. It seems not to be inherited, but only acquired and learned
from an older man. Many men live all their lives without having *kunda*.
I know little about its value and importance, but did learn that men
with *kunda* are said to be able to control the weather—to bring or repel
rain clouds. Also, it is men with *kunda* who have a ritually important
"garden heart" in their taro-yam grounds.

1. A *Hibiscus manihot-Xanthosoma* garden (*kem-kong nduk*). In August and September 1964 Tamo and his brother Nek cut down the secondary forest that had grown up on this plot since their father had cleared it of virgin forest fifteen to twenty years before. Tamo and Nek do not remember the earlier garden; Ndwimba and other older Angoiang men told them that the plot was theirs. In October and November 1964 they fenced the garden and burned some of the debris; then with their female garden partners they planted the crops. By June 1965 sweet potatoes, *Saccharum edule*, taro, *Xanthosoma*, *Hibiscus manihot*, and *Oenanthe* were being harvested. Manioc, sugar cane, bananas, and the yams were not yet ripe. When he planted this plot, Tamo thought the land was suitable for a taro-yam garden; but, because he and Nek lacked *wump* [2] for that sort of garden, they made the plot a "garden nothing" with the emphasis on the edible-leafed *kem* and the tuber-bearing *Xanthosoma*. It is, Tamo says, not proper to ask other gardeners for *wump*, especially of the ritually potent taro and yams; if you do, they will demand payment.

The two women who agreed to be Tamo's and Nek's garden partners were Yema, who was Ndwimba's wife, and Manepna, who was one of the two wives of an Angoiang man called Nakemba. Each woman chose a part of the clearing for her own. Tamo and Nek then laid or pointed out "marks" along

---

2. *Wump* is any kind of planting material, be it cucumber seeds, sweet potato vines, manioc stems, or the tops of taro tubers. Nek had little *wump* because he was one of the young men who had returned in February 1964 from two years of labor on a coconut plantation. In late 1964 he was still in the process of establishing a set of gardens.

Some *wump* can be taken directly from an old garden to a new garden, as needed; other kinds of *wump* require advance planning and storage. In the former class are banana suckers, *Xanthosoma* and taro cuttings and spouts, cuttings of sweet potato vines, and stem sections of the *Saccharum* species, *Hibiscus manihot*, and manioc. In the latter class are yams and the seed-planted crops, such as corn, cucumbers, pumpkins, and *Brassica*. Seeds are stored in packages above the hearth, where the smoke protects them from insect damage. Yams are stored in the garden under stumps and in other sheltered spots, where they dry until ready to sprout. In their casual treatment of yams, especially *D. esculenta*, the Bomagai-Angoiang are quite different from their neighbors the Fungai-Korama. (See *Dioscorea esculenta* in Appendix C.)

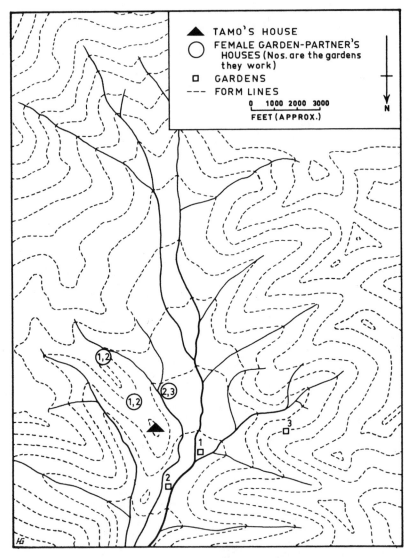

Map 7   Tamo's Gardens, June 1965

the line of division: rocks, stumps, logs, or piles of trash. The
men planted mostly the tall "male" crops of sugar cane, *Saccharum edule,* and bananas; the women planted the shorter
"female" crops, especially the sweet potato. Men may plant
almost any crop, and they know the varieties of—say—taro and
Hibiscus manihot, but only the women know all the many
varieties of sweet potato.

Tamo and Nek feel this garden to be theirs *yingomongo*, that is, jointly owned; they do not see particular sections as the private property of one man rather than the other. When it is time for the male task of tying supports around the sugar cane, they will do it together. The women, on the other hand, work only in their own sections. In return for their allotment of cleared land, the women give food to Nek and Tamo almost every day, if not from this garden, from plots given to them in other men's gardens.

2. A taro-yam garden (*ndang-wan nduk*). Tamo cleared this plot *yingomongo* with Sekwoi, a fatherless sixteen-year-old Angoiang, who lives in the same men's house as Tamo. Before they cleared it, Ndwimba is reported to have said to Tamo: "I am going to clear some land in Mbembria where my father once had a garden; next to it is some *ap ngɔni* ["large"or "well developed forest," either primary or secondary]. You clear there, and the land will be yours."

This garden was planted about June 1964 by Tamo and Sekwoi with three women, Manepna, Yema, and Kange, who is Sekwoi's widowed mother. A year later in June 1965 the taro was said to be finished; only taro *wump* remained. Cucumbers and pumpkins had been gone for months. Most yams had been harvested. Sweet potatoes, whose vines still made a solid cover across the garden, had been being taken out for many months, but some tubers were still available. Manioc, *Saccharum edule*, *Hibiscus manihot*, a *Dolichos* bean growing along the fence, and *Xanthosoma* were all yielding. Bananas and sugar cane were beginning to yield.

A year before this garden was planted, Sekwoi had set out a small trial garden, but the garden shared with Tamo was his first real garden. Tamo agreed to clear *yingomongo* with Sekwoi because the boy, who belonged to the same subclan as Tamo, had no father to teach him gardening techniques and because Tamo was a close associate of Kunbun, Sekwoi's half-brother.

3. A sugar cane-*Saccharum edule* garden (*mbo-mungap nduk*). This garden is part of a large enclosure, cleared and fenced jointly by several Angoiang men. The land is Bomagai-Angoiang *yingomongo* territory that belongs to Wut, a Bomagai

man, who gave the Angoiang men usufructuary rights to plant there. Once the plot was cleared, each man chose a particular section for his own and marked it off from his neighbors' sections with subtle "marks" of logs and trash.

After the clearing, Tamo and his mother, who was his initial garden partner here, wanted to burn the trash, but for several weeks it was not dry enough. Finally, Tamo said, "Forget about burning," and called together several persons who helped him throw the trash over the fence at the bottom of the garden. He and his mother planted the garden in October and November 1963; then his mother died, and Sekwoi's mother, Kange, took over her work.

In June 1965 the garden produced *Rungia klossii*, sugar cane, *Saccharum edule*, bananas, and *Hibiscus manihot*. The *Saccharum* species dominated the view, with *S. edule* six to seven feet high and some sugar cane tied into bundles fifteen feet high. In some places sweet potato vines still covered the ground, but there were no large tubers left to harvest; in other places the ground was covered with the two-foot-high weedy grass *Paspalum conjugatum*.

Details of the size, shape, and site of each of Tamo's gardens are given in Figure 7.[3] If half the square footage of each of the shared gardens (1 and 2) were combined with the square footage of his individual garden (3), the total would be 52,200 square feet, or 1.2 acres, in operation in June 1965. Shortly after June, Garden 3 was completely abandoned, but the loss was counterbalanced by the establishment of another taro-yam garden with *wump* from Garden 2. Tamo shares with Nek a total of about 0.7 acre of *Pandanus* orchards planted in various places by their father. After Tamo and Nek marry, they will come to an agreement about dividing their joint orchards into individual holdings. Tamo also plans fairly soon to plant a new *Pandanus* orchard of his own.

---

3. The gardens were measured in the field with tape and compass. A variety of obstacles and the often steep topography lent inexactness to the figures.

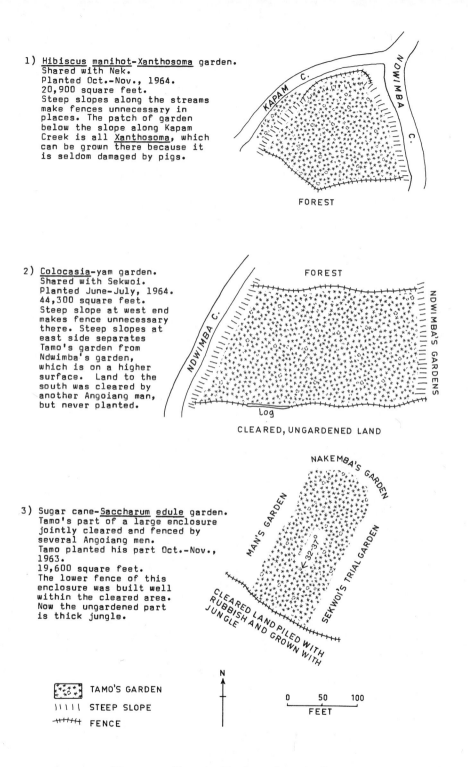

1) <u>Hibiscus manihot-Xanthosoma</u> garden.
Shared with Nek.
Planted Oct.-Nov., 1964.
20,900 square feet.
Steep slopes along the streams
make fences unnecessary in
places. The patch of garden
below the slope along Kapam
Creek is all <u>Xanthosoma</u>, which
can be grown there because it
is seldom damaged by pigs.

KAPAM C.

NDWIMBA C.

FOREST

2) <u>Colocasia</u>-yam garden.
Shared with Sekwoi.
Planted June-July, 1964.
44,300 square feet.
Steep slope at west end
makes fence unnecessary
there. Steep slopes at
east side separates
Tamo's garden from
Ndwimba's garden,
which is on a higher
surface. Land to the
south was cleared by
another Angoiang man,
but never planted.

FOREST

NDWIMBA C.

NDWIMBA'S GARDENS

Log

CLEARED, UNGARDENED LAND

NAKEMBA'S GARDEN

MAN'S GARDEN

32-37°

SEKWOI'S TRIAL GARDEN

3) Sugar cane-<u>Saccharum edule</u> garden.
Tamo's part of a large enclosure
jointly cleared and fenced by
several Angoiang men.
Tamo planted his part Oct.-Nov.,
1963.
19,600 square feet.
The lower fence of this
enclosure was built well
within the cleared area.
Now the ungardened part
is thick jungle.

CLEARED LAND PILED WITH
RUBBISH AND GROWN WITH
JUNGLE

TAMO'S GARDEN

||||| STEEP SLOPE

+++++ FENCE

N

0   50   100
FEET

Figure 7   Tamo's Gardens, June 1965

Example 2: Kunbun. Kunbun is a young, energetic married man about twenty-three. His mother has been dead for many years; his father, for about ten years. His closest consanguineal relatives are two half-brothers, the children of his father and his stepmother, Kange, who is still living. Kunbun's wife, Rameka, has one child, an infant boy.

In June 1965 Kunbun said that he had two gardens in operation; but because both of these spatially defined gardens, which I describe below, were divided into two or more parts of different ages, he had more than two gardens in a functional sense.

1. A sugar cane-*Saccharum edule* garden (*mbo-mungap nduk*). Kunbun began clearing his newest garden (Map 8, 1) in unclaimed *ap ngəni* between March and May 1964. He fenced, and he and Rameka planted, part of the garden in May and June 1964. Then in September 1964 he extended the clearing out from the existing garden, and he and Rameka planted an area that only partially filled the new clearing. In May 1965 he filled in about 800 square feet of the unplanted area with bananas and *Saccharum edule*; but there still remains more unplanted, cleared land, which Kunbun says he will plant later. The planted area totaled 25,000 square feet in June 1965.

2. A taro-yam garden (*ndang-wan nduk*). This garden is in the same large enclosure on Bomagai-Angoiang *yingomongo* land as Tamo's Garden 3. After receiving his section following the joint clearing and fencing, Kunbun with Rameka planted the upper part of it in September and October 1963. Several months later Kunbun cleared the lower part of the jungle growth that had grown up since the initial clearing. Then he planted *Saccharum edule* and *Xanthosoma* along part of the edge of the clearing and taro farther in; Rameka planted sweet potatoes throughout much of the garden but not adjacent to the *Xanthosoma*, which, if concentrated in a patch, casts a dense shade when mature. When I asked about the part of the clearing still unplanted, Kunbun replied that he might plant it later with cuttings of sweet potato vines taken from his clansman Nakemba's adjoining garden when it was abandoned. In

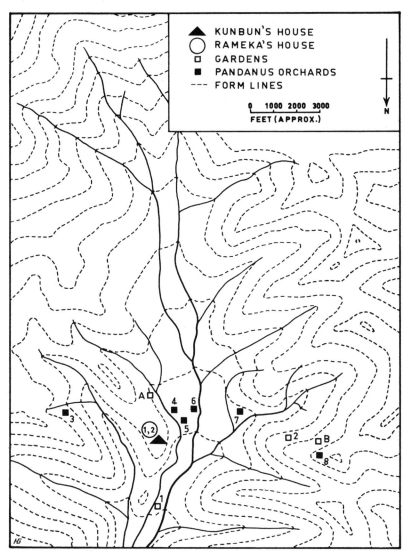

KUNBUN'S HOUSE
RAMEKA'S HOUSE
GARDENS
PANDANUS ORCHARDS
--- FORM LINES

0   1000 2000 3000
FEET (APPROX.)

N

Map 8   Kunbun's Gardens, June 1965

June 1965 the planted parts of this garden totaled 15,400 square feet.

Kunbun had in all in June 1965, 40,400 square feet of garden in operation, although the upper part of Garden 2 was yielding only *Hibiscus manihot*, bananas, and the *Saccharum* species.[4] He also had a garden abandoned to regrowth (Map 8, A) except for the occasional forays that he and Rameka made there for sugar cane, because the garden was convenient to their houses and to the route between their houses and Garden 2. In June 1965 Kunbun was clearing land (Map 8, B) inherited from his father in Bomagai-Angoiang *yingomongo* territory. There he will establish a taro-yam garden.

It is clear from Kunbun's situation that, within what initially appears to be a single garden surrounded by a fence built at one time, there may be several lesser gardens of different ages, each with a different mixture of crops. Because of this division within a single fence and because of the way in which planting and harvesting crest and diminish over a long time even in a single subdivision, only ambiguous agricultural calendars can be made for the set of gardens belonging to a Bomagai-Angoiang man. That it is difficult to construct such a calendar points out the organic complexity of the people's agriculture. Neither in space nor in time are the gardens neatly mechanical —either on or off. Instead they are often conceived on impulse, develop slowly, reach their primes, decline, and are diverted along the way like the living things they are. Despite the impossibility of accurate representation, I have tried in Figure 8 to show what I know of the approximate lifetimes and overlap of production of Kunbun's more important gardens during four years. At any time he had at least two gardens in some stage of fairly high production and generally had another garden or two coming in or going out of production. The tendency to plant taro-yam gardens during the dry season is also apparent.

---

4. This upper section was then more than eighteen months old and would have been used less, had it not been conveniently located next to the newer section.

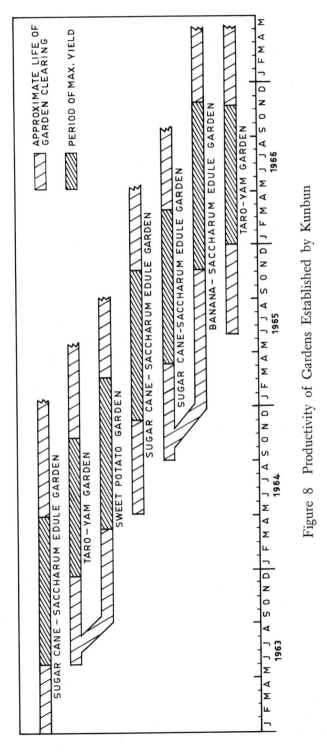

Figure 8   Productivity of Gardens Established by Kunbun

Before I arrived in the basin, Kunbun had a small pig that he had bought with feathers and that he cared for for several months while living in a little house in the middle of one of his gardens. As nearly as I could understand, his motive in staying there was to keep the pig from falling sick through sorcery. Eventually he gave the pig to a friend belonging to a clan located several hours' walk up the Simbai Valley. Later, he expected to receive a piglet in return.

Rameka now works only Kunbun's gardens. Probably as she becomes more integrated into the clan, she will become a garden partner to another Angoiang male, perhaps one of Kunbun's half-brothers. Because of the distance between Kunbun's gardens, she usually goes to only one in a day. Rising near dawn, she begins her day slowly by feeding her baby and putting wood on the embers in her hearth. She eats either food already cooked and stored overnight in leaves or else tubers cooked that morning on the hearth. Some mornings Kunbun asks her for food; other days he cooks tubers for himself on the hearth in the men's house. After she has eaten, if it is sunny, Rameka joins a group of women sitting outside at her hamlet or the nearby hamlet gossiping, making thread or net bags, and picking lice from each others' heads.[5] After an hour or so of sitting in the sun, she gets ready to leave the hamlet with her digging stick and two net bags, one a cradle for her baby, the other a carryall for garden produce. The walk to Garden 1 takes half an hour, that to Garden 2, nearly an hour. In the gardens she works at weeding and harvesting. Light weeds she pulls up by the roots and lay on stumps, rocks, or logs to dry; heavier weeds she pries out with her dibble or cuts with the bush knife she

---

5. On rainy mornings people stay inside their houses. If the rain continues later in the day, they make quick trips to nearby gardens for greens, bananas, pumpkins, and sugar cane, or else they collect food from the hamlet's household plants. Little digging is done for tubers in the rain. Consequently, after a rainy day everyone says "I haven't eaten anything today," meaning that they have not eaten any root crops, or "real food." On rainy days Kunbun would not expect Rameka to bring anything from the distant gardens; on other days, unless she were ill, he would chide her if she did not bring him food from the regular gardens.

sometimes carries. She harvests concurrently with weeding; as she moves about the garden, she gradually fills the net bag, digging up a sweet potato here and taking a handful of greens there. Frequently she stops to rest and play with or feed her baby. For lunch she eats a cooked tuber brought from home; or, if Kubun is near, they may make a fire and cook tubers in the garden. When Kunbun is in the gardens to plant or to tie sugar cane or to mend a fence, he weeds and harvests, too, but seldom for as long a time as Rameka. Between two and three in the afternoon Rameka starts home with her baby and the net bag, now full of tubers, greens, and other produce weighing at least twenty or thirty pounds. On the way home she may pick up some firewood from an *Alphitonia* tree felled earlier by Kunbun

Rameka in her garden. The bag on her lap serves as a cradle. The bag to her right she fills with food as she combines harvesting with weeding.

A midday meal in the garden. Tubers are roasted in the fire
in the foreground. The boy is holding a catfish he has just
caught in a nearby stream.

so that it would dry. When she reaches the hamlet, she lays
aside her burdens and fetches water if necessary or sends a young
boy for it. (See Map 6 n.) Then together with Kunbun and
others she begins the preparation of the day's main meal.

Kunbun's days are less regular. He may do other garden
tasks for himself or clansmen. He may go on a collecting trip.
He may loaf. He may set out to do one thing and end up doing
another, as when he comes across a feral pig and takes up the
hunt. On his way home he often collects firewood, too, or
harvests and cores a *Pandanus* fruit or gathers fern leaves,

bananas, and sugar cane to take to the hamlet. On arrival he frequently eats two or three stalks of sugar cane or several bananas rapidly. Then, if a feral pig has been taken, he and Tamo and any visiting men clean it and build a fire of cross-stacked wood on which to heat the rocks for the earth oven.

Meanwhile, squatting about the fire and the oven pit, the women prepare the food from the gardens. When the rocks are hot and the oven pit lined with fresh leaves, the greens, tubers, fern leaves, pig or other meat, pumpkins, and *Pandanus* are put in the pit alternately with the hot rocks, which are picked from the fire between the halves of a partially split stick. When full, the oven pit is sealed with leaves, and more rocks are laid on top. In about an hour and a half the oven is opened, sauce is made from the *Pandanus* seeds, and the food is distributed,

Kunbun displays a young feral pig he has just shot.

some to the immediate group and some in leaf-wrapped packages carried by boys to people in other hamlets.

It is nearly dark by the time the meal is over. The people,
especially the men, may sit for a while talking around an outside fire, but before long they usually go into their houses. On
some nights, however, men may go eel fishing or, when it has
been prearranged, unmarried adolescent girls visiting from
another clan may meet with bachelors and young married men
in a nearby house to rub noses with each other—a pan-Highland
form of courtship. On other nights men may travel some
distance to a nose-rubbing party in another clan's territory.

The spatial and temporal arrangement of Kunbun's six
Pandanus orchards (*komba-naenk nduk*) is fairly typical of the
Bomagai-Angoiang. His Orchard 3 (Map 8) is in primary forest

This 120-pound feral boar is being prepared for the earth oven. Its
entrails will be cooked separately after washing.

on a steep slope to the east of the basin settlements. Alone in this orchard are four old *Pandanus* trees, planted before Kunbun's birth by his father when he found a place in the forest where a large tree had fallen and left a clearing with soft soil. Kunbun harvests the fruit if he is in the vicinity, but he will not plant more trees there. When the yield of the present trees starts to decline, he says that he will forget about this orchard and think about his new orchard (7).

Orchard 4 was also planted by his father before Kunbun was born. It contains about thirty-five *Pandanus* trees, ten *Gnetum gnemon*, ten *Ficus wassa*, and seven breadfruit. Some of the trees are close to death; others will yield for a long time. Kunbun and Rameka weed the orchard by slashing the grass, ferns, and saplings with bush knives.

Late afternoon in Ndembikumpf hamlet brings the main meal and social hour.

Orchard 5 is his largest orchard now, but it is close to being abandoned because so many of the trees, which were planted by his father before Kunbun's birth, are past their prime. Weeded only slightly, the orchard is a jungle of tall grasses and the fern *Dicranopteris linearis*. After the orchard is abandoned, some of the cultivated trees will serve as "marks" to ensure the claim of Kunbun and his son to the plot where the orchard has stood.

This orchard covers about 19,000 square feet and contains seventy to a hundred *Pandanus* trees of many varieties. Between the *Pandanus* grow the usual lesser numbers of *Gnetum*, breadfruit, and *Ficus wassa*, as well as: a clump of bamboo belonging to the Angoiang man Nakemba (planted with Kunbun's permission) and surrounded by a stake fence to protect it from pigs; *Cyathea* tree ferns from which Kunbun and Rameka collect leaves; a few ten-foot shoots of bamboo sprouting from the roots of a large clump planted by Kunbun's father and cut by Kunbun for house construction; an eighty-foot *ap krm* (*Lauraceae*) left uncut when the orchard was established because of its flexible bark, valued for making belts; a *Ficus dammaropsis*, valued for its large leaves and edible buds; and about sixty square feet of the bamboo *Bambusa forbesii* planted, says Kunbun, by his father when Kunbun was a boy, so that when Kunbun grew up he would have roofing material.

Orchard 6 was planted by his father while he was a young, unmarried man. About twenty trees still bear. Here, as in the other orchards, the *Pandanus* fruits are harvested by knocking them down with a bamboo pole left in the orchard leaning against a tree. The breadfruit can be harvested the same way or by climbing the tree. The *Gnetum* and *Ficus* leaves are taken by climbing the trees.

Orchard 7 is only incipient. In December 1964 Kunbun began to clear forest on Bomagai land previously owned by his cousin Wun, who gave the land to Kunbun, saying, "We are cousins, so I give you this land for a *komba-naenk nduk*. It will always be yours and then your son's." Kunbun says that because he and Wun are cousins Wun expects no direct repayment of this favor. By June 1965 Kunbun had still not felled all the trees or begun planting on this plot, but he will in time plant a sugar cane-*Saccharum edule* garden in which he will include *Pandanus* cuttings and *Gnetum* seedlings. After the short-lived crops have been harvested and the garden fence has rotted, the trees will remain, and the *Pandanus* orchard will come into full existence. Orchards are often started this way on the basin floor. On the lower slopes in the sheltered gullies that are especially favored as orchard sites, the orchards are more often established immediately without a preliminary phase as part of a garden of short-lived crops. The common practice of planting at least a few *Pandanus* trees while establishing a regular garden tests that site's suitability for an orchard, while providing quick gain from the yield of the short-lived crops.

Orchard 8 is a small group of immature trees that Kunbun planted in 1962 not far from the government rest house at Tabapi. This land belonged to a Bomagai man, who let Kunbun establish the orchard because Kunbun wanted to have a supply of *Pandanus* close at hand when he stayed at Tabapi for the annual census and other events connected with visiting Europeans, in whom he is intensely interested.

All told, Kunbun manages more than three-quarters of an acre of *Pandanus* orchards, which contain one hundred and thirty to one hundred and sixty trees. Because all his currently productive orchards were established by his father, Kunbun's half-brothers and his stepmother have a claim on the produce, which Kunbun dutifully distributes to them. The new orchards (7 and 8) that he planted or will plant will be his alone. In return for the *Pandanus* fruit, meat, and other things he brings her, Kunbun's stepmother Kange gives him food from the plots she gardens for other men (for instance, Tamo's Gardens 2 and 3). However, now that Kunbun is married and no longer apportions cleared land to his stepmother, she is not expected to give him much.

Example 3: Nakemba. All Bomagai-Angoiang men profess a loyalty and a sense of responsibility to their clan and clan cluster; Nakemba goes further than most—he could be described as chauvinistic. He proclaims frequently that there are too few people in the clan cluster, that there must be more men in the basin, that all the men there now must care for the women and children so that the Bomagai and Angoiang clans will grow. In part he may do so because several years ago the Simbai patrol officer appointed him *tultul* of the Bomagai-Angoiang.[6] But his motives extend further than his official position: in part, I think he truly feels responsible for widows and young fatherless males; in part, I think he sees his concern for clan welfare and growth as a road to becoming a "big man." But, no matter what his motives, he carries his words through into actions that exemplify the essence of the Bomagai-Angoiang ethos of reciprocity.

About twenty-eight years old, Nakemba is still young, but he already has two wives, Uri and Manepna, and was previously married to a Bomagai woman who died. Uri is childless; Manepna has by Nakemba a girl about four years old and an older boy from a previous marriage. Nakemba and both wives live in the eastern hamlet on Ndembikumpf Ridge—Nakemba in a men's house, each wife in a separate woman's house. Gaiok, Nakemba's widowed father, and his young daughter sleep in Uri's house. This somewhat aberrant situation is explained by saying that "it is not right that Gaiok's daughter cry alone." Because he sleeps there, Gaiok is obligated to keep the house supplied with firewood. Uri tends three of Nakemba's four pigs: two big sows and a male adolescent. One big sow lives with Manepna and her daughter. Sleeping in Nakemba's men's house, which is the most crowded in the basin, are Kong (a recently married young man), Menga (an old widower), Nek (Tamo's brother, who says he sleeps in Nakemba's house because Nakemba provided for him when he was a fatherless boy),

---

6. After initial contact in an area the patrol officers appoint in each population cluster a government representative called a *luluai*. To assist the *luluai*, at least one *tultul* is also appointed. It is the duty of these officials to report trouble to the patrol officers and to see that the people maintain the government rest houses and work on the government trails in their vicinity. The *luluai* of the Bomagai-Angoiang is Wun, a Bomagai, who treats his office with less regard than does Nakemba.

and sometimes as many as six boys—three of them the sons of widows, two of them the sons of Gaiok and thus younger brothers of Nakemba, and one of them the son of a man now living with his wife in a family house, where it is not proper that a boy older than five or six sleep. Sometimes Ngɔni, a young married man, also sleeps in Nakemba's house. Man, another young married man, slept there until Nakemba shot and killed his pig when it got into one of Nakemba's gardens. Angry at Nakemba for this, Man moved from Nakemba's house so that he would not have to look at him until his anger left him, which it did in about a month.

In June 1965 Nakemba had four gardens, two of them producing, one going out of production, and one being planted. The location of these gardens is shown on Map 9, and they are described below in order of age from the youngest to the oldest.

1. Sugar cane-*Saccharum edule* garden (*mbo-mungap nduk*). When I arrived in the Ndwimba Basin, I had the idea from reading and from what I had seen of shifting cultivation in Middle America that among shifting cultivators the activities of clearing, felling trees, burning, and planting were separate and fairly short-term processes.[7] After five months of watching the work on Nakemba's incipient *mbo-mungap nduk*, I knew that the Bomagai-Angoiang practice often differed from this ideal, as the following edited excerpts from my field notes illustrate.

---

7. For instance, Conklin (1957:49–57) writes that the Hanunóo (who do have a more clearly defined cycle of gardening than the Bomagai-Angoiang and a quite different major crop in dry rice, but who fall with the Bomagai-Angoiang into the class of shifting cultivators who have what Conklin (1957:3) calls an "integral system of established swidden farming") begin clearing the underbrush in the middle of February and, when finished, start felling trees. Most swiddens are completely cut during March, although felling operations occasionally continue to almost the end of April. Felling is followed by definite periods of burning and planting.

Perhaps more like Bomagai-Angoiang horticulture is the extensive shifting cultivation of the Kapauku of West Irian. As Pospisil (1963:90–102) describes this method among the Kapauku, who have the same crops as the Bomagai-Angoiang, there are clearly defined, separate stages of clearing the underbrush, felling the trees, burning, and planting.

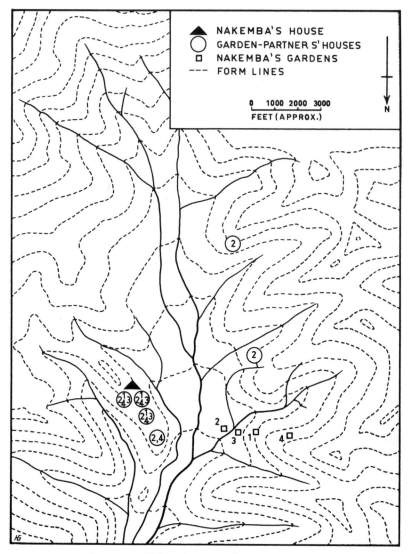

Map 9   Nakemba's Gardens, June 1965

January 10, 1965. Nakemba began clearing in old secondary forest on lower Kəlamakai Ridge. He says he is making an *mbo-mungap nduk.* By clearing he will establish rights to the unclaimed plot, which is covered with *ap ngəni* (well advanced secondary forest) at least forty years old. Some men say the plot has never been gardened; others say that unknown ancestors used it once. The initial clearing consists of slashing with a bush knife or pulling up the undergrowth of forbs, ferns, bushes, and saplings by hand.

January 12 and 16. Further clearing of underbrush.

January 24. There has been still more clearing of underbrush. Several thousand square feet are now clean of growth under the canopy of the high trees.

February 9. Today for the first time large trees were felled on this plot. Nakemba, Kong, and Ndinga (a young bachelor) came to do the work. The plot will belong to Nakemba, Kong, and Man;

These men are clearing underbrush from old secondary forest prior to felling some trees.

Felling an *Elmerrillia papuana*. Including the building of the scaffold, the operation took about 40 minutes.

Ndinga came simply to help. Man did not come at all today. Nakemba had announced earlier that he would leave for Kumoints today to fix a pig-damaged fence, but—as he put it—he thought about the wet trash in this plot and decided to cut trees to let the sun in. As the three men worked at felling, other men, both Bomagai and Angoiang, who passed stopped to help for half an hour or so. This was not, I think, from a sense of obligation but because they very much enjoy the excitement and accomplishment of felling trees. As a tree rends and begins to topple, every man around stops his work and shouts "*oo-a, oo-a, oo-a, oo-a*," a wavering cry of delight that ends only when the noises of the crashing tree have died away amid the fluttering of torn leaves over the now unshaded ground.[8] Men stand on the ground to cut small trees; for larger trees they build a light scaffold of poles and vines so that they can reach the bole clear of the buttresses. Because it was sup- ported by many prop roots, the most difficult tree to fell was a ninety-foot *Pandanus papuanus*; it was also the most valuable, and the Bomagai man who felled it claimed the leaves and prop roots for use in building a new house. After about two hours of work, ten large trees had been felled and an area of from two to three thou- sand square feet, opened to sunlight. Then felling was over for the day, and Nakemba, Kong, and Ndinga went to work piling debris against trees or on small scaffolds of sticks to dry. I asked Nakemba if he intended to fell more trees later. He replied that he did and that there was still much work to be done: the felled trees had to be trimmed, and some of the logs had to be cut up. To get this done, Nakemba said he would talk to his kinsmen thus:

> I am clearing a garden. I have cut the trees. Many logs must be cut to make a fence. Come help me. I will prepare a meal in the earth oven and *komba ndur* [the sauce made from the seeds of the cultivated *Pandanus*]. We will eat and afterwards go to our houses.

Nakemba, Kong, and Ndinga left the plot about three in the afternoon. Before he went, Nakemba planted several stem cuttings of sugar cane in the tract which had been opened to sunlight only a few hours before.

February 15. After a five-day interval, work was recommenced on this plot by Kabang (a Bomagai man and close associate of Nakemba), Tamo, and Ndinga. They are cutting the undergrowth but not large trees. Somewhat unusually, all three men have only bush knives; they left their axes at home. They work up the slope in three parallel zones about forty feet wide. The shrub and field layers are completely removed by slashing and pulling. Tree seedlings are pulled up; saplings two to three inches in diameter are cut three to four feet about the ground, the branches are trimmed, and the boles, cut into several segments. All the trash is spread on the ground. Later, says Kabang, after the large trees are felled the trash

---

8. Conklin (1957:58, 61) for the Hanunóo in the Philippines and Freeman (1955:41–43) for the Iban of Sarawak record a similar feeling. Freeman notes, "Tree felling is the one activity of the farming year in which the young men revel . . . ."

Burning trash in February in a recently cleared plot. The trash was
piled on sticks to dry before burning.

will be piled up on scaffolds and against stumps to dry as in the
opened tract up the slope. With the men are Kabang's seven-year-
old son and another boy; they help with the work and play in the
forest. When the men stop work to rest, talk, and smoke, the boys
squat with them about a little fire.

Instead of working in the plot today, Nakemba spent the
morning cooking greens and *komba ndur* at his house. In the afternoon he had planned to come to the plot, but, when it started to
rain, he sent two boys with the food enclosed in leaves and bamboo
tubes to the workers, who ate it in the men's house on Kəlamakai
Ridge.

February 16. Today the owners of the garden, Nakemba, Kong, and
Man, are working at clearing underbrush in a tract downslope from
the area cleared yesterday by other men. They work close together,
unlike the workers yesterday. Because they are at the bottom of the
garden-to-be, instead of spreading the cut trash on the ground, they

Scattered burning in June. The upper part of the clearing is Na-kemba's Garden 1, described in the text.

are throwing it down a steep slope that will not be planted. Nakemba says that people burn trash only in the middle of a garden.

I discovered today that the final area of this garden-to-be will include two small patches of land previously cleared of forest, one patch by Nakemba in September, the other by Man in December 1964.

February 19. Today Nakemba, Ndop (a Bomagai man), and 'Ren (Nakemba's fourteen-year-old stepson) are working at clearing undergrowth in still another spot within the boundaries of the garden-to-be, which is now a mosaic of recently felled trees, standing forest cleared of undergrowth, forest where the undergrowth remains, and the patches where trees were felled months before and weedy regrowth covers the ground. Today the men again cleared in separate strips while moving upslope. Three young boys—working, watching, playing—accompanied the workers. At noon everyone came together for a meal of bananas cooked in a fire in the forest, *Xanthosoma* tubers roasted in the morning at home, and cooked *komba* seeds carried in a bamboo tube. Work continued till three in the afternoon.

February 20. No work was done on the plot. Nakemba spent the day visiting with me while diligently weaving a belt of the inner stems of the fern *Dicranopteris linearis*.

February 22. Today the three owners of the garden and another man are felling trees and clearing undergrowth concurrently in a previously unworked part of the plot. By noon several large trees were down and the associated undergrowth cut and piled. In the afternoon the men cleared only, moving upslope into unfelled forest. More sugar cane and some *Saccharum edule* were planted today amid the unburned debris of the tract opened on February 9.

February 23. Nakemba felled trees by himself today.

February 28. During the past four days no one had done any clearing or felling. Nakemba did casually plant more of the *Saccharum* species and manioc cuttings in the tract opened on February 9. The ground there is littered with piles of trash and logs, above which rises a light forest of tall stumps of large trees and several smaller, uncut trees. These uncut trees will be felled later or pollarded and left standing as poles which yams will twine around and which the men can use as supports for sugar cane. I asked Nakemba about a cultivated *Pandanus* cutting growing in the opened tract. He said that some passerby had stuck it in the ground there, thinking to pick it up later, and then had forgotten it. Now it becomes Nakemba's. If it does well, he may plant more, so that the garden site will develop into a *Pandanus* orchard; if it does not do well, he will not plant more *Pandanus* but will abandon the garden to fallow.

March 1–15. In this period several thousand more square feet of undergrowth and trees were cut down by several men. There was also more planting of sugar cane, *Saccharum edule*, manioc, and *Rungia klossii* among the debris of the tract opened on February 9. For instance, on March 12 on his way from Tabapi to Ndembi-kumpf, Nakemba seized a handful of *Rungia* from his old garden (Map 9, 4) and planted slips of it in his new garden. A few days earlier Kunbun had planted several cuttings of sugar cane. When I asked why he planted in a garden that was not his, he replied that he and Nakemba were subclansmen.[9]

---

9. Frequently men pointed out to me plants that they had

March 16–May 12. During this interval clearing and felling continued spasmodically until, by May 12, the opened tracts had coalesced into a single plot of at least two acres. Also by May 12 the three owners had designated "marks" dividing the garden into three parts. Nakemba planted in his, the upper, part more sugar cane, *Saccharum edule,* manioc, and *Rungia,* as well as *Xanthosoma,* taro, bananas, and *Hibiscus manihot.* His female garden partners will plant sweet potatoes later. By May 12 Man and Kong had not yet planted anything; and the whole plot remained unfenced and unburned. Nakemba says that he has not built a fence because he has been busy hunting in Kumoints. If pigs do any damage, he says, the three owners will build a fence from the supply of wood strewn everywhere in the plot. Near the center of the plot they have accumulated an eight-foot-high heap of logs and poles, which will be taken away slowly for use as firewood in their hamlets.

May 16. Nakemba planted bananas and sugar cane with *wump* from his old garden up the ridge.

May 17. Today, Togma, a widow who is one of Man's garden partners, began burning in her section of Man's part of the plot. She heaps some of the leaves and small pieces of wood that litter the ground onto the piles of trash gathered earlier by the men. After a pile is burning well, she spreads the burning material and ash over the surrounding ground with her digging stick. Much undecomposed litter remains unburned, and only about 30 percent of the surface gets covered with ash. Concurrently with the burning, Togma plants *Hibiscus manihot* and the "male" crops of *Saccharum edule,* sugar cane, and bananas—all where there is no ash. She says that later she will plant root crops in the ashy places because burning will have killed the weeds there.

May 19. Nakemba's wives are burning trash and planting *Coleus* (both *nimp* and *amami*), sweet potatoes, and taro in Nakemba's part of the garden. The small, separated fires do no harm to the crops already planted and in some cases already sprouting. Man's wife is planting and burning in her husband's part of the garden.

May 28. For the past week planting and burning have been going on almost every day. Togma as well as Man's half-sister, Man's wife,

---

started in gardens belonging to other men, but not always subclansmen or even clansmen. They expected no return for this, but seemed proud of being part of a life-supporting process and used the plant they set out as a kind of commemoration of the event of establishing a garden.

Kong's mother, Kong's bride, and Nakemba's wives have all taken part, each in her own section except for Kong's bride who works with his mother. Yams and taros have predominated in the planting. Because this is an *mbo-mungap nduk*, there is no "garden heart" and no ritual associated with planting. The women come with the *wump* in their net bags and begin burning and planting. To plant they dibble a hole with a stabbing, then a rotating motion, place the *wump* in the hole, and pat the earth back with their hands.

June 12 (the last day of observation of this garden). Now the planting and the partial burning have been almost completed. The plot remains unfenced.

2. Taro-yam garden (*ndang-wan nduk*). This garden was part of a conterminous aggregation of several men's gardens (Figure 9a). By May or June of 1964 Ngɔni had cleared and

A woman planting.

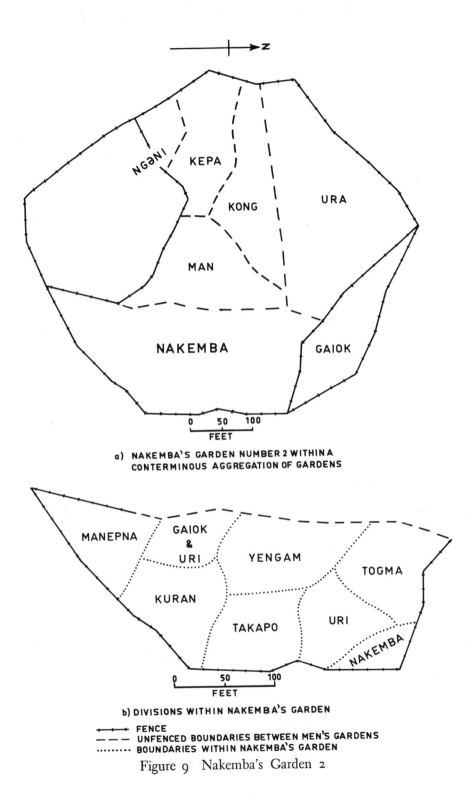

a) NAKEMBA'S GARDEN NUMBER 2 WITHIN A
CONTERMINOUS AGGREGATION OF GARDENS

b) DIVISIONS WITHIN NAKEMBA'S GARDEN

●——● FENCE
— — — UNFENCED BOUNDARIES BETWEEN MEN'S GARDENS
··········· BOUNDARIES WITHIN NAKEMBA'S GARDEN

Figure 9 Nakemba's Garden 2

fenced a plot on the basin floor where his father had planted a garden twelve to sixteen years before. Nakemba said that, when he saw Ngɔni's clearing, he decided he would like a garden adjoining Ngɔni's on land that his father had cleared when Ngɔni's father was gardening in this place. While Ngɔni was helping Nakemba clear, they found a big *Cordyline* that reputedly had served as a "mark" between their fathers' gardens. They also exposed a breadfruit belonging to Ngɔni because his father had planted it while helping Nakemba's father clear for his garden of more than a decade before.

Kepa, Kong, Ura, and Man joined Ngɔni and Nakemba and also cleared adjacent to Ngɔni's garden on land used before by Ura and his father. Ngɔni helped Ura and Kepa clear, getting in return a parcel of land beyond his original fence (Figure 9a). Later, after Nakemba and the other four men who joined Ngɔni had built a fence enclosing their gardens and connected with the original fence around Ngɔni's garden, Gaiok (Nakemba's father) decided to plant adjacent to Nakemba. Because Gaiok was old and losing strength, he asked Tamo to build the fence around his garden. In return, Tamo received food from Nakemba's wives, who worked Gaiok's garden. The size of the final aggregation of gardens was four to five acres within the outer fence; but many cultivated plants also grew just outside the fence. By Gaiok's fence was a patch of pumpkin vines spread over a jumble of logs. Beyond Ngɔni's fence on the west was a small orchard of *Pandanus* and breadfruit mixed with *Heliconia* and bamboo planted by his mother and father during the previous gardening of this plot; on the south in a small stream was a patch of watercress and next to the fence, a dozen or so *Hibiscus manihot* planted by his mother during the current clearing. Among the *Hibiscus* Ngɔni has planted *Pandanus* cuttings.

As shown on Figure 9b, Nakemba divided his part of the aggregate plot into eight sections, each individually gardened. His wives (Manepna and Uri) had one plot apiece. Uri shared another with Gaiok, who could still weed and harvest but often spent the day in the hamlet looking after children. Kuran, who lived at Mwarmbong, was the widow of a Bomagai. Nakemba and two Bomagai men cleared gardens for her, so that she would stay in the basin with her three sons. Yengam was Nakemba's sister, now gone in marriage to a Bomagai man. Takapo was a natal Angoiang, now a widow. When her Bomagai husband died, she returned to Angoiang land with her one child, a daughter. Later the daughter went in marriage to a Jimi River clan who "backed" Uri, one of Nakemba's wives. Nakemba brought Takapo *Pandanus* (she also had rights to her dead husband's *Pandanus* on Bomagai land), built a house for her when needed, and assigned space to her in all his gardens. Takapo also received space in the garden of Ngirapo, a Bomagai "big man." Togma, the widow of an Angoing man, was given garden space by several Angoiang men—again, with the stated motive of keeping her male children in the basin. Nakemba also had one small section that he tended by himself, saying, "I have this garden so that I won't go hungry when my wives are angry with me and won't bring me food." His worry seemed unnecessary inasmuch as his other four female garden partners also brought him food. Many times in the afternoon at Ndembikumpf I saw Togma and Takapo hand food to Nakemba, either raw tubers or a combination of greens and tubers or *Xanthosoma* paste cooked in the earth oven.

Nakemba and his garden partners planted this garden by August and September 1964. By June 1965 everything had ripened but bananas, and the garden was yielding heavily. *Wump* from this garden will originate Nakemba's next taro-yam garden, which he plans to establish near Ndembikumpf in July or August 1965. The total size of the garden is about 47,500 square feet.

3. Sugar cane-*Saccharum edule* garden (*mbo-mungap nduk*). This garden was cleared of secondary forest on a plot used about fifteen years before by Nakemba's father. Planted by about September 1963, it was close to going out of production of short-lived crops in June 1965, when it was a forest of sugar cane and *Saccharum edule* growing over weeds and shorter crop-plants. Because Nakemba plans to turn the plot into a

Pandanus orchard, he has already planted some *Pandanus* cuttings and will clear the weedy growth and plant more *Pandanus* when the short-lived garden is abandoned. The area of this fenced plot is 28,000 square feet, but about one-quarter of it—grown with a jungle of wild bananas in June 1965—was never gardened, because, explained Nakemba, the woman to whom he gave the section decided not to work it.

4. Taro-yam garden (*ndang-wan nduk*). This garden was planted a few months earlier than Garden 3, about June and July 1963. It is part of the same large enclosure on Kɔlamakai Ridge where Tamo, Kunbun, and several other Angoiang men have gardens. By June 1965 this garden was abandoned except for the harvesting of a few crops and as a source of *wump* for Garden 1. Such harvesting as there was, was done in passing. For instance, once when Nakemba accompanied me through

The woman is carrying home the cultivated *Pandanus* fruit. In the right center is a *Pandanus*-breadfruit orchard.

An Angoiang woman arrives home with a load of garden
produce in her net bag and water in the bamboo tubes.
The roughness of her skin is the result of tinea.

this garden, he dug out to take his pigs the large "mother"
corm of a giant *Xanthosoma* plant growing in a moist gully; he
would not have made a special trip to get it. Later, if Nakemba
moves his wives from Ndembikumpf to Kəlamakai, he says his
pigs will forage in this garden for the small sweet potatoes that
remain unharvested.[10] I know that Takapo, Togma, and both

10. In more densely settled parts of New Guinea the pigs are
often taken to the old gardens to root out the remaining crops. In the

Nakemba's wives worked this garden, which had a total area of 54,000 square feet. Other women may have had sections there, too. I am not sure of this because I measured only the outer boundary of the garden and know from other experience that to discover all the female workers in a man's garden it may be necessary to question informants while walking over virtually every square yard of the garden.

In June 1965 the total area recognized as Nakemba's gardens was large—from three to four acres; but because Garden 1 was not in production yet and Gardens 3 and 4 were passing out of production, I estimate the actively productive area to be 60,000 square feet, or less than an acre and a half. Nakemba also had a bush garden in Kumoints, as did Kunbun and Tamo; but, because the area gardened there was small and none of the produce was brought to the basin, I have excluded the Kumoints gardens from my estimates of total land in production by each man.

Generalizations About Subsistence Behavior

Population Density and Amount of Sustaining Land per Person. The Bomagai-Angoiang feel that the basin is under-populated, that every man has more land than he needs. The population density in the area now subject to cultivation is eighty to ninety persons per square mile, which means that there are 7 or 8 acres per person; but this figure has no great meaning because, whenever they wish, the people can claim more land from beneath primary forest or recultivate some 200 acres of Bomagai-Angoiang land now lying fallow and unused under secondary forest just to the west of the basin. The number and size of the plots that a man clears are, therefore, limited by his energy and discretion, not by a shortage of land. The amount actually gardened depends in part on the energy and discretion of his garden partners. I estimate that on the average each fully active man has 1.2 acres of productive garden. If there is

---

Ndwimba Basin if the pigs find the old gardens, that is all to the good; but if they do not find them, no one shows them the way.

the equivalent of thirty fully active men in the basin,[11] there are 36 acres in production at any time, or 0.23 acre per person, a figure in accord with Barrau's (1958:25) estimate of 0.2 to 0.3 acre of garden per person in Melanesian rain forest foothills and mountain ranges. Rappaport (1967a:20) estimates somewhat less acreage (between 0.15 and 0.19) per person for the Tsembaga, the Maring clan cluster which lives a day's walk up the Simbai Valley from the basin. Besides the Bomagai-Angoiang 0.23 acre per person of gardened land, plant food sources also include about 0.16 acre per person of *Pandanus* orchard and an abundant supply of spontaneous plants with edible parts.

Fallow Period. For purposes of calculation, I can estimate that there are about 1,150 acres of land now subject to cultivation in the basin. Of this total area, 1,114 acres are under secondary vegetation or *Pandanus* orchards, and 36 acres are in cultivation. I take fifteen months (1.25 years) as the life of a garden because after that the secondary vegetation is allowed to develop, even if some food is still being removed. Calculating from these figures:

$$\frac{1,114}{36} = 30.9$$

$$30.9 \times 1.25 = 38.6 \text{ years average fallow period}$$

This period of about forty years for the average fallow period is higher than the range of fifteen to twenty years of fallow that I obtained by averaging the estimated ages of the vegetation actually cleared for the gardens while I was in the basin. I can suggest two reasons for the discrepency beyond the crudity of my measurements and the small size of the sample of vegetation that I observed being cleared. First is the decline in population that occurred because of the dysentery epidemic of the 1940's. The larger population that existed before the epidemic would have necessitated a fallow period shorter than forty years

---

11. There are thirty-four men over fourteen in the basin. Six of these are in the incipient nonproducer class (Figure 2), and two are just becoming producers. I estimate the aggregate productive capacity of these eight males to be the equivalent of four fully active men.

unless the area cultivated was larger then. The present condition of the fallow vegetation may still reflect this inheritance. Second, I may have judged some of the secondary communities to be younger than they were because their development had been slowed by the people's activities. As the men walk about the basin, axe or bush knife in hand, they casually whack and slash at any trees or shrubs within reach. Particularly in the *Alphitonia-Cyathea-Geunsia* woodland, they fell trees for firewood, thus opening the canopy and maintaining conditions favorable to sun-loving plants. Such disturbances must slow the succession toward incipient lower montane rain forest. But whether the average fallow period is forty years or less, it is sufficiently long to ameliorate the soils used for gardening and to inhibit rapid retrogressive succession from forest and wood- to grassland.

Selection of Garden Sites. Because of the easy availability of large amounts of unclaimed land, together with inherited land and land granted by friends or relatives, any Bomagai-Angoiang man has a wide variety of sites to choose from when he decides to clear land for a garden. Certain principles determine his choice. I have already touched on the slight preference for land fallowed under *Albizia falcataria* or land that is on slopes facing north and have also mentioned the decided dislike of land fallowed under grass.

Another principle of garden-site selection is connected with the distinction between the *kamunga*, or high-elevation land, and the *wora*, or low-elevation land. The people say that yields are less in *kamunga* than in *wora*,[12] but gardens are made in *kamunga* up to about 3,800 feet because, say the men, "Our fathers gardened there; it is our place." Another reason for cultivating in the *kamunga* is, or was, that the two altitudinal

---

12. I have only one measurement of the presumed difference in yield between gardens in *kamunga* and gardens in *wora*: 20 *Xanthosoma* tubers from a *wora* garden weighed 22 pounds, 20 *Xanthosoma* tubers from a *kamunga* garden weighed 13 pounds. There are no varieties of *Xanthosoma*, but it is possible that differences in soil or age between the gardens could as well account for the variation in tuber size as the differences in temperature and light that go with differences of elevation.

zones have different ritual meanings and are said to be inhabited
by different kinds of spirits. Before warfare was prohibited,
there were times during the fighting when food from *wora*
gardens was taboo to warriors. When they do plant in the
kamunga, the men establish *Hibiscus manihot*-sweet potato
gardens (*kem-koia nduk*) or sugar cane-*Saccharum edule* gardens (*mbo-mungap nduk*) rather than the ritually more significant gardens of taro and yams (*ndang-wan nduk*) because, say
the men, taro and yams do not grow well in the *kamunga*.
Neither do the men plant taro-yam gardens on low-elevation
wora land which is newly cleared of very old secondary or primary forest; they believe the soil on such sites to be "too strong"
for these ritually important crops. When such a site is reused
some years after the initial clearing, a taro-yam garden may be
established if the few taro and yams that would have been
planted in the first garden did well. In other words, as with the
Pandanus orchards, the site is tested before being fully planted.
A similarly conservative approach is used with land that has
been through several periods of fallow vegetation and garden:
sites where taro-yam gardens have yielded well before are used
again for the same crops. This empirical choice parallels the
pleasure and comfort that the men seem to gain from repeat-
ing the subsistence behavior of their fathers or of themselves
when younger.

About 10 percent of the gardens now in use were newly
cleared in what the people considered virgin forest. The men
who select such sites are mature, "strong" men who for some
reason want to expand their holdings or who are taken with the
idea of having a garden in a certain locality where they previously have had no holdings. Adolescent, old, or otherwise
"weak" men do not clear in primary or very old secondary
forest because the large trees are hard to fell and, once felled,
are hard either to cut up for fence posts or to dispose of so that
they take up minimum space in the garden.

Garden Management. Early in their lives Bomagai-Angoiang
boys and girls begin to be educated in the tasks and planning
connected with gardens. They accompany and imitate men and

women on the adults' daily rounds. The men and women both
instruct the children about the proper work of each sex and
what must be done so that everyone has food. A child is
watched and encouraged to learn subsistence skills until, as one
man said about his younger brother, "he begins to think like a
man." With respect to gardens, "to think like a man" means
to know how to clear land, build fences, plant, weed, and tie
sugar cane; it also means knowing how to initiate through time
a series of gardens at least one of which is always adequately
productive.

Although the Bomagai-Angoiang have no clear agricultural
year with a beginning and an end, as "time belong sun" (the
drier period from June through September) approaches, the
people talk about the impending hard and time-consuming work
of preparing gardens even if they are in the midst of an
extended preparation like that described for Nakemba's new
mbo-mungap nduk (Garden 1). What they mean is that "time
belong sun" is a time of concentrated work, for the taro-yam
gardens, most of which are started then, are usually cleared
and fenced more quickly and burned more thoroughly than
other gardens, which may be started at any time of year. The
workers hurry to clear taro-yam gardens because they want to
have the trash ready to burn whenever a dry spell comes and
because, I think, they feel a psychic pressure, lacking from their
work with other gardens, to get these gardens into production.
They fence the taro-yam gardens quickly to give these most
important, these true gardens maximum protection from pigs.[13]
They say that unusually thorough burning, although it is still
quite incomplete, is necessary for taro-yam gardens because: the
fires kill insects that would eat the young leaves of taro and
yams; the fires kill weeds that would compete with the crops;
and the tubers would not grow large unless planted in ash.

---

13. The Bomagai-Angoiang have no material crop-protection devices other than fences and pitfalls, although the rituals that some
men perform in the "garden heart" at the time of planting taro-yam
gardens do reflect still further concern for the success of this type of
garden.

A garden fence. One man can build 50 to 60 feet of such a fence in a day.

Considering the relative intensity of the work of preparing gardens during "time belong sun," it is not surprising that the leisurely and pleasantly sporadic gardening activities of the rest of the year hardly seem like work at all—at least for the men.

Unless there has been a long delay between clearing and planting, the first weeding occurs four to six weeks after planting, by which time the soil between the crops is usually covered with a tiny forest of weeds, especially *Crassocephalum, Ageratum, Homalanthus,* and the wild banana.[14] If the gardeners

14. The only disadvantage that I can see to the relaxed extension of clearing over several months is that it necessitates an extra weeding at or before the time of planting. On the other hand, as John Street (personal communication) suggested to me, clearing before the rainier season ends cuts down transpiration and assures that soil moisture reserves are at their maximum when the crop plants are set out. Street reports that in another part of the Maring area he found a marked

neglect this initial weeding, it is said that the roots of the cultivated plants do not develop properly. No further weeding is done for about two months, or until the cucumbers are ripe and the second stand of weeds is two or three feet high. If necessary, crops are thinned along with the second weeding. Some people, who say they are lazy, skip the first weeding and wait until the garden is three or three and a half months old and the crops are almost hidden by weeds. As with burning, I think that weeding is done more thoroughly in taro-yam gardens than in other gardens. The people have separate names for what seems to be a formally conceived sequence of stages of weeding, but my impression is that, from the time the cucumbers ripen, weeding and harvesting are done concurrently, and the stages merge into each other. Neither men nor women ever go into a garden, whether theirs or another's, without pulling up at least a few weeds. Weeding continues until the garden is fifteen to eighteen months old; but because of the practice of selective weeding (removing forbs and grasses, leaving tree seedlings), the fallow period really begins with the planting of the crops. This practice naturally increases the chances of a rapid regeneration of woodland and forest, and the shading effect of the young saplings may inhibit the growth of forbs and grasses, thus reducing the labor of weeding during the later life of the gardens.

The harvest, which begins with cucumbers two to three months after planting, lasts without interruption for as long as twenty months. It consists of a succession of crops that yield like waves rising to crests and then subsiding. After the cucumbers have been ripe for a month, the greens (*Setaria, Hibiscus, Rungia*) become available, followed closely by maize, beans, and pumpkins. When sweet potatoes begin to mature at five or six months, the cucumbers are gone. In the next few months taro, *Xanthosoma, Saccharum edule,* and yams rise in

---

difference during the drier season between soil under well developed forest and soil from which the vegetation had been cleared—the forest soil being considerably drier. That forests transpire more than herbaceous vegetation is well known from observations and watershed experiments in other parts of the world.

importance as the beans, maize, and pumpkins decline. By now the sugar cane has been tied (always a man's job) and the leaves of some varieties, removed (Appendix C). Other men's tasks are fence-mending and the removal of dried banana leaves, which, if left on the plant are said to inhibit further growth. The last crops to become ripe are manioc, bananas, and sugar cane, which are not available as food until the gardens are eight or nine months old. Because banana suckers sprout from the original planting stock and the cane ratoons, both these crops continue to yield after their first harvest. The manioc tubers, which can remain in the ground after reaching a harvestable size, are removed slowly, mostly for food for domestic pigs. By the time the garden is ten months old the yield of taro and yams is falling, but that of sweet potatoes and *Xanthosoma* continues copiously. Of the greens, the perennial *Hibiscus manihot* remains the most important until the garden is abandoned. When weeding ceases, many sweet potato tubers remain in the ground, but because they become increasingly hard to harvest, the garden in its senescence supplies mainly bananas, *Hibiscus manihot*, the *Saccharum* spp., and lesser amounts of *Xanthosoma* and manioc. Long before a garden is totally surrendered to jungle, the prudent gardener has taken out *wump* and seen to the birth of other gardens.

The Bomagai-Angoiang, like most shifting cultivators who have a similarly free choice, always choose to establish new gardens on new sites rather than immediately replanting on the sites of old gardens. That to reuse an old site would result in lower yields is one way the people explain their shifting. Nye and Greenland (1960:75) list six consequences of cropping that lead to the decline in yields that induces the farmer to shift from one site to another: (1) deterioration in the nutrient status of the soil; (2) deterioration in the physical status of the soil; (3) erosion of top soil; (4) changes in the numbers and composition of the soil fauna and flora; (5) increase of weeds; and (6) multiplication of pests and diseases.

I have discussed the first two already. The third, erosion, which is negligible now in the basin and of no concern to the

Bomagai-Angoiang, might increase with an extension of cropping on one site. Neither the Bomagai-Angoiang nor I can judge
the presence or effects of the fourth, changes in soil flora and
fauna. The fifth and sixth are definitely reasons for shifting
garden sites in the Ndwimba Basin. As the garden ages, the
composition of the weed flora changes. The initially prevalent
soft forbs *Crassocephalum* and *Ageratum* are succeeded by
grasses, ferns, vines, and a variety of tree seedlings. Because the
selective weeding favors trees of several species, by the time
the garden is fifteen months old, saplings six to eight feet high
are common and are beginning to shade the lower crops. But,
more to the point, the firmly rooted grasses and ferns are harder
to weed than the soft forbs that first invade young clearings.
Rodents find a hospitable niche in the older trash-littered gardens and compete increasingly with the people for food as the
garden ages. Diseases and insect pests do only a little damage in
the intercropped gardens of the Bomagai-Angoiang, but would
presumably become a more serious threat if garden sites were
immediately reused.

In summary, two important reasons for shifting gardens
from site to site in the basin are a decline in soil fertility and
an increase in labor costs for weeding if the same site were to
be reused without an interval of fallow. Two other reasons for
shifting are the decay of fences and the predilection of the men
to move about within their territory. Within twenty months
after being put up, fence posts are half rotten and the bindings
that hold them together are coming apart. Because pigs can
easily get through fences in such condition, it would be necessary to completely rebuild the fence around a plot that was to
be reused. But in an old garden there is no ready supply of
wood, a lack that one man gave as his principal reason for shifting sites. "I am lazy," he said. "If I regardened in my old garden, I would have to search around and fell trees elsewhere on
land of mine or of friends of mine and then carry the posts and
poles to the garden; it is easier to clear in a new place." Beyond
the immediate economic reasons, the men also shift garden
sites because they enjoy having gardens that are variable in time

and space. As they walk about in the basin, the men like to note their past and future garden sites—a set of places with which they have psychic connections. The way that they scatter their gardens also has economic and social meanings.

Location of Houses and Gardens. Given their present economy, the Bomagai-Angoiang need to have the following resources within an accessible range of their houses: water, cultivable land, foraging land for pigs, materials for construction of houses and other artifacts, hunting and fishing grounds, wild plant sources of food, and firewood. No houses are located beside streams or springs, because the advantage of having water just outside the door is outweighed by the disadvantages of noise, valley fogs night and morning, and the lack of view and of freshening winds. Besides, even the ridgetop houses are nowhere more than fifteen minutes from water, and the need for water at the houses is small because the people neither wash there nor use more than a few pints in preparing the evening meal. The energy cost of walking to fetch water is often incorporated into trips to and from gardens: the bamboo tubes used to carry water are left by the source of water on passing in the morning and filled and carried home in the afternoon.

Disregarding rights of use for the moment, I think it essentially accurate to consider the basin to be a region where all necessary resources except water, fishing grounds, and certain high-elevation resources are evenly distributed—or at least are not concentrated in a particular place. The inhabitant's choice of the specific place from which he extracts a resource or in which he uses it is, therefore, unrestrained by a zonation of resources. But, once he chooses a particular place to live or a particular plot to cultivate, he partially rigidifies his lines of activity. An obvious question follows: Are the gardens and houses located on the basis of some economic principle? Certainly not, if the principle is that of simple minimization of the cost of distance. Every man has established at least one garden at a distance of forty-five minutes or more from his house; and the motive for moving from one house site to another never

seems to be to achieve proximity to gardens. In several cases
the same distance between house and garden was maintained in
a move. For instance, in June 1965 Nakemba was in the process
of moving from Ndembikumpf to Kɔlamakai, to a site adjacent
to a garden he had just abandoned; at the same time he was
starting to clear for a taro-yam garden on a plot close to his
old house at Ndembikumpf.

Figure 10 shows four examples of the spatial distribution of
men's houses and gardens. The patterns for women are similar,
except that some women have as many as five plots to work at
one time. When the distribution of a man's *Pandanus* orchards
is taken into account along with the distribution of his gardens,
it is seen that his network of necessary travel is still further
amplified. Of course, the set of inherited sites owned by a man
determines in part where he locates his gardens, orchards, and
house. However, the idea of consolidating holdings by trade is
not unknown: while I was in the basin, the Angoiang traded an
isolated and unused parcel of their land near the Fungai clan's
settlement of Ngunts for some Fungai land adjacent to currently
used Angoiang land to the northeast of Tabapi. In theory, then,
the men of a clan could consolidate their holdings by trading
land with each other. In fact, however, such an undertaking
would be inhibited by the attachment each man feels for the
several places where he or his father have already gardened or
lived. Besides, the people, especially the men, benefit from the
circulation made necessary by the scattered and ever-changing
distribution of houses, gardens, and orchards. Taken together,
these benefits, of which I see four, outweigh the cost of distance,
which in several cases in the Ndwimba Basin exceeds the rough
kilometer that Chisholm (1962:148) sets as the distance beyond
which some adjustment in pattern of settlement or land use becomes necessary.

First, by traveling to and fro the men constantly refresh
their store of knowledge about their habitat. If a man is to make
a successful living in the basin, his mind must be a reservoir of
information about potential garden sites and other resources.
If he traveled far from his house only rarely, detailed memory

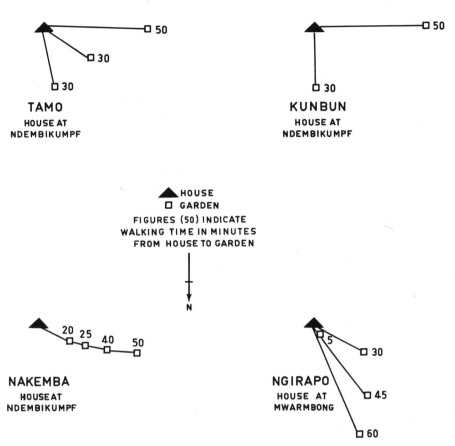

Figure 10 Examples of Time and Direction of Gardens from Men's Houses

about the rest of the clan territory would fade from his mind like the pages of a seldom-opened book. But if almost every day he walks about widely, he has the opportunity to reread the pages of his environment, consciously or unconsciously to perceive and assess the condition of the vegetation on his holdings, the ripeness of his *Pandanus*, the location and development of wild plant sources of food and materials. Second, as a man walks about, he can define and interpret the clan's territory and the place of himself and his fellows within that territory. When shared by all men of the clan, it is this constant process of definition and interpretation that maintains the corporate identity of the clan within its territory. The communication—gained by continuous circulation—of the men with their environment and their fellows seems of particular importance in a community with dispersed settlement. Third, the men and, to a lesser extent, the women like to travel and do so for the sake of interest as much as for material gain.[15] Frequently in the morning someone will say, "Today I am going to go visit so-and-so or go see such-and-such a place." And off they go, incorporating into an economic trip an enjoyable detour that invigorates social and ecologic ties. Fourth, while walking with their bows and arrows through the diversified environment of the basin, the men often incidentally come upon and take marsupials, snakes, and birds. But the men never set out deliberately to hunt with the object of obtaining meat unless they already have strong hints of the location of an animal; I believe that this is because to spend time simply hunting for meat would result in an expenditure of energy greater than that gained. But it is worthwhile for the men, while walking about on other tasks and on different routes from day to day, to be ready, as they usually are, to shoot animals that are seen by chance or that are roused by the dogs. To hunt birds for their plumes is a different matter, because the take has a high economic and emotional value that makes the long journey to Kumoints or the hard climb to the leech-thronged montane crest forest amply rewarding.

Reciprocity. Reciprocity pervades the lives of all Melanesians; but—as seems true of many of the activities of the Bomagai-Angoiang—the reciprocal process is a comparatively casual affair in the Ndwimba Basin. Like other Maring-speakers, the Bomagai-Angoiang do have the sporadic pig-slaughtering cere-

---

15. Several Europeans with long experience in New Guinea express similar ideas about the fondness for travel of the New Guineans in general. The Chimbu of the Central Highlands are especially noted for their long trading journeys throughout Australian New Guinea. (See, for example, R. Bulmer, 1962.) And Pouwer (1961:13) writes of coastal Papuans in southern West Irian: "Besides, as a result of the dispersion of his areas of food-supply (including hunting and collecting areas), the Papuan is fairly mobile and is very attached to the travelling and moving about that is involved."

monies at which allies and ancestors are compensated for their help in wars; but, to my knowledge, Maring-speakers lack the more formalized cycles of ceremonial-exchange festivals that take place in many other parts of Melanesia. Among the Bomagai-Angoiang, the exchanges other than those connected with war seldom extend above the level of individuals or very small groups and are relatively informal.

Reciprocity has obvious economic functions. Simple exchanges may save labor, as when one man asks another bound for the montane forest to bring back fern cordage or *Dendrobium* orchid stems and promises to give the traveler food on his return. When several men develop a joint plot, they can save the labor of building the greater length of fence that would be necessary if they had separate plots. However, it is obvious from my description of the garden shown in Figure 9 that reducing the labor of building fences is not the only motive for aggregating gardens. When a feral pig or wild cassowary is killed, the wide distribution of the meat, which rests on the ideal of mutual giving and receiving, makes possible the immediate use of all the food, which would otherwise quickly spoil and be wasted.[16] The grander distributions of pork that occur at the pig-slaughtering ceremonies serve the same function (Vayda, Leeds, and Smith, 1961:70). The reciprocal relations of brother and sister and the ideal that all men should clear land for widows and give sections in their gardens to any related woman expand for the participating men the number of female garden partners. This benefits the men by spreading the risk of a failing food supply connected with poor planning of the overlap of gardens and with a woman's anger or death. For everyone, the scattering of women's gardening places through several men's gardens provides a relatively steady supply of food throughout the year, because each woman has access to several gardens, each at a different stage of growth. When a man gives

---

16. The Bomagai-Angoiang do have a method of temporarily preserving meat by hanging it over hearth fires; but even there the meat lasts only a few days because they store it in bulky chunks rather than cutting it into thin strips.

a pig to a friend in another clan, he knows that later there will be a counterpresentation. In the interval between giving and receiving, the original giver in a sense still owns the pig but need not care for or worry about losing it. Finally, the ideal of reciprocity ensures that everyone is cared for throughout his life. It is explicit that children are provided with food when young, so that they will reciprocate to the erstwhile providers when they are mature. The father of the one young man who, for unknown reasons, did not return from the lowland coconut plantations in 1964 with the other contract laborers once declaimed to me with tears running down his face, "If my son does not come back soon and marry and plant gardens, there will be no one to take care of me when I am old and weak." His rhetoric seemed a little overdone, as he had four other sons, but the essence of his concern was real.

Besides bestowing economic benefits, the Bomagai-Angoiang ethos of reciprocity bears on social relations. It would seem theoretically possible that a Bomagai-Angoiang man or nuclear family could be economically independent. But humans are never socially independent. All human groups have mechanisms whereby social coherence is maintained. I have suggested that shared territory is one such mechanism among the Bomagai-Angoiang; their system of reciprocity is another. Where equality of personal status prevails, the ideals and processes of reciprocity can take the place of a hierarchy of authority as a socially integrating principle.

Reciprocal economic relations, which rest on debt and credit, create cohesive bonds of expectation. A man gives a woman land in his cleared plot; he expects to be given food in return. His investment in the labor of clearing links the woman to him for the life of the garden. If she should try to withdraw from the relationship, the man will condemn her impropriety and may beat her. The link between garden partners is commonly further articulated by go-betweens who carry food from women to men. Often the go-betweens are children, who thus learn the principles and operations of the reciprocal system. Between men, gifts of land, labor, pigs, axe blades, feathers, and other goods require countergifts at a later date. The unbalanced accounts tie the men together, institutionalizing a social structure in which every man has a place because of his debts and credits.

Usually it is either materials or energy in the form of labor that moves through the reciprocal network. But to become a "big man" in the basin rests in part also on drawing prestige from the reciprocal system. All "big men" have commanding personalities and skill at oratory, but they are also men who give away rights to land and who actively support widows and orphans without expecting tit-for-tat repayment. Instead, they gain reputations for helping people and having people dependent upon them; and all the "big men" I knew stressed to their clansmen the merits of mutual support. Nakemba sometimes preached of a communism that was or should be, saying that the land belonged to the clan as to an organism and that all clan members worked so that all could eat. At first it seemed to me paradoxical that men who expressed such a view, as most Bomagai-Angoiang men do, also had strong feelings for private property and became righteously angry if a clansman took garden produce without permission. But, on second thought, I saw that any threat to individual control of rights of use was a threat to the reciprocal system, for it is necessary to possess in order to be able to give. If property were truly communal, acts of exchange would lose most of their power to bind the people together. Transactions that resolve or create inequalities of indebtedness are far more pleasurable and memorable than merely taking from or giving to a truly common pot. Because the element of fun also disappears if inequalities of debt and credit become too one-sided, accumulation by a few people of uncommonly large amounts of property is also a threat to the operation of the reciprocal system. Thus, if a man has many pigs while his clansmen have few, his pigs become objects of sorcery designed to make them sicken and die. As one man explained, "It is not right for a man to have many more pigs than the other men."

Other than bride payments, bride exchanges, and war

(which is a social and economic exchange of a death for a death), most exchanges take place within the clan. However, there are other and more informal reciprocal links across clan lines, as when men present pigs and other goods to friends or relatives in foreign clans—always with the expectation of an eventual counterpresentation. Such exchanges, aside from the economic benefits, give reason for travel and social relations beyond the clan—just as reciprocity among the Bomagai and Angoiang helps to give form and reason to the need for social relations within the clans.

Labor Input, Yields, and Consumption

Considering the nature of Bomagai-Angoiang behavior and gardens, I decided in the field that attempts to collect what have been called statistically meaningful amounts of quantitative data on labor input, on consumption, and especially on yields would not be worth my time. Had I to do it again, I would try to gather more such data because it is essential for any study that is to approach being a full analysis of an ecosystem. For now, I can only say that in most cases my figures are based on a small number of samples and on possibly inaccurate estimates.

Labor Input. For comparison with my estimates of the Bomagai-Angoiang agricultural labor input (Table 8), I also give the estimates of Freeman (1955), Conklin (1957), and Pospisil (1963), all of whom studied groups of shifting cultivators living in environments not greatly different from the Ndwimba Basin. The Iban of Sarawak, described by Freeman, and the Hanunóo of Mindoro in the Philippines, described by Conklin, are dry-rice cultivators who have low population densities (Iban, 23 per square mile; Hanunóo, 26 per square mile) and practice forest-garden rotations in hilly or mountainous tropical regions. The Hanunóo have a crop mixture as richly varied as the Bomagai-Angoiang; the Iban seem more dependent on rice. The Kapauku of West Irian, described by Pospisil, have a "low density of population" (Pospisil, 1963:197) and practice —along with other types of cultivation—an "extensive shifting cultivation" of sweet potatoes on forested land with fallow periods of from eight to twelve years.

My attempt to calculate validly comparable totals of the man-days per acre put in by each of the four groups proved a baffling and perhaps fruitless exercise. But, bearing in mind the different percentages of primary forest cleared as well as several unknowns and complicating conditions, I did estimate the following totals: the Bomagai-Angoiang, 165 man-days per acre; the Iban, 70; the Hanunóo, 140; and the Kapauku, 200. Expressed in this form the agricultural labor input of the four groups covers a wide range. But if their labor input is expressed in terms of the agricultural work that a gardener puts in during a year, the four groups appear to be much closer together.

Table 8. Time Expended on Agricultural Work
(In Man-Days per Acre) [a]

	Bomagai-Angoiang	Iban	Hanunóo	Kapauku
Felling Secondary Forest	6–7	4–5	12	32
Felling Primary Forest	12–16	12–14	24–32	
Slashing	3–7	5–6	4–16	46
Fencing	16–18 [b]	30 [c]	12	32
Burning			11	
Planting	18 [d]	9	11	5
Weeding	35	12–20	24–48	27
Tying sugar and miscel. garden tasks	25			
Harvesting	55	14–20	40	60

a. My "man-day" represents five hours, which is the most that the Bomagai-Angoiang usually work in a day. Pospisil (1963:422) and Conklin (1957:150) presented their figures in hours, which I converted to five-hour man-days. Freeman (1955:89–90) presented his figures in unconvertible "man-days," defined as "a normal day's work for either a male or a female."

b. Includes the two or three days spent in collecting cordage

c. Includes the time spent building fences, traps, and field huts and in keeping watch—per farm, not per acre. The average Iban farm is 4.5 acres in extent (Freeman, 1955:92).

d. Includes the time spent burning and in collecting wump.

This is true because the differences in area worked per worker compensate for the differences in labor input per acre. However, comparisons are made difficult and perhaps inaccurate because the sexual division of labor differs from group to group. I say "gardener" instead of "man" or "woman" because the figures cited represent an attempt to combine men's and women's work.

I estimate that, on the average, a Bomagai-Angoiang gardener put 1,070 hours of work a year into gardens and an additional 80 hours into *Pandanus* orchards—a total of 1,150 hours. Conklin (1957:151) estimates 1,200 hours per year for the average Hanunóo. Using data from Pospisil (1963), I estimate that the Kapauku put slightly more labor time into their extensive gardens than do the Bomagai-Angoiang. The Iban appear to work the least—fewer than 1,100 hours per year. Although I have no easily comparable data, I believe that, if the ratio between labor costs and yield is considered, garden-forest rotation such as that practiced by the tribal Bomagai-Angoiang, Iban, Hanunóo, and Kapauku is more efficient than the more intensive methods of hand labor in permanent fields used by peasants elsewhere. When draft animals are introduced into the sedentary systems, the human labor cost declines, but the total energy cost of production increases; thus, in terms of the relationship of energy input to yield, shifting cultivation gains still more in efficiency in comparison with sedentary agriculture. I find support for these ideas in Conklin (1957:152) and Leach (1949). Freeman (1955:90), on the other hand, argues that in Sarawak, if the time expended in guarding a dry-rice swidden is included in the labor costs (as he says it must be), a swidden requires as much, if not more, labor than a wet-rice field.

Bomagai-Angoiang men work most steadily during the time of clearing and fencing plots for their taro-yam gardens. During the rest of the year labor demands on the men are intermittent, and they seldom work at a single task for more than a few days at a stretch. The women work much more steadily throughout the year at their weeding and their almost daily harvesting. The men spend roughly 40 percent and the women, 60 percent of the time necessary to maintain the gardens and orchards. When not busy at agricultural tasks, the people spend their time at home during bad weather or sickness, in preparation of food, on trips to the Kumoints or elsewhere, on local visits, at dances, in fishing for eels, at building houses,[17] and in local travel which includes considerable opportunity for hunting and for collecting firewood. I should note that collecting and transporting firewood take a good deal of energy, if not much time. Men and women often pick up wood on their way home from the gardens, and boys may be sent specifically to fetch wood. In both cases the vine-bound bundles of sticks and logs, which often must be carried uphill weigh at least twenty pounds and more frequently over thirty pounds. I saw one boy weighing eighty pounds carrying a thirty-seven pound bundle; and Kunbun's wife, Rameka, who weighs ninety-four pounds, once arrived home with forty-six pounds of wood, partly on her head, partly in her net bag. Including the wood used to heat the rocks for the communal earth ovens, seventeen to twenty-two pounds of wood are used daily by each household.

Before the men had steel axes and bush knives, they had to work longer than they do now. With considerable effort I persuaded some of the older men who had grown up with stone axes to use them again at tasks of felling and slashing.[18] On the average, work with stone axes took four times as long as the same work with steel axes, a difference nicely in accord with that obtained by Salisbury (1962) from his Siane informants of the eastern Central Highlands.[19] Even though their work

---

17. A work-group of three or four men can build a house in two to three days if the women help, as they usually do, by collecting roofing material.

18. In order to slash grasses, bushes, and small saplings with a stone axe, the man had first to bend the stems down against a pole laid on the ground as a solid cutting surface. With bush knives only a simple slashing motion is necessary.

19. Salisbury (1962:109) writes: "The major effect of steel tools has been to shorten the time needed to clear and fence gardens. Informants say it took three or four times as long to do these jobs with stone axes, and that instead of going to garden sites every second or

hours were longer, however, it is clear that the stone-age men were not drudges with no time for war or ceremonies. Still, the older men who have used both types of tools speak appreciatively of the benefits of the new axes. One man told me, "Once I had to work all day every day; now I work a little before midday, and then I have time to sit and talk with you."

Another way by which to represent agricultural labor input is by the ratio in calories between the yield of the gardens and the energy expended in garden work. Rappaport (1967a:19–20), who did this for the nearby Tsembaga, estimated energy ratios of 17:1 for the Tsembaga "taro-yam gardens" and 16:1 for their "sugar-sweet potato gardens." He (Rappaport, 1967a:29, n. 5) also cites estimates by Marvin Harris of other energy ratios (10:1 for Dyak rice swiddens and a range at Tepotzlán from 13:1 on poor land to 29:1 on the best land) and suggests (1967a:20) that Tsembaga energy ratios compare favorably with figures reported for swidden cultivation in other regions. I spent several weeks among the Tsembaga and have no reason to think that the Bomagai-Angoiang ratios would not be quite similar to those of the Tsembaga.

Yields. The harvesting of a constantly changing assortment of crops over a period of more than a year makes measurement of yields from Bomagai-Angoiang gardens so cumbersome that, as already noted, I collected only slight data that bear directly on yields. Rappaport (1967a and 1967b) for the Tsembaga, Barrau (1958) for Melanesia as a whole, and Pospisil (1963) for the Kapauku of West Irian, are among those who have estimated yields of several crops that are also common in Bomagai-Angoiang gardens; however, I see little value in citing these figures because Barrau's have a wide range and represent potential yield, and Rappaport's and Pospisil's represent the amount actually harvested by the groups that they studied. Because the Bomagai-Angoiang have a surplus production and always leave unharvested some of all their crops, potential yield

---

third day for one month and working ten to fifteen days, they went every other day for about two months and worked between thirty and forty-five days preparing each garden."

has little meaning. And, from what I know of the Kapauku and the Tsembaga, I believe that both of them harvest more thoroughly than the Bomagai-Angoiang.[20] Consequently, yields are better approached indirectly by way of consumption.

Consumption. In Table 9 are my estimates of the average food consumption of Bomagai-Angoiang adult males. For comparison I also give figures for two peoples of the Central Highlands, the Siane (Salisbury, 1962:80) and a Chimbu group (Hipsley and Kirk, 1965:77). Some of their foods may have been left out of the lists for the Siane and the Chimbu group, but it is apparent, on comparing the amounts of sweet potatoes eaten, that the diet of the Bomagai-Angoiang is more varied than that of the highlands people, who are noted for their extreme dependence on sweet potatoes. Two things account for this dietary difference. First, the greater elevation (5,000 to 9,000 feet) of the highlanders' gardens discourages sweet potatoes less than it does many of the other crops that are common in Bomagai-Angoiang gardens. Second, the greater density of the highland population[21] and the associated retrogression of forest to grassland clearly result in a shift toward sweet potatoes as the dominant crop at the expense of a variety of minor crops.

---

20. Indications of Bomagai-Angoiang surplus production are that: (a) during the phase most productive of tubers, people take only the large tubers and discard the small ones that they extract accidentally; (b) the large amount of food (150 to 300 pounds) that I could buy each week (from the Kono and Fungai clans as well as the Bomagai-Angoiang) for myself, my staff, and my guests; and (c) the large amounts of food, especially sweet potatoes, *Xanthosoma*, and manioc left unharvested in old gardens. Tubers in older gardens are particularly likely to be unharvested because new gardens are coming into production and the weeds in the old gardens raise the labor cost of digging the tubers. The most thoroughly harvested crops are such early bearers as cucumbers, beans, and maize. Among the root crops, yams (the least important quantitatively) are the most completely harvested.

In having a sizeable surplus the Bomagai-Angoiang are not unusual among bush-fallow cultivators. On the contrary, as Lea (1969:174) notes of such groups, "huge surpluses appear to be usual."

21. Siane density is 80 persons to the square mile (Salisbury, 1962:11). The Chimbu group described by Hipsley and Kirk (1965) live in a zone with about 400 per square mile (Brookfield and Brown, 1963:122, map).

The total daily intake of calories of the adult Bomagai-
Angoiang male is 2,650,[22] compared with 2,927 (Salisbury, 1962:
80–81) for the Siane male, who weighs on the average 31
pounds more than the Bomagai-Angoiang man, and 2,360 for
the Chimbu male, who weighs on the average from 9 to 18
pounds more than the Bomagai-Angoiang man (Hipsley and
Kirk, 1965:79, 90). Rappaport (1967a:20) estimated on the
basis of much more thorough records than mine that Tsembaga
males, whose average weight is 101 pounds, or 8 pounds less
than the Bomagai-Angoiang males, take in 2,600 calories daily.
According to figures recently established by the United Nations
Food and Agriculture Organization and other agencies (Wilson,
Fisher, and Fuqua, 1965:14–15), the Tsembaga and Bomagai-
Angoiang diets are adequate in calories for their body size and
climate.

I estimate the daily protein intake of Bomagai-Angoiang
males to be 52 grams each, a figure in accord with Rappaport's
(1967a:20) estimate for the Tsembaga of between 43 and 55
grams. As I have noted, Rappaport and I both saw occasional
symptoms of what appeared to be protein deficiency, and Rappaport has suggested that the protein intake of the Tsembaga,
although adequate for everyday life, is probably insufficient for
times of stress. Certainly, the complete use the Bomagai-Angoiang make of the soft parts of the animals they kill indicates
that there is no excess of protein and that there may be a shortage. When a feral pig is taken, for instance, nothing is wasted.
Brains, tongue, eyes are eaten, as well as all the flesh and internal organs; the guts and stomach are washed and steamed
with leaves, separately from the flesh; the blood that flows
during butchering is collected in a banana leaf and heated,
gently suspended over a fire until it congeals into a chocolate-
like mass that can be sliced and distributed.

---

22. The caloric values of the Bomagai-Angoiang foods listed in
Table 9 are derived from Hipsley and Kirk (1965:39) and Watt and
Merrill (1963).

Young boys are said to like to move from their mothers' houses into men's houses because there they get more meat, sharing with the hunters bits of birds, marsupials, lizards, grubs, eels, and eggs; in the women's houses they get only frogs and

Table 9. Daily Food Consumption
(In Grams of Edible Portion)

	Bomagai-Angoiang Adult Males	Siane Adults	Chimbu Adult Males
Sweet potatoes	510 (663) [a]	1,903 (1,890)	1,326 (1,990)
Xanthosoma	520 (754)		
Colocasia	100 (145)	142 [b] (135)	111 (161)
Yams	28 (30)		
Beans	30 (29)		13 [c] (14)
Maize [d]	— —	114 (105)	
Pumpkins	140 (62)		37 (16)
Cucumbers	199 (21)	312 (31)	
Pandanus sauce	80 (134)		
Greens	800 (240)	398 (90)	147 (44)
Bananas	110 (103)		95 (90)
Saccharum edule	40 (9)		
Sugar cane	582 (338)	456 (305)	8 (5)
Manioc	14 (18)		
Seeds (pumpkin, Gnetum, breadfruit)	10 (10)		
Papaya, figs	30 (14)		
Meat [e]	28 (80)	77 (371)	9 (40)

a. Figures in parentheses represent calories. The apparent discrepancies among some of these figures for caloric content result from the use of different caloric values in different sources. All of the figures for caloric content are tentative.

b. Includes yams.

c. Includes maize.

d. Little maize was grown while I was in the basin because of a government prohibition intended to stop the spread of a corn smut.

e. Figures for Siane and Chimbu include meat from domestic pigs eaten irregularly at ceremonies; Bomagai-Angoiang figure includes only the more regular supply of meat from wild animals and feral pigs.

This is one of the many types of marsupials in the basin.
Both the flesh and the fur are used by the people.

the rats that the women catch in the gardens.[23] Children also
gain small amounts of protein from the insects and spiders
that they catch. As shown in Table 9, I estimate that a man's
average daily consumption of meat from other than domestic
sources is 28 grams, or about an ounce, which contains about
10 percent of the total daily intake of protein. On the occasions,
either of feasts or of sickness or death, when domestic pigs and
tame cassowaries are killed, everyone connected with the event
has considerably more meat, and at the time they probably
need it most.

---

23. When a rat's nest is found in a garden, one woman waits
along the trail leading from the nest while another woman or a child
disturbs the nest so that the animal flees toward the waiting woman,
who tries to seize it by hand.

Wut is displaying a lizard that he shot with a three-
pronged arrow and cooked wrapped in a leaf in hot ashes.
Rotted teeth like Wut's are common among the Bomagai-Angoiang.

Ninety percent of their protein intake comes from vegetable
sources. Of that, a remarkably high percentage (40 percent of
the total intake) comes from green leaves, which, because they
are usually eaten when young, contain a relatively large amount
of protein—two or three times as much as the tubers.[24] Inter-

24. Hipsley and Kirk (1965:39) estimate that a combination of
greens eaten by the Chimbu group that they studied contains 2.7 grams
of protein per 100 grams of weight; 100 grams of sweet potatoes were
estimated to contain 0.9 grams of protein, and 100 grams of taro, 1.4
grams of protein. Beans contribute only a small percentage of the
people's protein because so few are eaten.

preting from the food-composition table in Hipsley and Kirk (1965:39–40), I judge that the leafy greens are also the people's major source of calcium, iron, carotene (a precursor of Vitamin A), and Vitamin C. According to my comparisons of their probable intake of vitamins and minerals (carotene, thiamine, riboflavin, niacin, Vitamin C, calcium, and iron) with Food and Agriculture Organization figures (Wilson, Fisher, and Fuqua, 1965:14–15), the Bomagai-Angoiang diet is adequate in this regard.

When questioned, the Bomagai-Angoiang say that no one ever goes hungry in the basin. On occasion they do say, "We have nothing to eat" or "Today I am going hungry." What they mean, as I have noted, is that there is little "real food," or tubers, available. However, there is usually plenty of other food, such as greens, *Pandanus*, pumpkin, sugar cane, or bananas. I would need to spend a longer time than I did in the basin to be sure of how much seasonality there is in crop production. On the basis of what the people say and the data that I could collect, there seems to be a time of relative shortage from July to November when the new taro-yam gardens are not yet in production. But, even then, only taro and yams are in short supply. Because of this seasonality, the ratio of tubers consumed is not always that given on Table 9; at times *Colocasia* and yams rise in importance at the expense of *Xanthosoma* and sweet potatoes, which are available more steadily throughout the year. Not much manioc is eaten at any time of year, although it is always available if needed. *Pandanus* and such minor crops as cucumbers and breadfruit are also subject to seasonal variation. Each of the many varieties of *Pandanus conoideus* comes ripe at a different time, so that yield is staggered through the year, though there is a relative shortage in the drier season. However, the Bomagai-Angoiang have an abundance of *Pandanus* trees and for most of the year eat the *Pandanus* sauce, their major source of vegetable fat, whenever they desire—on the average, three to four times a week. Cucumbers are scarce from December to the end of the drier season, when those planted in early taro-yam gardens begin to mature. The breadfruit ripens in September and October.

By weight harvested, sugar cane is the most important crop throughout the year. Women frequently come back to their houses bearing twenty or more pounds of sugar cane. One woman's burden that I weighed included forty-two pounds of cane, twenty pounds carried tied together on her head, and twenty-two pounds in her net bag along with eleven pounds of *Xanthosoma*, four pounds of sweet potatoes, and three pounds each of taro and greens. Much of the sugar cane is waste; according to my measurements, 54 percent of the total weight of a cane is either skin or fiber that is spit out after chewing. Of the material taken in, 80 percent is water and the rest, nothing but carbohydrate except for quite small amounts of protein, calcium, and perhaps other minerals. But the people would not be without sugar cane and frequently eat it as a snack while gardening or walking about and almost always eat large amounts on returning home tired and hot. In addition to giving quick energy, the cane may also meet a significant part of the people's need for water, for they drink little directly.

Trends

As a formal analysis of an ecosystem, my account of the relations between the Bomagai-Angoiang and the components of their environment has been rudimentary. I could not give detailed quantitative information about the flow, accumulation, or loss of energy and material relevant to the ecosystem; undoubtedly I missed many of the pertinent linkages between parts of the system. It follows that my conclusions about the trends of the ecosystem must be openly intuitive and only tentative. I organize these conclusions around a theme suggested by F. R. Fosberg. Drawing words, I hope without violence to his thought, from several of Fosberg's papers (1958; 1963; 1965) I summarize this theme as follows:

There is a tendency toward diversity in natural ecosystems; there is a tendency toward uniformity in artificial ecosystems or those strongly influenced by man. Diversity is a component of the organized complexity of an ecosystem. Generally, the greater the degree of diversity and complexity within an ecosystem, the greater the stability of the system. A reduction of complexity usually leads to changes in the direction of an increase of entropy within the system. An ecosystem wherein entropy is increasing must be considered to be, at least to some extent, unhealthy.

Because ecology and geography are the foci of a consideration of man's ultimate well-being as an inhabitant of the face of the earth, a student following ecologic or geographic lines in a study of man should be concerned with the stability of human ecosystems. Stability means that what has been called the carrying capacity (the level of population at which a steady state is possible in a given ecosystem) of the ecosystem is not exceeded. Stability or loss of stability and an increase of entropy can be determined by observing the system's diversity, for it is a reflection of the entropy level.

The Past. That to the east and northeast of the Ndwimba Basin lies a large extent of habitable but unpeopled land, that the Maring language spoken by the Bomagai-Angoiang and their neighbors is found along the northern edge of the area occupied by the East New Guinea Highlands Stock, and that many Maring-speakers including the Bomagai have myths of having originated in the Jimi Valley all point to a movement of people into the Simbai Valley from the south. The time of entry and whether the area had been occupied before are unknown. The pioneer location of the Bomagai-Angoiang and the lack of grassland within their territory suggests particularly recent movement into the vicinity of the Ndwimba Basin. However, the discovery in the basin of a stone implement of a type and with a use unknown to the present-day inhabitants suggests occupation of some duration. The implement, which was uncovered by a gardener while I was in the basin, is a double-edged, polished stone blade that is two inches wide and would be, if not broken at the ends, about eight inches long. Useful as neither an axe nor an adze, it can be imagined that the blade was a dagger point, a scraper, or a spear point. Since I left the basin in 1965, two more blades of a similar type have been found nearby, one in Simbai Valley (Bulmer and Clarke, 1970), the other in the Jimi Valley.

There are, however, many other evidences in highland New Guinea of a prehistoric technology that differed from the technology found by the first Europeans who entered the region in the twentieth century. (See, for example, S. Bulmer, 1964; S. and R. Bulmer, 1964). Stone mortars and pestles have been found in many parts of the Central Highlands as well as in the mountains to the north and—outside of highland New Guinea —on the north coast of the great island and in the Bismarck Archipelago and other islands to the east. With one exception (Chappell, 1964), there are no reports of contemporary manufacture of the mortars. Many present-day New Guineans know of no use for the prehistoric utensils, whose manufacture they attribute to spirits or ancestors; other people use them now, but never with real intensity. Chappell (1964:147) and R. Bulmer (1964:147) list the contemporary uses to which the mortars have been put: as fertility- and other cult objects and in various forms of magic, water-filled as mirrors, in the preparation of medicine, and in crushing certain types of leaves to make a potion (magical, but apparently not poisonous) to smear on battle arrows. To judge by the extensive wear on some mortars and pestles and by the presence of crude undecorated mortars (S. and R. Bulmer, 1964:70), there seems little doubt that the mortars had other original practical uses. The Bulmers suggest, and it seems likely, that an important use could have been for the grinding of wild nuts and other seeds for food. Several uncultivated plants in highland New Guinea have seeds that could be processed in this way. R. Bulmer (1964) lists several, including the seeds or nuts of *Castanopsis acuminatissima* (eaten now by the Bomagai-Angoiang and other New Guineans), at least three species of *Elaeocarpus* trees (eaten now by some New Guineans), and *Coix lachryma-jobi* (perhaps eaten in parts of New Guinea and widely reported as a food plant in southern and southeastern Asia). On the basis of archaeological and distributional evidence, S. and R. Bulmer (1964:72) posit "a rather late date" for the introduction of mortars and pestles into the highlands:

The implements date from a period in Highlands prehistory when root crops (taro, yams, and *Pueraria*) or bananas were being cultivated, but when the natural vegetation of the area still provided an important part of the diet, ar d before sweet potato cultivation permitted the extensive settlei .ent of the higher-altitude areas. Possibly, the wide-spread manufacture and practical use of mortars and pestles ceased with the general improvement in food supplies brought about by intensive sweet potato cultivation, though the destruction by agricultural clearing of uncultivated or semicultivated nut and seed bearing plants could also have rendered this technology obsolete.

Because, to my knowledge, no mortars or pestles have been found in the Ndwimba Basin, it is uncertain whether this unknown technology penetrated the basin. But in light of the stone blade and the presence of mortars nearby in the Simbai Valley as well as in the Jimi and Kaironk valleys, it seems probable that mortar-users could have been in the basin. Even if they were, it remains impossible to know what effects they and their technology had on the basin environment. I further suppose, however, that the past populations were too small to cause retrogression of forest to grassland; but they may have altered the forest vegetation considerably, either by clearing for gardens or by favoring certain species of trees. For instance, in places in the midmountain rain forest *Castanopsis acuminatissima* grows together in suspiciously concentrated stands. It also occurs with a spreading habit in open areas. Bulmer (1964:148), if I read him correctly, restricts the tree to "disturbed forest." The easily noticed, red-barked *Dillenia* tree—of a genus that contains pioneer species in parts of Asia—seems only to occur in potentially cultivable areas of the midelevation rain forest; and it too is sometimes suspiciously common for an ordinary species of the true primary rain forest. The nut-bearing *Pandanus* of the crest forest, as I have already mentioned, also grow in groves that may be natural but that look as if they were induced by man.

Following the Bulmers' hypothesis that sweet potatoes and an increased dependence on food from gardens overlays the mortar (and blade?) technology,[25] I can imagine several generations of post-mortar cultivators clearing the basin with stone axes, interplanting sweet potatoes with their other crops, and slowly replacing the altered primary forest with the types of secondary forest and woodland that I have described. The coming of the steel axe a few decades ago made an easy acceleration of this process possible.

The Present. An approach now popular in research on shifting cultivation is the determination of "carrying capacity," or "critical population density."[26] Fosberg (1963:5) has defined

---

25. As the Bulmers themselves imply, their hypothesis fits the basin's elevation and diversified agriculture less well than it does the higher elevation and less diversified agriculture of the Central Highlands. Furthermore, as noted, I believe that the Bulmers and Watson (1965a; 1965b) exaggerate the revolutionary impact of sweet potatoes on agricultural methods and production in New Guinea.

26. See, for instance, Allan (1949), Conklin (1959), Carneiro (1960), and Brookfield and Brown (1963). I applied Conklin's and Carneiro's formulas to the situation of the Bomagai-Angoiang, using the values listed below.

Conklin (1959:63): $\dfrac{L}{AT} = Cs$

L (the maximum cultivable land available) equals about 587 hectares, which is the equivalent of 1,450 acres, a modest figure that I derive by adding to the basic 1,150 acres sometimes cultivated in the basin the 200 acres of unused secondary-forest land immediately west of the basin and 100 acres of easily available virgin-forest land out of the much larger area actually available to the Bomagai-Angoiang.

A (the minimum average area required for clearing, per year, per individual) equals 0.093 hectare (0.23 acre).

T (the minimum average duration of a full agricultural cycle) equals 39.85 years (38.6 years fallow plus 1.25 years cropping). Cs represents the critical population size.

Carneiro (1960:230): $\dfrac{\dfrac{T}{(R + Y)} \times Y}{A} = P$

T (the total area of arable land [in acres] within practicable walking distance of the village) equals 1,450 acres.

Y (the number of years that plot of land continues to produce

carrying capacity as "the level of population at which a steady
state is possible in a given ecosystem." Allan's (1965:89) definition is more commonly used: "the maximum population density
the system is capable of supporting permanently in that environment *without damage to the land.*" The concept of carrying
capacity is fruitful, but the determination of carrying capacity
is difficult. To begin with, what is damage to the land? Allan
(1949:1) describes land degradation as "a process which results
in radical changes in the whole character of the land; loss of
mineral foods, oxidation and disappearance of organic matter,
breakdown of soil structure, degeneration of vegetation; and the
setting up of a new train of land and water relationships." It
is because land degradation is a process that the determination
of carrying capacity is difficult. Most studies of ecosystems are

---

before it has to be abandoned) equals 1.25 years.

R (the number of years an abandoned plot must lie fallow before it can be recultivated) equals 38.6 years.

A (the area of cultivated land [in acres] required to provide the
average individual with the amount of food that he ordinarily
derives from cultivated plants per year) equals 0.23 acre.

P represents the population that could be supported permanently
in the basin under the present system of horticulture.

Using Conklin's formula I estimate that Cs for the Bomagai-
Angoiang is 158 persons, or 4 persons more than the present population
of 154. Beyond that number, if the amount of cultivable land were not
increased, the population and the land (or resources) would, according
to the formula, be out of balance. Using Carneiro's formula, P is 198
persons, with the same proviso that the amount of cultivable land
remains constant. The Conklin and Carneiro figures convert, respectively,
to 70 and 87 persons per square mile of cultivable land. At the same
figure of 1,450 acres of cultivable land, the actual density of the basin
is 68 persons per square mile.

Freeman (1955:135) wrote of Sarawak that, when the Iban
population rises above 51 persons per square mile of cultivable land,
there is danger of land degradation. Conklin (1957:146) estimated that
a Hanunóo area could support a maximum of 124 persons per square
mile of available swidden land under existing conditions. Spencer (1966:
15, n7) cited the widely quoted figure worked out by van Beukering
(on the basis of a detailed study of shifting cultivation in Indonesia)
of 130 persons per square mile as the upper limit for a long-run carrying
capacity. Pelzer (1945:23), on the basis of van Beukering's then unpublished study, agreed that shifting cultivation could be maintained
at densities of up to 130 persons per square mile.

synchronic; formulas are established to determine carrying capacity on the basis of conditions during a short time; the values used for the variables in the formulas represent current events, not processes of change. John Street (1969) has considered the problems connected with quantitative determination of carrying capacity. Among other points he noted the following:

1. New crops and tools and different agricultural techniques are readily adopted by many primitive peoples. Such changes may increase or decrease environmental degradation.
2. As crops change, even if the land is not affected, the quantity and nutritive quality of food consumed may change.
3. In determinations of carrying capacity, many students have gratuitously taken the actual length of fallow to be equivalent to the length of fallow required to prevent gradual soil impoverishment or changes in spontaneous vegetation.
4. Deterioration of the land is a cumulative process; current changes may be so slight as to be exceeded by errors in measurement.

It is easy to find examples of these points. (1) For instance, the introduction of steel axe heads into the Ndwimba Basin not only lessened labor requirements but also increased, if not the size of the area gardened, the size of the area cleared of trees each year. Also, Bomagai-Angoiang informants say that now with steel axes they fell large trees that they would have only pollarded with stone axes. Because most of the pollarded trees resprouted, the regeneration of mature forest was more rapid before the introduction of steel axes than it is now. Steel axes also encourage the clearing of primary forest. (2) The recently introduced crops of *Xanthosoma* and maize, respectively, correspond fairly closely in behavior and use to the older Bomagai-Angoiang crops of taro and *Saccharum edule*, and I do not see that either of the new crops has much affected the character of Bomagai-Angoiang gardens. But the maize has bettered the quality of the people's diet, and, I suspect, the *Xanthosoma* has increased the quantity of carbohydrate available. In contrast, a shift to a high consumption of manioc, which has occurred

in many parts of the tropical world, would deteriorate the diet.
(3, 4) As Street pointed out, there is a tendency among re-
searchers (most of them anthropologists) who have worked on
the determination of carrying capacity to make the unlikely assumption that, because "their people" seem to be in harmony
with nature, their agricultural techniques are not changing the
environment. However, with the Bomagai-Angoiang, as with
almost any group of shifting cultivators, even if a formula
showed that the population could double without damage to
the land, an increase in the population of 10 percent would
change the cycle of rotation of garden and secondary regrowth,
bringing subtle changes in the cover of vegetation. A walk
through the Jimi and Simbai valleys, where population densities
vary from group territory to territory, clearly shows the correlation between vegetation and population density; even where
there is scarcely any retrogression to grassland, the secondary
cover of taller plants in territories more densely populated than
the Ndwimba Basin has less diversity and a simpler structure
than that in the basin. For example, in the more densely
populated places, there is more jungle and almost solid stands
of the weedy tree *Dodonaea viscosa* and tree ferns. The solid
stands could result partly from accidents of seed availability,
but I believe that they represent a movement of the vegetation
away from the diversified stands of primary and incipient primary forest.

In sum, I think that carrying capacity should be thought
of as a gradient rather than as a critical limit. Any change in
population density along the gradient will prompt environmental change; at most points along the gradient some environmental change will be going on, even if the population
remains constant. It follows that measurement of carrying
capacity requires knowledge not only of the length of actual
fallow and cropping periods, the amount of land needed to feed
each person, and the total amount of land available, but also
of the rate of the processes of erosion, leaching, retrogression of
vegetation, and changing yields. Information about these processes can be gained only by careful long-lived or comparative

experiments. In lieu of such experiments, the amount of biological diversity within an ecosystem serves as a partial indicator
of the current relations between the human population and
the other parts of the ecosystem.

Judged by its diversity, the ecosystem of the Ndwimba
Basin is now in good health. Large amounts of lower montane
rain forest are present, and it is a truism that tropical rain
forests contain great diversity. The secondary vegetation is
relatively diverse and complexly structured, compared with the
secondary vegetation of much of New Guinea and the rest of
the tropical world. This layered, diverse plant cover efficiently
appropriates solar energy, accumulates organic matter, and maintains soil fertility—all with little work by the few members of
the human species that now inhabit the basin. The people and
their environment are close to being in a state of internal equilibrium, in the sense that the people maintain themselves within
their ecosystem with virtually no imports of matter or potential
energy and no exports or "production" in the form of harvests
of materials to be removed by man. Such a harvest in most
man-dominated ecosystems depends either on a constant drain-
ing-off of the system's resources or on imports in amounts sufficient to counterbalance the exports.

The Future. Certainly the Bomagai-Angoiang have, as C.O.
Sauer (1952:3–4) put it for all mankind, "prospered by disturb-
ing the natural order." Their gardens and orchards are more
productive of food than the rain forest; their domestic pigs give
them, if not an abundance, a supply of meat that is available
when needed; their artifact, the secondary vegetation, is more
fruitful of materials and food than the primary forest. In short,
they have created from the natural elements of the environment
a habitat they understand and can manipulate so that it gives
them sustenance.

But Sauer went on to say that man often "overreaches himself and the new order he has introduced may end in disaster."
Of course, I see no self-induced disaster in the near future for
the Bomagai-Angoiang, but there are seemingly inescapable
processes at work that will reduce the natural diversity of their

environment and—if the environment is to continue to sustain the resident population—require a greater input of energy.

The most immediately certain of these processes is an increase in population. The medical facilities of the government and the missions have already begun to reduce the mortality rate of the Bomagai-Angoiang. The government's prohibition against warfare and ambush has had the same effect.[27] If the Ndwimba Basin were to remain as isolated as it is now, part of an expanding population could move to Kumoints or beyond. But such migration would provide only temporary relief; and when feeder roads are extended outward from the planned Highlands-to-Madang highway (to pass through Bundi about forty miles east of the basin) and the newly opened road into the Jimi Valley from the Central Highlands, peoples from the crowded highlands may colonize the empty lands, thus restricting the Bomagai-Angoiang population to the vicinity of the basin. Under the current system of agriculture, an increase of population in the basin would inevitably lead to a retrogression of the vegetation toward grassland. Seen in the light of Fosberg's ideas regarding entropy and diversity, this means that, as the amount of diversified forest lessens, the large and organized biomass that is the forest is lost, being replaced by grass communities that appropriate relatively little energy, much of which is periodically dispersed by fire. The seeds and cuttings of cultivated plants rapidly increase their useful biomass when planted in forest-fallowed soil because of the organized matter and potential energy accumulated there by the forest; in effect, the people channel the "work" of the forest into their crops. When crops are planted in grass-fallowed soil, the men themselves must somehow make up the energy deficit. That is, as the capi-

---

27. It has been suggested (Vayda, 1961b:1968) that warfare among men has ecologically adaptive functions similar to the hypothesized population-regulating and resource-distributing activities of animals, as described by Wynne-Edwards (1962). Although warfare doubtless has recurrently resulted in deaths and caused migration in New Guinea, thereby slowing population growth, its population-limiting function has not been efficient enough to prevent the formation of immense tracts of anthropogenic grasslands.

tal, or diversity, of the ecosystem diminishes, input by man must increase. This input can be effected by tilling the soil or by a combination of tilling and fertilization.

Indisputably, it is harder to work grassland soils than forest soils. I have traced elsewhere (Clarke, 1966) what I believe to be a succession of ever-increasing labor costs that accompanies the increase of population densities and the associated retrogression of vegetation. Harding (1967:11), in his work on the gardening practices of a community of grassland farmers on the northeast coast of New Guinea, writes:

Tilling was the most demanding operation, absorbing, by rough calculation, about 4 percent of the total man-hours of labor available annually. If a five-man team plus their wives worked one day to prepare a standard plot, and there were three annual plots totaling a half-acre or less, then 60 man-days/acre were required annually. In labor expenditure, tillage in grassland farming is comparable to clearing in forest cultivation.

Harding then adds that, according to Clark and Haswell (1966:32), sixty man-days of labor amounts to twice the time needed to clear heavy rain forest with steel tools in Ghana. Harding's comparison shows grassland cultivation to consume less labor than it actually does, for tillage in grassland soil is a task additional to any of the tasks connected with the preparation of forest-fallowed soil. The grassland operations comparable to clearing forest are the pre-tillage clearing, burning, and firebreaking that by Harding's (1967:10) estimates take eight to sixteen man-days per acre among the people that he is describing. The labor necessary for these operations must be added to that for the tillage before the grass-fallowed soil is ready for gardening, which is a total labor cost much higher than that of preparing forest-fallowed soils. The whole matter can be summed up by rendering the words of Vicedom and Tischner (1943–1948 1:185), early ethnographers of a Central Highlands people who had to prepare gardens in man-made grasslands: "It is not easy work."

Besides the work connected with clearing and tilling grass-

land soil, many New Guinean peoples who live in grass-domi-
nated regions put energy into planting trees in an attempt to
reproduce at least partially the missing spontaneous woodland
and forest. *Casuarina* trees are widely planted as fallow vegetation and wood for fuel and fences; *Albizia* trees are also planted,
though less widely, for their ameliorative effects on the soil;
and several species spontaneous in the basin, such as the nut-
bearing *Pandanus* and the edible-leafed *Ficus dammaropsis* and
ap tse (? *Acalypha* sp.), are planted as supplementary sources
of food. Many of the basin's other food-bearing secondary
plants, however, are nowhere cultivated and do not grow spontaneously in grasslands, so a loss of variety of edible leaves and
fruits also accompanies a growing domination of grassland over
forest. The variety of garden crops also diminishes, to be replaced by an increasing monotony of sweet potatoes, with a
consequent impoverishment of the diet. The diversity of wild
birds and other animals decreases, too, as expanding gardens
and grasslands destroy forest habitats and as the numbers of
human hunters increase. Hunting pressure on wild animals also
increases, as more males go to work on plantations and, in the
light of their new Western schooling, abandon the taboos that
provide seasonal protection to particular animals. For instance,
the Bomagai-Angoiang have a taboo against eating eel during
the planting and early life of the taro-yam gardens. It is believed
that if a person who has eaten eel (in theory, within the same
"moon," in practice, within three or four days) enters a young
taro-yam garden, the taro and yams, instead of ripening, will
become "soft" because "eel is soft." This taboo means that the
people take almost no eels during the several months of the
drier season when taro-yam gardens are being established. If eel
hunting were to increase during this period, the total take for
the year would probably diminish. Goggles (to help in seeing
eels) and fish hooks have already been introduced into the
basin. Further new pressures on wildlife will result from the
inevitable coming of the shotgun.

Up to now, however, aside from a small increase in the
felling of primary forest with the coming of steel axes, the

influence of the outside Western world has been slight on the
environment of the Bomagai-Angoiang. But they, as is often
said of all Melanesians, are materialists. They like things, they
like to trade them and to acquire them; they will be eager to
participate in the revolution of rising expectations, to possess
some of the flood of manufactured goods. They will be able to
earn money only by selling their labor, mostly on plantations,
or by planting cash crops, most likely the coffee or tea that is
already grown commercially in highland New Guinea. Each
man who remains in the basin—if he continues to raise all his
own food, as well as a cash crop—must increase the acreage
that he cultivates each year. If this increase in cultivated area
per man is not balanced by an emigration of plantation laborers
or people drawn along the new roads to towns, it will have the
same ecologic effect as an increase in population density.

As outside influence increases, the people will drift from
the integral independence and near-stability of their diversified
native system of existence toward the commoner human system
that feeds ever more hungrily on the earth's capital accumulation of organized matter and potential energy. By this drift, the
Bomagai-Angoiang will become more completely a part of that
process that Lévi-Strauss (1961:397) describes so vividly:

From the day when he first learned how to breathe and how to keep
himself alive, through the discovery of fire and right up to the
invention of the atomic and thermonuclear devices of the present
day, Man has never—save only when he reproduces himself—done
other than cheerfully dismantle millions upon millions of structures
and reduce their elements to a state in which they can no longer be
reintegrated. No doubt he has built cities and brought the soil to
fruition; but if we examine these activities closely we shall find that
they also are inertia-producing machines, whose scale and speed of
action are infinitely greater than the amount of organization implied
in them. As for the creations of the human mind, they are meaningful only in relation to that mind and will fall into nothingness as
soon as it ceases to exist. Taken as a whole, therefore, civilization can
be described as a prodigiously complicated mechanism: tempting as it
would be to regard it as our universe's best hope of survival, its true

function is to produce what physicists call entropy: inertia, that is to say.

If a more limited view is taken, some aspects of the Bomagai-Angoiang future can be seen in a more encouraging light. Contact with Europeans has or will remove the burden of some diseases and the fear of local war and ambush. And, although for most Bomagai-Angoiang there will be the frustration of a low income linked with the increasing need and desire for money, for some there may be joy and excitement in the wider world to which they will have access. Before contact, the way of life of an individual in the Ndwimba Basin was limited to a single path. Now, some individuals will at least have an opportunity for wider freedom of action. But—to return to the ecologic theme—in the outside world, or what has been called the developed world, that freedom often rests on the rapid expenditure of environmental capital. It is an irony that while the Bomagai-Angoiang still live in a relatively stable ecosystem they are becoming so impressed and intrigued by the artifacts of the outside world's plundering economy that they feel that they can only learn from that world, that they have nothing to teach it in return.

Appendixes

Theoretical Considerations and Practical Problems

Man and milieu, land and life, place and people—such has been the essential content of all studies in human or cultural geography. But the choice of principle around which to organize this content has varied from student to student. Some have seen the relation of man and land primarily in terms of man's modification of his habitat. Viewed in this light, human activities, issuing from cultural history, are agent or cause, and the cultural landscape, molded from the passive environment, is effect. Others have seen the opposite flow of influence and have written of the determinative and controlling power of environment over man.[1] In recent years, often under the banner of human or cultural ecology, there have been attempts by anthropologists and by geographers to subdue the conceptualized duality of man and environment by considering the two as parts of a single interacting system. Such an attempt has been the unifying thread of my study of the environment and people of the Ndwimba Basin.

Of course, the word "ecology" and some tenets of the biological discipline of ecology are not new to the literature of the social sciences. Decades ago Barrows (1923) designated geography as human ecology; sociologists (for example, McKen-

---

1. I will not detail here the often-told story of argument and over-response among proponents of environmental determinism, possibilism, and what could be called cultural determinism. Clarence Glacken in his *Traces on the Rhodian Shore* (1967) thoroughly delineates the earlier history of thought on these matters. H. and M. Sprout (1965) make a close examination of the more recent literature and ideas. O. H. K. Spate (1968) and C. Geertz (1963: Ch. 1) provide briefer reviews. All these works will lead the reader to the classics of environmental determinism and the opposing views. *Man's Role in Changing the Face of the Earth* (Thomas, 1956) is the best single collection of works on the theme of its title.

zie, 1926; Park, 1936; and Hawley, 1950) have used the same term in their works; and the anthropologist Steward (1955: Chapter 2) developed a concept and method of research that he termed cultural ecology. But Barrows's interest was in man's adjustment to what he presented as a static environment. The sociologists were scarcely thinking of the environment in a material sense; to them human ecology had to do with the spatial aspects of human interdependencies. And to Steward, cultural ecology was a tool for explaining cultural traits through the study of the adaptation of a culture to its enivronment. That is, none of these scholars was considering human activities and the physical environment as truly interdependent parts of a single system. Now the conceptual path to such an explicitly interactionist position has been smoothed by the formal adoption into the social sciences of the idea of the ecosystem—a term and idea first proposed in 1935 by Tansley and more recently propagated in 1956 by Evans (1956), both biologists.[2]

As it is now applied to human life by anthropologists and geographers, the idea of the ecosystem, which stresses the circularity of the relationship between organism and environment, make it easy to consider that environment as both a result of and an influence on human behavior. Man affects the environment; in turn, the changed environment requires new responses from man and acts to rearrange man's image of his surroundings. Considered thus as components of an ecosystem, both man and environment are seen as parts of a single unit, the whole of which is worthy of study. Concern shifts from which part most influences the other to the structure of the whole system and how it operates and changes. This is not to say that the ecosystem approach divinely illuminates all the mysteries of the relations of man and land, but as a point of view it does relieve the observer of fruitless preconceptions of unilinear influence. Further, it removes the fear of the heresy of

---

2. Other works on nonhuman ecosystems that have influenced my thought have been Fosberg's (1961) description in qualitative terms of the important features of the ecosystem of a coral reef and Odum's works (1959; 1962; 1963) in which he defines ecology as the study of the structure and function of ecosystems.

determinism in considering some human behaviors as adaptations to environmental conditions.

Outstanding among the recent works in which data on man and environment have been joined systematically are studies by anthropologists. Conklin (1957), with a stress on ethnoecology, described as a system the shifting cultivation of the Hanunóo of the Philippines; Geertz (1963) used ecosystem analysis in his study of agricultural involution in Indonesia. Rappaport (1967b) analyzed the functioning of ritual in the environmental relations of a Maring community living close to the Bomagai-Angoiang. Geographers have also made substantive contributions to this field. Clarkson (1968) wrote on the cultural ecology of a Chinese settlement in the highlands of the Malay peninsula. Several geographers contributed essays to a recent book titled *Geography as Human Ecology* (Eyre and Jones, 1966); and several others—with anthropologists—took part in a 1961 symposium on "Man's Place in the Island Ecosystem" (Fosberg, 1963). Aside from the works treating specific environments and peoples, there have been several theoretical papers and reviews of literature on human and cultural ecology. Important among these are papers by the geographers Mikesell (1967) and Stoddart (1965, 1967) and the anthropologists Vayda and Rappaport (1968).

A kind of systematic analysis related to the concept of the ecosystem and the theory of general systems is an approach known to anthropologists as functional analysis, the meaning of which has been discussed by the philosopher Collins (1965) in his consideration of the use of functional analysis in several of the papers presented at a 1960 symposium on "Man, Culture, and Animals" (Leeds and Vayda, 1965). In essence, all of the papers classed by Collins as functional analyses were attempts to analyze and specify systems of operationally defined behavioral, demographic, and environmental variables. Acquaintance with these and other works in functional analysis influenced my writing and my field research, even though I did not formally apply the approach. The most relevant example of such a formal application is R. Rappaport's (1967b) analysis of the functioning of ritual within a Maring community. Specifically, Rappaport tried to show how ritual, rather than being a part of culture that produced no practical effect on the external world, functioned to mediate critical relations of the community with its environment and its neighbors. Studies such as Rappaport's are exciting and usually convincing, although I think anthropologists have sometimes put too much emphasis on homeostasis as a static condition and too much trust in the unfailing operation of systems of negative feedback. No life system is stable in the sense that it is unchanging. Cultural behavior may act to counterbalance environmental changes, but there is always a net change in the system. Certainly, ecosystems as evolutionary entities are self-maintaining, but they are self-transforming, too. Rather than a homeostat, a gyroscope may be the suitable analogy for regulatory mechanisms in ecosystems.

There are problems in my use of the ecosystem concept: some of them are matters of theory; others arise from shortcomings in my field data. One problem of theory is the ancient one of epistemology: How can I be certain what the relevant components of the system are, or even that in reality there is a system? The answer is simple: I cannot be certain. The cybernetician Beer comments significantly on this matter (Beer, 1961:7–8):

What after all *is* order, or something systematic? I suppose it is a pattern, and a pattern has no objective existence anyway. A pattern is a pattern because some*one* declares a concatenation of items to be meaningful or cohesive. The onus for detecting systems, and for deciding how to describe them, is very much on ourselves. I do not think we can adequately regard a system as a fact of nature, truths about which can be gradually revealed by patient analytical research. A viable system is something we detect and understand when it is mapped into our brains, and I suppose the inevitable result is that our brains themselves actually impose a structure on reality.

And the geographer H. C. Darby (1962:4) writes:

It is true that a contrast has sometimes been drawn between the subjective impression of the artist and the objective description of the geographer. But is the geographer objective? Can he be? In describing a landscape, is he not committed by his past training and his past experiences—by his prejudices, if you will? Just as the portrait an artist paints will tell you much about the artist as well as about his sitter, so the description of a countryside will tell you a great deal about a writer.

Darby (1962:5) also quotes from George Perkins Marsh's *Man and Nature:* "Sight is a faculty; seeing an art. The eye is a physical, but not a self-acting apparatus, and in general it sees only what it seeks." In sum, even though we cannot be sure we see or know reality, we can search for better ways to examine what lies before us and within us. Explicit in this study is the hope that the use of the concept of the ecosystem is one such way.

As a partial solution to the uncertainty about what is relevant and operative in a given human ecosystem, some anthropologists have advocated the use of ethnoscience or, more specifically, ethneocology. Frake (1962:52) said that the ethnographer must "describe the environment as the people themselves construe it according to the categories of their ethnoscience." By means of such a procedure, the investigator "learns, in a rather meaningful and precise sense, what role the environment plays in the cultural behavior of the members of a particular society." A similar view is implicit in Conklin's papers on shifting cultivation and Hanunóo agriculture. To know something of an alien people's cognition of their world is fascinating in itself and, of course, fundamental to any understanding of their decisions; but if the goal of a study is a description of a human ecosystem, a strict adherence to the method of ethnoecology would raise difficulties. Burling (1964) and Vayda and Rappaport (1968) have discussed some of these difficulties: (a) an observer cannot be sure from a people's verbal behavior what is going on in their minds; (b) consciously or unconsciously, people do not always tell the truth or the whole truth, especially if the right question is not asked; and (c) the method of ethnoecology does not point out the latent consequences of a people's current behavior.[3] For a geographer interested in human ecology—and Vayda (1965:4) suggests the same for anthropologists—a more profitable major concern than a people's perceptions of their environment is their behavior as it relates to their environment.

Another problem of the ecosystem approach relates to quantification: how to measure the amounts and rate of flow of energy and matter and how to express exactly the relationships between the components of the ecosystem. There is no dispute that numerical measurements and mathematically exact statements of relationships are desirable; practically, however, in a system even as uncomplicated as the small human ecosystem of the Ndwimba Basin, they are difficult to obtain. Because of field conditions and my own inclinations and background, I did not even attempt to collect quantitative data beyond simple measurements of location, aspects of soil, agriculture, labor input, food consumption, and climate. With regard to measurement, then, my description of the Bomagai-Angoiang and their environment can only be considered a qualitative sketch. In this quantifying age I find consolation for my numerically flimsy data in Beer's (1961:21–22) persuasive remarks:

Let us agree that quantification is paramount in science. But it is high time that we advanced beyond the crude concepts of "objective" measuring rods and clocks (the quotes have had to go on since Einstein's work) and looked to the brain for advice. How often does the brain produce an output in numerical form when not actually asked to do arithmetic? And when it does, how accurate is the answer? "Half a mile down the road," "7 inches long, dear," "he was in there a good half hour," says the brain when asked "how much further?" (2 miles), "how long is this knitting?" (5.9 inches), "how long did you wait?" (42 minutes precisely). And yet we pick our way across fast-moving traffic streams without getting killed. Conclusion: *there is more to quantification than numeration.*

Such faith that intuitive quantification can be accurate, even if not precise, would seem unjustified in a geographic

---

3. *Man, Culture, and Animals* (Leeds and Vayda, 1965) contains several discussions of latent ecological functions.

study on the usual regional scale. But because the population and area of my study were tiny by most geographers' standards (though more normal for anthropologists') I felt that the operation of the Ndwimba Basin ecosystem could be as comprehensible without as with buttressing by intense numerical measurement. Further, because my study lacked time depth, the figures I did obtain probably do not represent average conditions.[4] I do not disparage measurement, however, for in the field the act of measuring has value beyond gaining numerical data. I found Lea's observation (1964:13), based on his work among lowland New Guinean gardeners, to be completely true for my work too: ". . . in attempting measurement, a fieldworker finds out much that he may have otherwise missed, for measurement demands regular attendance and constant supervision."

Geographic studies of microregions have been criticized for being too restricted in scale to yield either useful generalizations or accurate views of larger regions. In reply to the first of these criticisms, Brookfield (1968:435) has argued that if the geographers' problem is the analysis of systems, "it is inescapable that we will formulate hypotheses on how these systems operate, and equally inescapable that they must then be tested in carefully chosen laboratory locations in the field where they must then be explored in as much depth as is necessary." Having studied a small area in considerable detail, even if not as rigorously as I might have, I of course agree with Brookfield. I have no quarrel with the second criticism that an aggregation of studies of microregions does not of itself give birth to a regional geography, but I do believe that microregion studies such as Waddell's (1968) and Lea's (1964) agricultural systems provide a vivid and accurate image of what is present and what is

---

4. Year-to-year differences in the pattern of rainfall and in the inclinations of the gardeners result in a different acreage under production each year. Before the Europeans came and stopped warfare, these year-to-year random differences had on top of them the cyclical increase and decrease in planted acreage that corresponded to the accumulation and mass slaughter of pigs that was part of the ritual cycle of warfare and truce. Rappaport (1967b) gives a full and fascinating description of the ecologic implications of this cycle among the Tsembaga, near neighbors to the Bomagai-Angoiang.

happening in parts of the wider region and thus lead to a deeper understanding of the diversity of life and environment in any region and make more meaningful the recognition of the important regional consistencies.

Certain possibilities for error and other deficiencies in my field data are recognized: First, having only a rudimentary knowledge of the Maring language, I had to communicate with the Bomagai-Angoiang mostly through Maring-speaking native interpreters. These people, because they came from the Jimi Valley where there had been longer contact with Europeans, spoke New Guinea Pidgin (sometimes called Neo-Melanesian)— a lingua franca that at times seemed poorly suited to detailed or subtle explanations. My lack of knowledge of Maring and of the habits of thought of the Bomagai-Angoiang must have led me often to ask the wrong questions and to fail to elicit complete information. Second, as is common in fieldwork in small primitive communities, the mere presence of an investigator upset the usual patterns of activity. Partly because of my presence, four families moved to a new location nearer to the place where I lived during most of my stay in the Ndwimba Basin; and many of the men spent considerable time visiting and watching me, in lieu of other diversions or chores. Third, the only aerial photograph of the Ndwimba Basin was taken from 25,000 feet in 1959, when none of the gardens that I investigated in 1964 and 1965 were yet in existence. When I had opportunities to fly over the basin, cloudiness made it impossible to take comprehensive photographs from a lower elevation of the contemporary scene. Consequently, my maps and my estimates of acreage are based mostly on ground observations and survey and are not as accurate as I would like.

Spontaneously Occurring Plants

Listed here are those Ndwimba Basin plants that I was able to have identified, with the most complete scientific names I could obtain. A few plants known to me only by the native names are also listed. The identifications are derived from plant collections that John Street, Roy Rappaport, and I made either in the basin or nearby. Initial identifications were made at the herbarium of the Division of Botany (Territory of Papua and New Guinea) at Lae. From there many of the specimens were forwarded to the specialists named in my Acknowledgements.

In general, Maring nomenclature is monomial, although there are some "big names" that include subtypes. The Maring term *ap*, which means tree, is usually prefixed to the names of arboreal species, except species of palms and *Pandanus*.

Scientific Name	Family	Native Name	Comments
Acalypha sp.	Euphorbiaceae	*ap tse*	Tree with edible leaves. Grows only in low-elevation secondary forest. Always spontaneous in the basin; planted in places in the Jimi Valley where population is denser than in the basin.
Ageratum conyzo-ides L.	Compositae	*kwiran*	Pantropical weed very common in the new gardens and other open places of the Ndwimba Basin.
Aglaonema sp. (?)	Araceae	*trlup*	Forest-floor aroid that occasionally comes up in gardens. A "wild taro," say the Bomagai-Angoiang.

APPENDIX B (continued)

Scientific Name	Family	Native Name	Comments
Albizia falcataria (L.) Fosberg	Leguminosae	ap kanam	Rapidly growing secondary tree said to enrich ("give grease to") the soil. Wood once used for shields.
Alocasia macrorrhiza Schott	Araceae	ndingum	Large aroid of secondary and primary forest. Leaves used to line earth ovens. In parts of Melanesia, but not in the basin, stem is eaten.
Alphitonia incana	Rhamnaceae	ap pokai	Common secondary tree often found in association with Cyathea angiensis. Important as firewood.
Alpinia spp.	Zingiberaceae	am'ne, kembor	Several species of Alpinia are present; the "big names" am'ne or kembor include most of them. Common in both primary and secondary growth at all elevations. Leaves used to line earth ovens, as roofing, and to wrap hot rocks and food to be placed in ovens.
Alstonia (?) brassii	Apocynaceae	ap kora	Tall forest tree.
Angiopteris cf. evecta	Angiopteridaceae	ndongai kunkun	Common secondary fern.
Ardisia sp.	Myrsinaceae	amengi	Understory shrub or low tree of montane forest.
Artocarpus fretissii T. and B.	Moraceae	ap amboka	Wild Artocarpus of lower montane rain forest. Cooked seeds eaten.
Arytera sp.	Sapindaceae	ap ngunts	Tree of lower montane rain forest.
Astronia sp.	Melastomataceae	ap kukair	Tree of primary forest. Ten-inch leaves used to line kont' mbint (special occasion, ritual, above-ground oven for cooking pig).
Begonia sp.	Begoniaceae	kond'rakmai	Herbaceous shrub common on forest floor.
Bidens pilosa L.	Compositae	ndambi	Weed of especially degraded sites.

Blumea riparia	*Compositae*	*ngopngawa*	Common secondary climber used for light tying. Another specimen of vine with the same native name was identified as *Microglossa pyrifolia,* also a *Compositae.*
Boerlagioden-dron sp.	*Araliaceae*	*ap mgimbadan*	Secondary tree.
Breynia cernua	*Euphorbiaceae*	*ap non'mant'*	Old-garden tree.
Buchanania ar-borescens	*Anacardiaceae*	*ap komara*	Tall forest tree. Flexible bark peels off easily; used for walls of houses.
Calamus sp.	*Palmae*	*gǝlo*	Rattan palm of primary and old secondary forest. Core of stem used for binding and for weaving into belts and armbands. (See *Dicranop-teris linearis.*) Was used for fire saw.
Castanopsis acu-minatissima (Bl.) Hack.	*Fagaceae*	*ap uram*	Forest tree. Nut eaten raw or cooked. Bulmer (1964:147) suggests that these nuts may have been an important source of food in pre-agricultural New Guinea.
Casuarina oligo-don	*Casuarinaceae*	*ap kepa*	Both the basin's *Casuarina* spp. (C. oligodon and C. papuana) come up spontaneously and are occasionally planted. They are known to be good for the soil; but—unlike much of New Guinea—not planted in gardens in the basin, because the Bomagai-Angoiang consider the soil good enough without *Casuarina.* Trees are planted near houses and at ritual pig-killing sites as markers and because the fallen "needles" make a pleasant ground covering. Also prized as firewood. Neither species is common in the basin.
Casuarina papu-ana S. Moore	*Casuarinaceae*	*ap n'demi*	(See *Casuarina oligodon.*)
Cephaëlis (?) sp.	*Rubiaceae*	*ap mblant*	Low tree or shrub of tall forest.
Chisocheton sp.	*Meliaceae*	*ap mburpi*	Primary forest tree, home to large numbers of *mburpi-kambo,* an insect of the *Hemiptera,* order, which is eaten by the Bomagai-Angoiang. Seeds eaten by phalangers. Possibly *Dysoxylum* sp.

APPENDIX B (continued)

Scientific Name	Family	Native Name	Comments
Coix lacryma-jobi	Gramineae	kuri	Coarse grass. In open secondary sites. Seeds used for necklaces. Reportedly eaten in parts of New Guinea (Barrau, 1958:49), but not in Maring-speaking area.
Coleus scutellarioides (L.) Benth.	Labiatae	amami	Decorative forb with multicolored leaves. Several varieties, wild and planted. In gardens and at houses, often derived from cuttings of wild plants. Mildly aromatic leaves are appreciated by the people who often grab a few in passing, crush them, and smell them for a while before discarding. Leaf eaten with salt. (cf. Plectranthus sp.)
Cordia sp.	Ehretiaceae	ap nduk'mant	Small (?) tree of primary and perhaps secondary forest.
Crassocephalum crepidioides (Benth.) Moore	Compositae	kubulkabuj	Very common weed of new gardens and other open places. In a breeze its plumed achenes are widely distributed. Said to be a recent arrival.
Indet.	Cunoniaceae	ap mbokant	Common secondary tree.
Cyathea angiensis (Zipp.) Domin.	Cyatheaceae	i-munt	Tree fern common in secondary growth, usually in association with Alphitonia incana. Young leaves cooked and eaten. Wood used for firewood and fence horizontals, not for houses. Basins cut from blocks of Cyathea wood used to give water to cassawarias.
Cyathea sp.	Cyatheaceae	kangup	Tree fern of both secondary sites and lower montane rain forest. Different from i-munt (C. angiensis), which only comes up in disturbed sites. The tender leaves, cooked in the earth oven, are one of the most important of the collected greens for the Bomagai-Angoiang.
Cyclosorus truncatus (Poir.) Farwell	Thelypteridaceae	aimo	Common secondary fern, also grows in forest. Leaves and tender shoots eaten.

Cyclosorus unitus (L.) Ching	Thelypteridaceae	*mbunga*	Common secondary fern.
Cypholophus sp.	Urticaceae	*ap anyugrek*	Secondary tree.
Cyrtandra sp.	Cesneriaceae	*werenje*	Shrub of the floor of dense forest.
Cyrtococcum patens	Gramineae	*arpepe*	Delicate grass, common as a garden weed. *Pseudechinolaena polystachya* has same native name.
Dendrobium (?) *regale*	Orchidaceae	*kant'gai*	Crest-forest orchid with a bright yellow stem used on headbands to hold the shells of a bright green beetle (*Cetoniidae*). Stem prepared by heating (to soften), then split and inner parts scraped off. This orchid is present in abundance in the basin's montane crest forest; men come from the Jimi Valley to collect it, because it is rare and small there.
			(See *Urena lobata*.)
Desmodium sequax Wall.	Leguminosae	*koraindindi*	Herb of forest floor.
Dianella sp.	Liliaceae	*riamai*	Low-elevation *mombo* (see *Gleichenia brassii*) common in jungle and grassland. The core of the larger stems of this sprawling fern is esteemed for weaving belts and armbands. The black *mombo* is often interwoven with lighter-colored strands of *Calamus*. Also used for binding.
Dicranopteris linearis (Burm.) Underw. var. *montana* Holttum	Gleicheniaceae	*mombo*	
Dillenia sp.	Dilleniaceae	*ap munduka*	Forest tree, sometimes very tall (120 feet).
Dioscorea sp.	Dioscoreaceae	*ndungwi*	Wild, edible yam with a thorny vine. Grows in secondary vegetation. Not sought after, but collected and eaten by people hungry in the forest—as on hunting trips. Occasionally brought to houses.
Dioscorea sp.	Dioscoreaceae	*tsukman*	Wild yam said by the Bomagai-Angoiang to be a wild kind of *man* (*D. bulbifera*). The leaves of the two plants are similar, and the stems of both twine to the left. Not eaten because it "fights the mouth." Perhaps poisonous, as the noncultigen types of *D. bulbifera* are said to be (Burkill, 1951:311).

APPENDIX B (continued)

Scientific Name	Family	Native Name	Comments
Diospyros sp.	Ebenaceae	ap wonum	Tree common in secondary sites. Leaves are chewed (they "fight the mouth") and the masticated mass is put on sores to heal them. Same or another Diospyros occurs as a tall tree in rain forest.
Diplazium sp.	Athyriaceae	tangɔroba	Common fern. Leaves cooked and eaten.
Dipteris sp.	Dipteridaceae	ngɔnt	Sprawling fern of montane crest forest.
Dodonaea viscosa Jacq.	Sapindaceae	ap ngra	Small weed tree common in many parts of the Simbai and Jimi valleys (and the rest of New Guinea, the East Indies, and mainland Southeast Asia). Light winged seed is easily dispersed. Present but not abundant in the basin. I believe Dodonaea's prevalence elsewhere—often in almost pure stands on old garden sites—points to retrogressive succession away from mixed forest.
Dysoxylum sp.	Meliaceae	ap kurukundu, ap mburpi	Tree of old secondary and primary forest. See Chisocheton.
Elaeocarpus sp.	Elaeocarpaceae	ap yimgur	Tall primary forest tree.
Elatostema sp.	Urticaceae	ngai-ngai, kor	Herbaceous shrub of primary and secondary forest floor.
Elmerrillia papuana	Magnoliaceae	ap mbank	Large primary forest tree, perhaps only present on basin floor.
Endospermum formicarium	Euphorbiaceae	ap auwongo	Secondary tree. Always inhabited by ants.
Eugenia pachyclada	Myrtaceae	ap angunong	Forest tree.
Eugenia sp.	Myrtaceae	ap ndumbi	Forest tree. Wood used in house construction.
Eugenia sp.	Myrtaceae	ap tringia	Forest tree.

Species	Family	Native name	Notes
Indet.	Euphorbiaceae	ap yingra	Secondary forest tree.
Euroschinus papuanus	Anacardiaceae	ap kang'gant'	Secondary tree widely scattered about the basin. Flushes of red, young leaves make the tree conspicuous. Milky exudate used as glue on arrow bindings. Before Western razor blades, exudate was also used to make the fingers sticky, so that facial hairs could be grasped and pulled out.
Ficus botryocarpa var. subalbidoramea	Moraceae	ap ngwingwi	Secondary forest tree. Leaf not eaten. Figs eaten occasionally.
Ficus itoana Diels	Moraceae	ap tak	Large Ficus of secondary and altered primary forest. Cauliflorous fruit eaten occasionally.
Ficus dammaropsis Diels	Moraceae	ap gambani	Mature leaves (30 inches long) used for lining earth oven and wrapping food. Young leaves cooked in earth oven and eaten. Fruits and cabbagelike apical bud eaten raw in the bush in emergency. Grows spontaneously in secondary and primary forest. Sometimes planted in more densely settled parts of New Guinea.
Ficus iodotricha	Moraceae	ap nimba	Riparian fig of primary forest. Young leaves eaten. Underbark used to make string.
Ficus nodosa	Moraceae	ap mbeka kiko	Leaves, but not fruit, eaten. Those trees in the forest away from houses belong to the whole clan; those near houses are private property of residents of the nearest house—called "the father and mother of the tree."
Ficus pachyrachis	Moraceae	ap kopenga / ap morung	Secondary and altered primary tree. Underbark of saplings made into string. Young leaves eaten. Rough leaf held in hand helps in seizing eels. Birds and animals attracted to fruit.
Ficus porphyrochaete	Moraceae	ap yamgoma	Ficus of secondary and primary forest. No use.

APPENDIX B (continued)

Scientific Name	Family	Native Name	Comments
Ficus pungens Reinw.	Moraceae	ap kobənum	Common secondary fig. Leaves eaten frequently, fruit occasionally. Bomagai-Angoiang recognize two varieties of F. pungens: ap kobənum təpəko and ap kobənum tingi. Tingi is more pubescent and has larger leaves than təpəka. Some men believe that this species is especially potent in restoring soil fertility.
Ficus trachypison	Moraceae	ap yamo ap kambuk ap poto ap rang'gant	Common tree of both primary and secondary forests. Leaf used as abrasive. Cloth for men's head covering made from bark. There is confusion over the native names applied to specimens that have been identified as F. trachypison; in some cases the native names given here may refer to species of Ficus other than F. trachypison.
Ficus wassa	Moraceae	ap rama ap mbeka	Secondary and primary forest tree. Young leaves and fruit eaten. In the Ndwimba basin this tree is usually spontaneous, but occasionally planted, in which case it is privately owned. Cloth for men's head covering made from bark.
Ficus sp.	Moraceae	ap amboka	Ficus, different from ap mbeka (F. wassa), said to grow in both secondary and primary forest. The leaf is eaten.
Freycinetia spp.	Pandanaceae	kleng'a, taka	There are at least two species (one called kleng'a and one called taka) of climbing Pandanaceae in primary and old secondary forests of the basin.
Garcinia sp.	Guttiferae	ap tandapa	Cassowaries, but not men, eat the fruit of this tree of the primary forest. Its wood is favored for axe handles.
Geunsia farinosa Bl.	Verbenaceae	ap ngon	Common secondary forest tree often associated with Alphitonia incana and Cyathea angiensis.

Scientific name	Family	Vernacular name	Description
Gleichenia brassii C. Chr. (*Sticherus brassii* (C. Chr.) Copel.)	Gleicheniaceae	*mombo*	Large, sprawling fern of the montane crest forest. It is used for heavy tying jobs, such as binding fence posts together. The men make special trips to the crest to collect mombo.
Glochidion philippicum	Euphorbiaceae	*ap mobo*	Large tree of the secondary forest.
Gronophyllum chaunostachys (Burret) H. E. Moore	Palmae	*kəmir*	Tall palm of the montane crest forest and lower montane rain forest. Wood used for arrow foreshafts; a sheathing leaf base from it serves as a container for making sauce from the cultivated *Pandanus* and as wrapping material. The cabbage is eaten raw or cooked and can weigh as much as six pounds.
Harmsiopanax sp.	Araliaceae	*ap mokopeng*	Small jungle tree.
Homalanthus sp.	Euphorbiaceae	*ap mgabani*	Common secondary forest tree.
Horsfieldia sp.	Myristicaceae	*ap tangan*	Tall primary forest tree. (See *Myristica hollrungii*, which has the same Maring "big name".)
Hydrocotyle javanica	Umbelliferae	*dokwipo, tina-kwipo*	Delicate creeping forb common as trailside and garden weed.
Impatiens sp.	Balsaminaceae	*korambe*	Common trailside and garden weed. Flowers are worn in hair. Leaves used as medicine on wounds. Plant held in fire, then fluid squeezed on fresh wound. Said to stop bleeding and promote healing. (According to Chopra et al, 1956:140, *I. balsamina* L. and *I. chinensis* are both used externally for burns in India.)
Imperata cylindrica	Gramineae	*korndo*	Common garden weed. Forms small grasslands on driest sites. Used for light cordage. Flower plumes serve as head decoration.

APPENDIX B (continued)

Scientific Name	Family	Native Name	Comments
Isachne myoso-tis Nees.	Gramineae	konchain, pingo	Tiny grass in gardens and near water.
Ischaemum digitatum and I. polystachyum	Gramineae	mbombak	Common garden weeds. Form small grasslands on somewhat moister sites than those dominated by Imperata cylindrica.
Laportea decumana	Urticaceae	nent	Stinging nettle, common on trailsides. Leaf used as counterirritant medicine: rubbed on sick person's body to the accompaniment of ritual chant, it is said to relieve a variety of pains.
Laportea (Fleurya) sp.	Urticaceae	ap fokwai	Riparian tree. Underbark used to make string.
Indet.	Lauraceae	ap krm	Primary forest tree with bark that strips easily off the trunk in flexible bands used as belts, above-ground ovens, and eel traps.
Lepidagathis sp.	Acanthaceae	mbarequingyu	Trailside forb.
Lepistemon urceolatum	Convolvulaceae	apop	Common vine used for light tying jobs.
Licuala sp. or spp.	Palmae	kembuka	Palm of primary forest. Wood used for bows and arrow points and foreshaft.
Lindernia antipoda	Scrophulariaceae	tinakwipo	Trailside and garden weed.
Lithocarpus sp.	Fagaceae	ap nong	Forest tree. Phalangers and wild pigs eat the acorns; people do not.
Litsea sp.	Lauraceae	ap ndəpai	Tall forest tree. Leaves used as decoration.
Ludwigia sp.	Onagraceae	nengyumguramai	Weedy forb.

Species	Family	Native name	Notes
Macaranga aleu- ritoides	Euphorbiaceae	*ap tseboi* *ap mondokumpf*	Small secondary forest tree. One of three *ap tseboi* recognized by Bomagai-Angoiang. Two are understory trees of the primary forest. *M. aleuritoides* grows only in secondary associations.
Macaranga sp.	Euphorbiaceae	*ap mbinjam*	Common secondary tree. Often in the *Alphitonia-Cyathea-Geunsia* woodland.
Macaranga sp. or spp.	Euphorbiaceae	*ap tseboi*	Shrub or low tree in understory of midelevation rain forest. There are two types of rain forest *ap tseboi*. Both were identified as *Macaranga* sp. or possibly *Mallotus*.
Maesa sp.	Myrsinaceae	*ap pia*	Appears in young secondary communities. Said to be a tree of well developed forest also.
Mallotus sp.	Euphorbiaceae	——	See *Macaranga* sp.
Mangifera sp.	Anacardiaceae	*ap wowi*	Forest tree. Fruit eaten occasionally in the bush, but not esteemed.
Maoutia sp. (or *Missiessya* sp.)	Urticaceae	*ap nungamba*	Small tree that commonly pioneers in gardens. Underbark the most important source of fibers for string. Seedlings spared in garden weeding so that saplings will be available for later use.
Marattia sp.	Marattiaceae	*ndongai*	Common secondary fern, smaller than *ndongai kunkun* (*Angiopteris* sp.).
Medinilla sp.	Melastomata- ceae	*aik'mbindi*	Primary forest liana or epiphytic shrub used for lashing fences together. Occurs in secondary vegetation also. May develop into tree. Native name also refers to other lianas.
Melanolepis sp. (or possibly *Acalypha* sp.)	Euphorbiaceae	*ap tse* *ap tsant*	Secondary forest tree. Tender leaves eaten.
Melastoma ma- labathricum L.	Melastomata- ceae	*ap wop'kai*	Shrub or low tree widely distributed from India to Australia. Common weed in gardens and—outside the basin—in degraded grasslands. According to Roy Rappaport (pers. comm.), produces a purple dye used by some Maring for dyeing string. I have no record of this use for the Bomagai-Angoiang, but—as the name of the genus suggests— the berry of *M. malabathricum* blackens the tongue.

APPENDIX B (continued)

Scientific Name	Family	Native Name	Comments
Melothria sp.	Cucurbitaceae	morup	Vine of secondary jungle. The lemon-shaped, green fruit is covered by a waxy powder in which patterns can be scraped. After making patterns, the people string several fruits together and hang the necklace down their backs as a decoration. With the coming of beads and cloth, this decoration is falling out of style.
Metroxylon sp.	Palmae	———	Species of sago palm. A rare moist-habitat plant in the Ndwimba Basin. Not used by the people.
Microglossa pyrifolia	Compositae	ngopngawa	See Blumea riparia.
Miscanthus floridulus	Gramineae	təpa	Tall grass common in jungle and some grasslands. Stem used to make arrow shafts.
Missiessya sp.	Urticaceae	———	Tall tree present in montane crest forest.
Missiessya sp.	Urticaceae	———	See Maoutia sp.
Musa (?) ingens Simmonds	Musaceae	norokome	Giant Musa (15-foot leaves) of the high-altitude forest. The species was not identified but is probably M. ingens, present in the mountains of northern central New Guinea (Simmonds, 1962:17).
Musa sp.	Musaceae	ndiki	Weedy heliophyte common in gardens and young secondary vegetation. Seed-filled, yellow-pulped fruit is edible, but seldom used.
(mushrooms)	———	mbai	Several varieties or species of edible mushrooms are present. Collected casually in forest or gardens, scorched in fire, eaten. Seldom carried home.
Myristica hollrungii	Myristicaceae	ap tangan	Forest tree. Underside of large (13 inches long) leaves is pale green ("white," say the Bomagai-Angoiang), deemed attractive as lining to above-ground oven.

Neonauclea (?) *schlechteri*	*Rubiaceae*	*ap mbor*	Tree of old secondary or primary forest.
Neophrolepis falcata (Cav.) C. Chr.	*Oleandraceae*	*nomabund'amai*	Common secondary ground fern.
Ophiorrhiza sp.	*Rubiaceae*	*keomaiquingyu*	Forb common on the forest floor.
Orania sp.	*Palmae*	*mgamba*	Short palm of the high-elevation forest. The wood is made into arrow foreshafts.
Indet.	*Orchidaceae*	*yibun*	Epiphytic orchid with a flattened fleshy stem that can be held in the mouth while inhaling in such a way that the resulting noise sounds like the distress cry of certain young birds—thus attracting adult birds to the waiting hunter.
Oreocnide sp.	*Urticaceae*	*ap rumen*	Common secondary shrub or low tree used for fence posts because the posts sprout and keep the fence strong.
Indet.	———	*ap paiem*	Forest tree with aromatic wood, bits of which are carried by some men and smelled for the reviving effect of the aroma.
Palmeria sp.	*Monimiaceae*	*ap tumbi*	Tall forest tree.
Pandanus danck-elmannianus K. Schum.	*Pandanaceae*	*mbuk*	*Pandanus* tree of lower montane rain forest. Leaves used in woven mats.
Pandanus (?) *floribundus* Merrill and Perry	*Pandanaceae*	*ndi*	Tallest high-elevation *Pandanus*. Cassowaries, but not men, eat the seeds. Leaves used for bush shelters. The species identification is tentative; *ndi* might be *P. aggregatus* Merrill and Perry.
Pandanus foveo-latus Kanehira	*Pandanaceae*	*pima*	High-elevation *Pandanus*. Small kernel eaten either cooked or raw. Leaves used to make bush shelters and woven mats.
Pandanus julian-ettii Martelli	*Pandanaceae*	*tapa, amare*	High-elevation *Pandanus*. Oily white kernel eaten cooked or raw by men on hunting and collecting trips to the crest. Some kernels may be

APPENDIX B (*continued*)

Scientific Name	Family	Native Name	Comments
			brought home to the lower basin. Leaves used to make bush shelters. Possibly *P. brosimos*.
Pandanus krauelianus K. Schum	Pandanaceae	*kunong*	Short *Pandanus* of the lower-elevation forests of the basin. Leaves used for weaving sleeping mats. Fruit not eaten by people, but is eaten by pigs, cassowaries, and marsupials.
Pandanus limbatus Merrill and Perry	Pandanaceae	*tramnowa*	*Pandanus* of lower montane rain forest. Leaves are woven into mats.
Pandanus papuanus Solms.	Pandanaceae	*miom*	Tall *Pandanus* of lower montane rain forest and secondary forest. Wood of prop roots used in house construction; long leaves (10 feet or more) used to make wall for houses. Slivers of prop roots used as torches for night traveling and eel hunting.
Paspalum conjugatum	Gramineae	*tamo*	Common secondary grass present in sunny and shady sites. Frequently dominates the field layer of *Pandanus* orchards and *Alphitonia-Geunsia-Cyathea* woodland and colonizes extensively in garden plots.
Phrynium sp.	Marantaceae	*mengin*	Understory plant of primary forest. Leaves used to line earth ovens, for roofing, and for wrapping food. Young unfurled leaves may be eaten raw in the bush.
Piper sp.	Piperaceae	*yikun*	Low, spreading tree common in jungle and other young secondary growth.
Pipturus sp.	Urticaceae	*ap kar'ma*	Common secondary shrub or low tree.
Pittosporum sinuatum	Pittosporaceae	*ap mbismbis*	Rain forest tree.

Scientific name	Family	Native name	Notes
Planchonella sp.	*Sapotaceae*	*ap kina*	Tall tree of primary forest. Hard brown seeds used in necklaces.
Plectranthus sp.	*Labiatae*	*amami*	Spontaneous garden forb. The people give the name *amami* to *Coleus* also.
Poikilogyne sp.	*Melastomataceae*	*ap karama*	Understory tree or shrub common in secondary vegetation.
Polypodium sp.	*Polypodiaceae*	*kwiop*	Secondary fern. Before the coming of trade salt, the dried leaves of this species were burned and the ash used for salt.
Polytoca macrophylla	*Gramineae*	*wandama*	Tall grass common in old gardens and jungle. When cut, it sprouts vigorously from underground parts.
Pometia tomentosa	*Sapindaceae*	*ap kinde*	Rain-forest tree.
Pouzolzia hirta Hassk.	*Urticaceae*	*yangurai*	Trailside and garden weed. Stem and leaves are cooked in earth oven and eaten.
Pseudechinolaena polystachya	*Gramineae*	*arpepe*	Recumbent weedy grass common in gardens. *Cyrtococcum patens* has the same native name.
Psychotria sp.	*Rubiaceae*	*ap mbangawa*	Tree or shrub of primary forest.
Pteris sp. (?)	*Pteridaceae*	*mbor*	Common secondary fern. After spells have been spoken over it, it is draped over boundary markers to prevent the passage of sickness.
Randia sp.	*Rubiaceae*	*ap kr*	Tree of primary forest.
Rubus moluccanus L.	*Rosaceae*	*krkr*	Common woody ground vine used as rope. Fruit is eaten occasionally, but not esteemed.
Saurauia spp.	*Actinidiaceae*	*ap tokɔnt, ap ngo-ngo, ap angrek*	Several small trees of this genus occur as pioneers in secondary re-growth. Wood used for fences and firewood.
Schefflera sp.	*Araliaceae*	*ap tumbum*	Small tree or epiphyte with a strangling habit.
Schuurmansia elegans	*Ochnaceae*	*ap alale*	Secondary forest tree.

Scientific Name	Family	Native Name	Comments
Scleria sp.	Cyperaceae	tri-ai	Common garden weed.
Selaginella sp.	Selaginellaceae	tokəmaikwipo, ngarambomai	Lycopod common on primary forest floor.
Setaria palmi-folia Stapf	Gramineae	kwiai	Wild variety of the cultivated plant. Cultivated kwiai, always planted by cuttings, has a thicker stem than the wild variety, which comes up spontaneously in gardens from seed. Inner stem of both cultivated and wild is eaten.
Sloanea papuana	Elaeocarpaceae	ap rim	Tall tree of rain forest.
Solanum nigrum L.	Solanaceae	ambek	In the basin, a garden weed, never planted. In some parts of New Guinea this species is a cultivated plant, grown for greens. In the basin the rather harsh-tasting leaves are cooked in the earth oven with other edible leaves.
Spathoglottis plicata Bl.	Orchidaceae	tiokum	Broad-leafed ground orchid common in young secondary vegetation. Purple flower worn in the hair as a decoration. Leaves used as wrapping material.
Spondias dulcis	Anacardiaceae	ap apan	Tall tree that probably only grows in the lower elevations of the basin. Fruit is recognized as edible, but seldom eaten.
Sterculia sp.	Sterculiaceae	ap ndukmbina	Tree that bears bright orange pods containing black-skinned seeds, edible when cooked.
Trichosanthes sp. or spp.	Cucurbitaceae	n'gən	There are two varieties or species of Trichosanthes vine in the basin. Both come up in disturbed sites. Seeds and the surrounding red flesh is eaten after being cooked. The outer, seedless flesh or rind is not eaten. The fruit ripens during the drier season.
Urena lobata L.	Malvaceae	koraindindi	Weedy garden and trailside shrub. The same native name also applies to a Desmodium sp. (Leguminosae) of similar habit.
Indet.	———	ap wombəna	Tree of secondary forest. Flexible bark is stripped from the trunk and coiled into a cylinder to make an above-ground oven.

ADDENDUM TO APPENDIX B

A small collection of specimens made during 1970 makes possible some refinements of the nomenclature and identifications in Appendix B.

Callicarpa spp. *Verbenaceae*   *ap ngon*

The trees known to the Bomagai-Angoiang as *ap ngon* and referred to in Appendix B and the text as *Geunsia farinosa* are perhaps better named *Callicarpa pentandra* Roxb. Other species of *Callicarpa* may be present also.

Ficus copiosa   *Moraceae*   *ap mbeka*
Steud.

The tree referred to in the text and in Appendixes B and C as *F. wassa* is probably better identified as *F. copiosa*. I am not certain whether the spontaneous tree and the planted tree belong to the same species. The people, who prize both trees primarily for their leaves, say that the planted tree has sweeter, more edible fruits than the spontaneous tree.

Homalanthus   *Euphorbiaceae*   *ap mgabani*
novoguineen-
sis (Warb.)
Laut. & K.
Schum.

The very common weed tree of the genus *Homalanthus* has been identified as *H. novoguineensis*.

Leucosyke sp.   *Urticaceae*   *ap kar'ma, ap*
or spp.   *reng'glench*

Small trees common in jungle and secondary woodland. One specimen with the same Maring name of *ap kar'ma* has been identified as a *Pipturus* sp.

ADDENDUM TO APPENDIX B (*continued*)

Litsea sp.	*Lauraceae*	*ap wombo*	Tree of secondary and perhaps primary forests. Paste made from its seeds is said to cure sores.
Mucuna stanleyi C. T. White	*Leguminosae*	*ngawa wiwa*	Jungle liana. Stem used to tie firewood.
Rhus taitensis Giull.	*Anacardiaceae*	*ap kang'gant'*	Specimens of the tree known to the Maring as ap *kang'gant'* and identified as *Euroshinus papuanus* in Appendix B have also been given the name of *R. taitensis*.
Saurauia congestiflora A. C. Smith	*Actinidiaceae*	*ap ngo ngo*	One of the Saurauia has been further identified as *S. congestiflora*.
Thelypteris cf. *glaucescens* Brause	*Thelypteri-daceae*	*mbunga*	Common fern of grassland and old gardens. Another specimen called *mbunga* by the people was identified as *Cyclosorus unitus*. What are probably several species of weedy ferns are encompassed by the compound name *mbunga-mbor*, and a single plant will often be given the individual name *mbor* (identified as *Pteris* sp. in Appendix B) by one man and *mbunga* by another.

Cultivated Plants

Scientific Name	Native Name	Common English Name	Comments
Acalypha sp.	*ap yingra məki*		Shrub planted near houses for decorative and ritual purposes. The serrate, red leaves are chewed with salt, and the resulting pulp is spit on pork for ritual presentation to allies at pig-slaughtering ceremonies. Planted by cuttings. The name means "red *yingra* tree." An unidentified tree with green leaves known simply as *ap yingra* is found wild in the forest.
Amomun (?) *polycarpum*	*ngun'ma*		Large herb planted at boundary markers as protective magic. The fruit is eaten raw by people who are hungry when passing.
Artocarpus altilis Fosberg	*aiyu*	breadfruit	Minor component of the *Pandanus-Gnetum gnemon* orchards. Unlike the breadfruit in parts of coastal New Guinea, where the fruit's flesh is eaten and the varieties may be seedless, the basin variety is grown only for its edible seeds. Planted by seedling. Said to grow wild also. Fruit ripens in September and October.
(Bamboos)	*mung*	bamboo	Several types of bamboo (*mung* is the native "big name") grow in the basin. Some is planted, some spontaneous; but in the lower parts of the basin, bamboo is usually associated with human activity. Bam-

APPENDIX C (continued)

Scientific Name	Native Name	Common English Name	Comments
			...boo used as fence posts often sprouts and in time radiates into large clumps that indicate past locations of gardens. When the men clear, they leave some of the bamboo uncut because of its many uses. One of the more important bamboos is the largest, *mung waiya*. Its stems, 4 inches or more in diameter, are used for fence posts, water containers, and the heavy jobs of house construction; its sprout used to be burned to make salt. Strips of *mung waiya* are used to make bows, but bamboo is considered inferior to palm wood for that purpose, except for toy bows for boys. Finely whittled strips of bamboo are used as bowstrings, and pieces of stem are carved into blade-shaped arrow points. The large-leafed *Bambusa forbesii* (*q.v.*) is used as roofing. Several bamboo varieties are used in light construction in houses and as tubes in which food can be cooked directly in the fire. The sprout of one of the basin bamboos is eaten. Before the introduction of trade razor blades and steel knives, slivers of bamboo were used for cutting and shaving.
Bambusa forbe-sii (Rdl.) Holttum	*mung kokambre, mung mgamp*		This species of bamboo has 20-inch-long leaves, which are made into shingles by breaking the midrib of one leaf about two inches from the base and pushing the broken end through another leaf near its midrib. The two-leaf shingle can then be hung over laths to make roofing. Small stems of *mung kokambra* are used to make arrow shafts.

Scientific name	Local name	Common name	Notes
Bixa orellana L.	*ap sipalon*	annatto tree	Time of entry unknown; the people say the plant is ancestral. Planted near houses. Seed pulp is used for face paint and for dying hair and string.
Brassica juncea	*ngombi*	leaf mustard	Crucifer, which is probably *Brassica juncea* but might be a *Rorippa* sp., grown for greens. Planted by seed.
Carica papaya L.	*kuramp*	papaya, paw paw	Papayas introduced to the basin 10 to 15 years ago from Jimi Valley. Usually eaten before fully ripe, often as a snack in the gardens. Planted casually by throwing down the seeds of eaten fruits.
Casuarina spp.	*ap kepa, ap ni'demi*	casuarina, iron-wood, she-oak	In many grassy parts of highland New Guinea groves of planted casuarinas are one of the most striking features of the landscape, and the fast-growing trees are very important as a source of wood for fires and fences and as soil-enriching fallow plants. In the forested Ndwimba Basin many other trees meet these needs, and the casuarinas lack the singular significance they have elsewhere; but the trees are occasionally planted as markers and for the dry, clean litter that accumulates beneath them. For more information see *C. oligodon* in Appendix B.
Celosia argentea L.	*amaruk, ngondiwan*		Planted by seed near houses and in gradens. The purple flowers are put in the hair for decoration. The plant serves as *yingpunt* ("house decoration") when set out around the hamlets.
Codiaeum variegatum Blume	*ngur*	croton	Planted by cutting at houses and pig-killing sites, where the green and yellow leaves serve as decoration. The plant also has meaning as protective magic. Said to grow spontaneously in secondary forest.
Coleus scutellarioides (L.). Benth.	*amami*	coleus	Interplanted by stem cuttings with garden plants, *Coleus* is appreciated for its aromatic and colorful leaves. It is said that its presence also makes *Colocasia* grow large—a belief similar to that in New Caledonia,

APPENDIX C (continued)

Scientific Name	Native Name	Common English Name	Comments
			where *Coleus blumei* Benth. is said to promote a good crop of yams (Barrau, 1965:291). *Coleus* is also planted near houses for decoration. The soft leaves may be eaten with salt and are used as a breech wiper and as bedding for babies when they are carried in net bags. *Amami* grows wild and in cultivation.
Coleus sp.	*nimp*		*Coleus* with purple stems and leaves, grown in gardens and near houses for decoration and for dye. The stem is crushed so that strings drawn over it are colored.
Colocasia esculenta (L.) Schott	*ndang*	taro	According to Barrau (1958:39, 41) there is argument as to whether *C. antiquorum* is also present in Melanesia or is simply a synonym for *C. esculenta*. Cobley (1956:182) writes that *C. antiquorum* lacks the subsidiary corms that are present on *C. esculenta* and on the *Colocasia* of the Ndwimba Basin. At least ten varieties of *ndang* are distinguished by the people, on the basis of differences in leaf and stem color and the size and shape of the tuber. *Colocasia* is not as plentiful as sweet potatoes or *Xanthosoma*, but, like *Dioscorea*, ritual may be associated with its planting, and it has, I believe, richer emotional associations as food than sweet potatoes or *Xanthosoma*. *Xanthosoma* is often known by the common name of taro or New World taro, but in my text I have used the word "taro" only to refer to *Colocasia*.

Scientific name	Local name	Common name	Description
Commelina cyanea	tampmanye		Trailing herb used for greens. Planted by stem cuttings like sweet potatoes. Grows as a weed also.
Commelina sp. (or Pollia sp.)	komeruk		Herb eaten raw with salt. Also serves as decoration in the gardens and as medicine for scabies. Planted by root cutting. Komeruk also occurs as a garden weed, in which case it is not eaten.
Cordyline fruticosa (L.) A. Chev. (C. terminalis Kunth)	rumbim	ti plant, palm lily (tanket, in Pidgin English)	This apparently ancient cultivated plant, found throughout Oceania, is important in the Ndwimba Basin for ritual and as decoration and clothing. Not used for food or fiber. Rappaport (1967b) describes its importance in the rituals related to now-forbidden war. It is still ritually significant as a plant placed as boundary markers and in the center of taro-yam gardens. Most houses have some, often many, Cordyline about them, serving as decoration and as sources of leaves, used by the men to cover their buttocks. The several varieties exhibit wide variation in shape and color of leaf. The red leaves of one variety are prized as a buttocks covering for dance ceremonies. The wide leaves of another variety are often used for wrapping food put into earth ovens. Cordyline is planted with stalk cuttings and grows, often untended, throughout the inhabited part of the basin.
Crinum macranthum	i-mani	a kind of amaryllis	When mounted on a scaffold, the white sheathing that surrounds the pseudostem serves as a signal to summon friends or relatives from a distance. It is said that i-mani does not grow wild. Once established, it continues to sprout for many years.
Cucumis sativus L.	pika	cucumber	Ancestral plant common in Bomagai-Angioang gardens. The first crop to mature in gardens. Eaten raw. Two varieties: pika, very like the commercial cucumber; pika mop, longer, thinner, seedier, and tougher to chew than pika.

APPENDIX C (continued)

Scientific Name	Native Name	Common English Name	Comments
Cucurbita (?) *pepo* L.	*ira*	pumpkin	Introduced within the last two or three decades. Two varieties: one with a round fruit like a Halloween pumpkin, the other with an elongated fruit. Flesh, leaves, and seeds eaten. Planted both by seed and by stem cutting.
(?) *Curcuma longa* L.	*andonk*	turmeric	Planted with tuber cuttings near houses and in gardens. String for net bags dyed by being drawn over the curshed yellow tuber. Said to come up wild too. A wild *Zingiberaceae* with the native name of *koma koma* was collected a few miles from the basin and identified as *Curcuma longa* (turmeric), but I have no record of it in the basin and do not know whether it is the wild form of what the Bomagai-Angoiang call *andonk*.
Dioscorea spp.	(see names of the separate species, below)	yam	The five species of yam grown in the basin are described separately below. Yams, especially *D. alata* and *D. nummularia*, are esteemed as food, but yams are not quantitatively important in the diet. Some Bomagai-Angoiang wives, immigrant from the Jimi Valley, say that yams are a commoner food there than in the Ndwimba Basin, "where people eat sweet potatoes and taro." Ritual is often associated with the planting of yams, as with that of *Colocasia*.
Dioscorea alata L.	*wan*	greater yam	*D. alata* and *D. nummularia* are classed together by the Bomagai-Angoiang under the single "big name," *wan*. Within the two species many named races (perhaps 25) occur in the basin. The races are dis-

Scientific name	Local name	Common name	Notes
			tinguished by size, form, and color (magenta or white) of the tubers. *D. alata* is planted with small segments of the tuber, the top of the tuber, or the bulbils borne in the axils of some races.
Dioscorea bulbifera L.	*man*	yam	All three to five varieties are magenta-fleshed and have a bitter taste. Not considered good food, compared with *wan*. The well developed bulbils are used as planting material.
Dioscorea esculenta (Loureiro) Burkill	*tukaia*	lesser yam	Probably the commonest yam species in the basin, but much less common there than just to the west, where the Fungai-Korama clan cluster plants special "*tukaia* gardens" and has "*tukaia* houses" where the tubers are dried. The Bomagai-Angoiang have neither the special gardens nor the "houses" (small, roofed platforms). In the basin *tukaia* tubers, like all yams, are dried simply by being left in sheltered spots in the gardens.
Dioscorea nummularia Lamarck	*wan*	yam	See *Dioscorea alata*.
Dioscorea pentaphylla L.	*ndinga*	yam	The least common of the yams. I think only one variety is present.
Dolichos lablab L.	*mbar pengar*	lablab, hyacinth bean	Bean, long-established in Melanesia. In the Ndwimba Basin, seeds and leaves are eaten, but pods are considered too tough.
(Euphorbiaceae)	*ap ngimbo'*		Shrub planted at boundary markers, in gardens, and about houses as a protection against sorcery. It is vegetatively reproduced like *Cordyline* and has ritual power. According to the staff of the Botanical Garden at Lae, it is widely planted in the highlands, where it is sometimes used as a fish poison. Because it never flowers, its genus has not been identified.

APPENDIX C (continued)

Scientific Name	Native Name	Common English Name	Comments
Ficus (?) robusta	ap kan'pam		The leaves are eaten, and bark cloth for the outmoded men's head coverings was made from this tree. The natives say it never comes up spontaneously.
Ficus wassa	ap rama, ap mbeka		See Ficus wassa in Appendix B.
Gnetum gnemon L.	naenk, ambian	tulip (Pidgin English)	Tree, widely distributed in Melanesia, cultivated for edible leaves, inflorescences, and fruits. In the basin, grown with cultivated Pandanus and breadfruit trees in orchards known as komba-naenk nduk. The inner bark of Gnetum gnemon is one of the many sources of fiber for string—a use to which several species of Gnetaceae are put throughout Malaysia (Markgraf, 1954). Planted in new places with self-sown seedlings. It is said to live considerably longer than the other orchard trees.
Heliconia sp.	kole		This relative of the banana is planted by sucker near houses for decoration and for the five-foot leaves, used to line earth ovens and to wrap food placed in the ovens.
Hibiscus manihot L.	kem		Shrub grown for its edible leaves, H. manihot has been characterized (Barrau, 1958:56) as "truly the traditional vegetable for all of Melanesia." In the basin the many varieties are the commonest garden plants grown solely for leaves, which are cooked in the earth oven before being eaten.

Homalomena   *ndu ndu*
sp.

The striped green and yellow leaves of this household garden plant are pleated accordion-fashion by married couples and given to bachelors to wear about their necks at dances to make themselves attractive to watching girls. The leaves' mild aroma, reminiscent of lemon, enhances their value. The plant is vegetatively propagated with cuttings from a sprouting rhizome.

Ipomoea batatas   *koia*
(L.) Lam.

sweet potato

Most authorities believe that the sweet potato originated in the New World. When it spread into the rest of the world is more moot; the common view is that it reached New Guinea in the sixteenth or seventeenth century (Nishiyama, 1963; Conklin, 1963). As for the highlands of New Guinea, all that is certain is that when Europeans arrived in the twentieth century, sweet potatoes were already grown everywhere, usually as by far the most important crop. Watson (1965b:440) estimates that the plant entered the highlands between two and three centuries ago. He cites (Watson, 1965a:300) the example of one highland people who has a tradition of a pre-ipomoean time ending about ten generations ago. The Bomagai-Angoiang, like most New Guineans, have no folk memory of a time without sweet potatoes. At least fifteen named varieties grow in the basin, differing in leaf form, size and form of tuber, and color of the tuber's skin and flesh (most tubers have white flesh, a few have yellow). Sweet potatoes are always propagated by stem cuttings, but many varieties flower and set seed. Bulmer (1966) suggests that new varieties arise from cross-fertilized seeds, which may be distributed by birds. Sweet potatoes are for the Bomagai-Angoiang the single most important source of carbohydrate, but they do not approach being the 90 percent of the diet as they are often reported to be in the Central Highlands; 40 percent

APPENDIX C (continued)

Scientific Name	Native Name	Common English Name	Comments
			is closer to the fact in the basin. Sweet potato leaves are not eaten in the basin, but some of the women report varieties with edible leaves in the lands of their natal clans. The leaves suffer some damage from disease and pests. Tubers often have a scab (*Elsinos batatas*, according to a government agricultural officer), but the infestation is not very damaging to the plant.
Kaempferia galanga L.	am'nen	galanga	Garden plant vegetatively reproduced by tuber cuttings. Only women plant it. The leaves have a mild smell similar to licorice. When the leaves are rubbed on the skin, put in the hair, or worn in woven armlets, the odor is said to make the bearer sexually attractive. Barrau (1958:60) says it has been imported into New Guinea by Indonesians who use the rhizome as a condiment. I have no record of whether the Bomagai-Angoiang regard the plant as ancestral.
Lagenaria siceraria (Mol.) Standley	yibona	gourd	Two varieties are grown, one with a round fruit, one with an elongated fruit. Leaves and young fruits are eaten. Salt and *Pandanus* oil are stored in the hard-shelled mature gourd.
Manihot utilissima Pohl	mbaundi	manioc, cassava	Manioc was introduced into the Ndwimba Basin about 30 years ago. According to Barrau (1958:47) it came to Melanesia in the nineteenth century at the beginning of European colonization. The crop is, however, listed in *Herbarium Amboinense* (Merrill, 1917:324). The single variety, which is sweet, now in the basin is common in Bomagai-

Musa (cultivar)	*yobai*	banana

Angoiang gardens, but the people do not esteem it as a food for themselves. Most is fed to the pigs.

Simmonds (1959: Chap. 3) has discarded the traditional names *Musa paradisiaca* and *M. sapientum* for edible bananas of the Eumusa series. He feels that all cultivated Eumusa had a bispecific origin in only two wild species: *M. acuminata* and *M. balbisiana*. For the present no one Latin name can be meaningfully applied to the cultivated Eumusa. In the Ndwimba Basin there are more than ten named varieties, with fruits that vary considerably in size and taste. A few varieties are "plantains" that must be cooked to be edible; a few other varieties are said to be eaten only raw. With the rest there is a choice: either the fruit is cooked when green or eaten raw when ripe. Bananas can be roasted in their skins in the fire or steamed in the earth oven, in which case they are skinned and the flesh made into a paste and wrapped in leaves before being cooked. The stalks of fruit are light in weight (I measured none that weighed more than 18 pounds), compared with those of commercial bananas. Bananas are planted in almost all gardens and also near the houses, so that leaves are easily available for wrapping material, for lining earth ovens, and for roofing material. Fruit-eating bats and some of the marsupials damage bananas on the plant, but they do not appear to be too serious a pest.

Nasturtium sp.	*ninkngombi*	watercress

The recently introduced watercress adds another green to the Bomagai-Angoiang's large supply. Planted by stem cuttings in shallow streams. The name is derived from *ngombi*, the term for dry-garden crucifers (see *Brassica juncea*), and *nink*, which means water.

Nicotiana tabacum L.	*yurf*	tobacco

All Bomagai-Angoiang say that tobacco is an ancestral plant that has always been in the basin. However, Watson (1965b:440) reports that

APPENDIX C (continued)

Scientific Name	Native Name	Common English Name	Comments
			at Kainantu in the eastern Central Highlands many of his older informants acknowledge a time when their people had no tobacco. Riesenfeld (1952), in his thorough review of the literature on tobacco in New Guinea, concludes that all cultivated tobacco there is derived from *N. tabacum* that through European agency reached the northwest coast of the island in the sixteenth century and then spread by native dissemination. In the basin, tobacco is dried in the smoky houses, rolled in leaves or now in newspapers, and avidly smoked by both sexes from toddlers on. Besides frequent everyday use, smoking is associated with a ritual that involves a deep inhalation of smoke, whereby spirits can be contacted. Tobacco is planted by seed or by transplanted spontaneous seedlings, almost always in ashy spots.
Oenanthe java-nica D.C.	kinipo		Forb used as greens. Propagated by stem cuttings.
Pandanus cono-ideus Lamarck, *sensu* Merrill and Perry	komba	marita (Pidgin English)	The cultivated *Pandanus* is the most important tree of the Bomagai-Angoiang orchards. The trees' large syncarps, which weigh up to 18 pounds when ripe, are cored and steamed in the earth oven. The cooked drupes may then either be eaten directly by sucking off the edible mesocarp and spitting out the seed or be made into a sauce (*ndur*) by mixing the drupes with water and expressing the mesocarps' fluid by hand. The sauce, which has a pleasing taste and whose

consistency is that of oily ketchup, is eaten with greens or pumpkin. Undoubtedly the oil-rich *ndur* is the people's major source of vegetable oil. If no water is added during the squeezing, the drupes yield a fluid called *wai*, which when analyzed was found to be more than 99 percent fat. *Wai* is used as hair and body oil and as polish for arrow shafts. Leaves of the cultivated *Pandanus* are sometimes used to make house walls but are not considered as suitable for that as the leaves of the wild *P. papuanus*. I recorded 36 named varieties of cultivated *Pandanus* in the basin. Three of these have yellow syncarps, said to yield the best *wai*, which are taboo for eating to the Bomagai-Angoiang. The other 33 cultivars all bear nontaboo red syncarps. They are distinguished by the form of the limbs and stilt roots of the trees, the characteristics of the syncarps, and the time of ripening. The fruits of cultivated *Pandanus* are available all year but are most abundant in January and February. I believe that the seasonal nature of the time of abundance of this significant and valued food gives the Bomagai-Angoiang their clearest way of stating the passage of years. They may, for instance, speak of "two *komba* past," meaning a time two seasons of abundance of *komba* ago. All varieties are propagated vegetatively by stem cuttings.

Small tree whose inner bark is used to make string for net bags. It is planted around hamlets and also grows spontaneously.

The lima bean is generally regarded to be a quite recent introduction into New Guinea (Keleny, 1962:83; Massal and Barrau, 1956:30). The Bomagai-Angoiang say it is ancestral with them. Burkill (1935, II:1709) records two races of lima bean in the Moluccas in Rumpf's time (1652–1692). Seeds, leaves, and occasionally pods are eaten after being steamed in the earth oven.

Phaleria marcrocarpa (Scheff.) Boerl.

ap puk'na

Phaseolus lunatus L.

mbar pengup

lima bean

APPENDIX C (continued)

Scientific Name	Native Name	Common English Name	Comments
Pollia sp.	komeruk		See Commelina sp.
(?) Polyscias sp.	ap koimang		Large-leafed small tree planted by cuttings at house sites. Leaves are chewed with salt, and the masticated mass is spit on pork, steamed phalanger, and cooked Pandanus. I did not have the plant identified, but to me it looked like a Polyscias. Burkill (1935, II:1795) writes that the leaves of Polyscias fruticosa are widely used in Malaysia as a flavoring for flesh and fish.
Psophocarpus tetragonolobus (L.) DC.	mbar pitsim	asparagus bean, yam bean, wing bean	Bean of wide distribution and apparently great age in New Guinea. In the Ndwimba Basin the leaves and beans are eaten; but the pod is rarely, and the tuberous "yam" is never eaten. According to Barrau (1958:58) the pods and tubers are commonly eaten in New Guinea.
Rorippa sp.	ngombi		See Brassica juncea.
Rungia klossii S. Moore	akemba		Low shrub grown in gardens for its edible leaves.
Saccharum edule Hassk.	mungap	pit pit (Pidgin English)	Common garden plant whose large, undeveloped inflorescences (which have been compared to asparagus) are eaten baked, steamed, or raw. Planted by stem cuttings, as sugar cane is.
Saccharum officinarum L.	mbo	sugar cane	Sugar cane is grown throughout New Guinea and was probably domesticated there (Warner, 1962:407). In the basin the people chew cane avidly when they are tired and thirsty, but do not consider it real food. The cane, a "male plant," is almost always planted and tended by

men, but often harvested by women. As cane grows, it requires more work than any other crop. When it is three or four feet high, the men begin tying it to tree trunks or poles to keep it erect. From some of the at least twenty varieties, the men must remove dead leaves to inhibit insect damage; on other varieties having especially hard stems a sheathing of dried leaves is left around the stem to keep it from becoming too hard to rip apart with the teeth.

Setaria palmi-folia Stapf	*kwiai*	pit pit (Pidgin English)	Common garden plant grown for the edible heart of the stem, which is cooked with leaves in the earth oven. Mature men with *kunda* (a magical power) do not eat *Setaria*. The crop is planted by stem cuttings, but it also comes up from seed as a garden weed.
Xanthosoma sp.	*ndang kong*	New World taro, Yautia	This New World aroid arrived in the basin about 30 years ago. Its name means "Chinese taro" (*ndang*: Maring for *Colocasia*; *kong*: Pidgin English for Chinese, an adjective attached to *Xanthosoma* in much of New Guinea). There is now only one variety in the basin. *Ndang kong* grows more vigorously, is less subject to pest infestation, and yields more than *Colocasia*. Unlike *Colocasia*, a single plant produces many edible-sized corms, auxiliary to what the natives call the "mother tuber." The auxiliary corms can be harvested one by one over several months. When the garden is near disuse, the mother tuber, which can weigh more than 5 pounds, can be harvested, cooked, and fed to the pigs. People do not eat it because "it fights the mouth." *Xanthosoma* has become second in importance to sweet potatoes as a source of carbohydrate in the basin. Tubers usually are roasted in the fire or steamed in the earth oven, but sometimes people grate them into a paste, which is wrapped in leaves and cooked into a pudding in the earth oven.

APPENDIX C (continued)

Scientific Name	Native Name	Common English Name	Comments
Zea mays L.	*tumbla*	maize	Brought to the basin about 30 years ago, it is considered an auxiliary vegetable, not an important food. It is cooked in the fire in its husk or steamed on the cob in the earth oven. There is little mention of maize in my text because, when I was in the basin, most people were observing a government edict against its cultivation, in an attempt to eliminate a corn smut that had been introduced into New Guinea on seed from the United States.
Zingiber sp.	ginger	*tango*	The leaf of this cultivated ginger is eaten cooked. The spicy root is eaten cooked or sometimes raw in the gardens as a snack.

Wild Animal Life

Birds

I have little knowledge of the many species of birds that inhabit the basin. I had no specimens identified and did not spend much time observing birds or questioning the people about them. I list here only a few species that I am fairly certain were present in the vicinity of the basin. Information provided by Ralph Bulmer about the birds of the Kaironk Valley was helpful in compiling my list. Mayr and Gilliard (1954), Gyldenstolpe (1955) and Rand and Gilliard (1967) all provide information on the birds of New Guinea.

The Bomagai-Angoiang eat almost all the birds that they succeed in killing. The usual cooking procedure begins with feathering the body and partially cooking it at the edge of a fire or in coals. Then the body is opened, the inner organs are removed, and the body is cooked further in the coals, while the inner organs are cooked on a hot hearthstone. The feathers of the dramatically plumed birds of paradise and the brightly colored members of the parrot family are especially favored for use in headdresses.

Aepypodius arfakianus	Brush turkey. Known as *komami* to the Bomagia-Angoiang. Flesh and large, white-shelled eggs eaten.
Astrapia stephaniae	Stephanie's bird of paradise, known as *kalants* to the Bomagai-Angoiang. Special hunting trips are made to its home in the montane crest forest to obtain its long black feathers, which are traded for pigs with the people of the Jimi Valley.
Cacatua galerita	The large white cockatoo of New Guinea and Australia.
Casuarius bennetti	Large flightless bird of the primary forest. Adult birds are sometimes shot by hunters. Wild chicks are sometimes caught, tamed, and kept for several years before being killed and eaten, always on special occasions. Further notes on the cassowary appear in Chapter 2.

Falco berigora	Brown hawk, know to the Bomagai-Angoiang as *mumung*.
Gymnophaps albertisii	One of the New Guinea pigeons, known to the Bomagai-Angoiang as *mak'ma*.
Magapodius freycinet	Scrub hen, known to the Bomagai-Angoiang as *koraki*. Flesh and large (3½ inches long) red-brown eggs eaten.
Neopsittacus musschen-broekii	Lory of high elevations, perhaps known to the Bomagai-Angoiang as *ngir*. Brightly colored feathers mounted on sticks used for head decorations.
Ninox sp.	Small owl, known to the Bomagai-Angoiang as *tro*.
Paradisaea raggiana	Raggiana bird of paradise. The entire skin and plumage of the males of this species make one of the most valued of feather headdresses.
Pteridophora alberti	King of Saxony bird of paradise.
Ptilinopus sp.	Fruit dove, known to the Bomagai-Angoiang as *parak*.
Rhipidura leucophrys	Common bird of the gardens.

Marsupials, Rodents, and Bats

Except for *Rattus* spp., all the identifications given here were made by H. M. Van Deusen of the American Museum of Natural History from skulls that I collected in the basin.

All these animals are eaten: the marsupials and the bat by the men who take them, the rodents in most cases by women and children. The Bomagai-Angoiang names are enclosed in parentheses below the scientific names.

Echymipera clara (*meya tambun*)	Spiny-haired bandicoot. Ground-dwelling, nocturnal, having low-elevation habitat. The coarse fur has no use, being—say the people —like that of a dog.
Phalanger gymnotis (*meya augwia*)	Ground-foraging cuscus, also at home in trees. Lives at all basin elevations. Fur used to decorate net bags.
Phalanger maculatus (*meya rakapo*)	The spotted cuscus. A tropical-forest, arboreal species that reaches into the lower elevations of the basin. Fur used as head ornaments.
Phalanger orientalis (*meya moiyamp*)	Low-elevation, arboreal cuscus. Present only in the *wora* in the basin. Fur used to decorate net bags.
Phalanger vestitus (*meya mamga*)	Common high-elevation (5,000 to 10,000 feet) cuscus of New Guinea. Fur used to decorate loin cloths; tail used as wrist ornament.

Thylogale bruijni browni
(*meya kumbudai*)

Wallaby found at both high and low elevations. Skin used for drumheads.

Pogonomys macrourus (?)
(*kamenda koi*)

Small arboreal rat. Sometimes enters houses and eats stored food.

Rattus spp.
(*kamenda . . .*)

Native informants say that there are four types of *kamenda* besides *kamenda koi* (*Pogonomys*). At least some of these are *Rattus* species, according to collections made by Ralph Bulmer in the Kaironk Valley, where Bulmer obtained the Maring as well as the Karam names for the specimens in question. One of these rats is a pest in old gardens, eating sweet potatoes, corn, bananas, and sugar cane. The others live in secondary woodland or in *Pandanus* trees. They are said to eat the fruits of the *Ficus* spp. and the wild *Musa*. The men may work magic against the species inhabiting the gardens by planting *Cordyline* along the fences and saying spells. Some rats enter the houses, where they may eat ripe bananas. It is said that rats do not like yams or taros. Rats are usually caught by hand.

Uromys caudimaculatus
(*meya makek*)

Lowland, arboreal rat that ascends to the lower elevations of the basin.

Dobsonia moluccensis
(*ma'dan*)

The black flying fox, a fruit-eating bat that sometimes damages cultivated bananas. It has excellent eyes and needs light to fly. Shot while asleep in trees. Wing bone used as a needle for sewing net bags.

Cold-Blooded Animals

The scientific names given here for insects and the snail were supplied by J. Linsley Gressitt of the Bernice P. Bishop Museum in Honolulu and were based on my small collection of specimens from the basin. Slater (1961:30) records the presence in the Chimbu Valley of the python *Chondropython viridis*; because specimens of the New Guinean *Chondropython viridis* that I saw in the Sydney Zoological Garden seemed to resemble exactly the basin's green python, I assumed that the basin snake might be the same species. The people said that there were poisonous snakes in the basin, but, as far as I could find out, no one then alive in the basin knew personally of anyone who had been bitten by one. The list is far from complete, but it does represent some of the variety of cold-blooded animals in the basin. The Bomagai-Angoiang names are enclosed in parentheses.

(*abredak*)   Small brown snake of the primary forest. Not eaten by mature males. Cooked by roasting in coals or in a bamboo tube.

(*aipor*)   Riparian lizard. One specimen was 18 inches long and weighed 8 ounces. Cooked by wrapping in leaves and placing in the hot ashes. Men eat it.

(*amja*)   Grasshopper. Eaten by children.

(*banamboi*)   Large hairy spider, which will bite when threatened. Caught and eaten by boys. Cooked at the edge of a fire.

(*beponamai*)   Beetle eaten by children. Cooked at the edge of a fire.

catfish   Occasionally caught in the streams. Eaten by men, women, and children. Cooked wrapped in leaves in a fire or the earth oven.

Chloritis sp.   Land snail. Eaten by children.
  (*gong-gant'*)

Chondropython viridis   Small python, harmless to man. Cooked in the earth oven. Esteemed as food by the men.
  (*dɔmenta*)

Cicadidae [family]   Insect eaten by children.
  (*ginge*)

Cetoniidae [family]   Beetle with a metallic green sheen. Several woven together with *Dendrobium* fibers are used as decorative headbands.
  (*mimaro*)

Pentatoniidae [family]   Insect that feeds in large numbers on the leaves of a species of *Meliaceae*. Collected and eaten by men, women, and children.
  (*mburpikambo*)

Hymenoptera [order]   Small stingless bee. No use. They rest in large and annoying numbers on sweaty skin.

(*kairok*)   Fresh-water, shrimplike crustacean 3 to 5 inches long. Caught in eel traps and by hand. Eaten by all.

(*kamp*)   Frogs of forest and stream. May be eaten or used as bait in eel traps. Cooked in the ashes, or in the earth oven if several are caught at once. Generally, men do not eat frogs. Usually taken by hand.

(*koraba*)   Terrestrial crustacean resembling a small crab. People dig them out of their holes. Cooked in ashes. Eaten mostly by boys.

(*kima*)   Larvae (perhaps of several species) that live under the bark of trees. Cooked in the earth oven, wrapped in leaves. The 2 to 3 inch grubs are relished by all. Noted as present on *Euroschinus papuanus*, *ap mgomp* (an unidentified tree), and an unidentified gymnosperm in the Kumoints. Some men deliberately girdle trees, so that the *kima* will have a suitable home in the decaying trunk.

(*kupf*) Grasshopper. Eaten by children.

(*machung*) Grasshopper. Eaten by children.

(*kobe*) The fresh-water eel. Of all the wild animals, *kobe* provide the Bomagai-Angoiang with the largest amount of meat. Taken by hook, trap, and spear. Most eel-fishing is done at night, once with light from torches of *Pandanus papuanus*, now with kerosene lanterns, if available. The longest eels are at least 40 inches and weigh up to 4 pounds. Cooked in earth ovens. After the oily flesh is eaten, the bones are heated on hot rocks until they become soft enough to eat. Taboos prohibit eel-fishing during planting and the first few months of development of taro-yam gardens.

(*muk*) Brown beetle. Eaten by children.

(*mənamən*) Grasshopper. Eaten by children.

(*ngana*) Large lizard that resembles the monitor lizard. Riparian; up to 4 feet long. Eaten by all.

(*tum*) *Tum* is the "big name" for lizards. Besides the two types already mentioned, several others are eaten. Lizard eggs are eaten also, cooked wrapped in leaves in the earth oven.

(*saunbina*) Larva collected in its cocoon from *Lithocarpus* trees. Eaten by all.

(*tangarompe*) Spider with a body 2 inches in diameter. Eaten by boys.

Tettigoniidae [family] Long-horned grasshopper. Eaten by children.

Xylotrupes gideon Rhinoceros beetle. Eaten by children.
(*kunt'kunt*)

Literature Cited, Index

Literature Cited

Allan, W.
　1949　Studies in African Land Usage in Northern Rhodesia.
　　　　Rhodes-Livingstone Papers 15.
　1965　*The African Husbandman*. Edinburgh: Oliver and Boyd.
Aufenanger, H., and G. Höltker
　1940　*Die Gende in Zentralneuguinea*. Vienna: St. Gabriel.

Bailey, K. V.
　1966　Protein Malnutrition and Peanut Foods in Chimbu. In
　　　　E. H. Hipsley, ed., *An Integrated Approach to Nutrition and
　　　　Society: The Case of the Chimbu* (New Guinea Research
　　　　Unit Bulletin 9) 2–30.
Baldanzi, G.
　1961　Burning and Soil Fertility. *Transactions of 7th International
　　　　Congress of Soil Science* (Madison, Wisconsin, 1960) 2:523–
　　　　530.
Barrau, J.
　1958　*Subsistence Agriculture in Melanesia*. Bernice P. Bishop
　　　　Museum Bulletin 219. Honolulu: Bernice P. Bishop Museum.
　1965　Witnesses of the Past: Notes on Some Food Plants of
　　　　Oceania. *Ethnology* 4:282–294.
Barrows, H. H.
　1923　Geography as Human Ecology. *Annals of the Association of
　　　　American Geographers*, 13:1–14.
Beer, S.
　1961　Below the Twilight Arch—A Mythology of Systems. In
　　　　D. Eckman, ed., *Systems: Research and Design*. New York:
　　　　Wiley.
Bierdrager, J., and H. de Rook
　1954　Gezondheidstoestand. In W. C. Klein, ed., *Nieuw Guinea*
　　　　3:121–177. The Hague: Staatsdrukkerijen Uitgeverijbedrijf.
Black, R. H.
　1955　Malaria in the South-west Pacific. *South Pacific Commission
　　　　Technical Papers* 81. Noumea: South Pacific Commission.
Brass, L. J.
　1964　Summary of the Sixth Archbold Expedition to New Guinea
　　　　(1959). *Bulletin of the American Museum of Natural History*,
　　　　vol. 127, art. 4, pp. 145–216.
Brookfield, H. C.
　1962　Local Study and Comparative Method: An Example from

Central New Guinea. *Annals of the Association of American Geographers* 52:242–254.

1966 An Assessment of Natural Resources. In E. K. Fisk, ed., *New Guinea on the Threshold*, 44–79. Canberra: Australian National University Press.

1968 New Directions in the Study of Agricultural Systems in Tropical Areas. In Ellen T. Drake, ed., *Evolution and Environment*. New Haven: Yale University Press.

Brookfield, H. C., and P. Brown

1963 *Struggle for Land: Agriculture and Group Territories Among the Chimbu of the New Guinea Highlands*. Melbourne: Oxford University Press.

Brookfield, H. C., and D. Hart

1966 *Rainfall in the Tropical Southwest Pacific*. Research School of Pacific Studies, Department of Geography Publication G/3. Canberra: Australian National University.

Brookfield, H. C., and J. P. White

1968 Revolution or Evolution in the Prehistory of the New Guinea Highlands: A Seminar Report. *Ethnology* 7:43–52.

Bulmer, R.

1962 Chimbu Plume Traders. *Australian Natural History* (formerly *Australian Museum Magazine*) 14:15–19.

1964 Edible Seeds and Prehistoric Stone Mortars in the Highlands of East New Guinea. *Man* 64:147–150.

1966 Birds as Possible Agents in the propagation of the Sweet Potato. *The Emu* 65:165–182.

1967 Why Is the Cassowary not a Bird? A Problem of Zoological Taxonomy Among the Karam of the New Guinea Highlands. *Man* (new series) 2:5–25.

1968 The Strategies of Hunting in New Guinea. *Oceania* 38:302–318.

Bulmer, S.

1964 Prehistoric Stone Implements from the New Guinea Highlands. *Oceania* 34:246–268.

Bulmer, S., and R. Bulmer

1964 The Prehistory of the Australian New Guinea Highlands. In James B. Watson, ed., *New Guinea: The Central Highlands* (Special Publication, *American Anthropologist* vol. 66, no.4, pt. 2) pp. 39–76.

Bulmer, S., and W. C. Clarke

1970 Two Stone Spear or Dagger Heads from the Bismarck Mountains, Australian New Guinea. *Records of the Papua and New Guinea Museum* (Port Moresby) 1:42–46.

Burkill, I. H.

1935 A *Dictionary of the Economic Products of the Malay Peninsula*. 2 vols. London: Crown Agents for the Colonies.

1951 Dioscoreaceae. *Flora Malesiana*, ser. 1, vol. 4, pp. 293–335.

Burling, R.
  1964 Cognition and Componential Analysis: God's Truth or Hocus-pocus? *American Anthropologist* 66:20–28.
Butterfield, I. H.
  1967 Endemic Goitre in Papua and New Guinea. *South Pacific Bulletin* vol. 17, no. 2, pp. 15–18.

Carneiro, R.
  1960 Slash-and-Burn Agriculture: A Closer Look at its Implications for Settlement Patterns. In Anthony F. C. Wallace, ed., *Men and Cultures*, 229–234. Philadelphia: University of Pennsylvania Press.
Chang, J.
  1968a Rainfall in the Tropical Southwest Pacific, *Geographical Review* 58:142–144.
  1968b *Climate and Agriculture: An Ecological Survey.* Chicago: Aldine.
Chappell, J. M. A.
  1964 Stone Mortars in the New Guinea Highlands: A Note on Their Manufacture and Use. *Man* 64:146–147.
  1966 Stone Axe Factories in the Highlands of East New Guinea. *Proceedings of the Prehistoric Society* 32:96–121.
Chisholm, M.
  1962 *Rural Settlement and Land Use: An Essay in Location.* London: Hutchinson.
Chopra, R. N., S. L. Nayar, and I. C. Chopra
  1956 *Glossary of Indian Medicinal Plants.* New Delhi: Council of Scientific and Industrial Research.
Clark, C., and M. Haswell
  1966 *The Economics of Subsistence Agriculture.* London: Macmillan.
Clarke, W. C.
  1966 From Extensive to Intensive Shifting Cultivation: A Succession from New Guinea. *Ethnology* 5:347–359.
  1968 The Ndwimba Basin, Bismarck Mountains, New Guinea: Place and People. Ph.D. dissertation, University of California Berkeley.
Clarke, W. C., and J. M. Street
  1967 Soil Fertility and Cultivation Practices in New Guinea. *Journal of Tropical Geography* 24:7–11.
Clarkson, J. D.
  1968 *The Cultural Ecology of a Chinese Village: Cameron Highlands, Malaysia.* Department of Geography Research Paper 116. Chicago: University of Chicago.
Cobley, L.
  1956 *An Introduction to the Botany of Tropical Crops.* London: Longmans, Green.

Collins, P.
  1965 Functional Analyses in the Symposium "Man, Culture, and Animals." In A. Leeds and A. P. Vayda, eds., *Man, Culture, and Animals—The Role of Animals in Human Ecological Adjustments*, 271–282. Pub. 78, American Association for the Advancement of Science, Washington, D.C.
Conklin, H. C.
  1954 An Ethnoecological Approach to Shifting Cultivation. *Transactions of the New York Academy of Sciences* Ser. 2, 17:133–142. (Reprinted in P. Wagner and M. Mikesell, eds., *Readings in Cultural Geography*, 1962. Chicago: University of Chicago Press.)
  1957 *Hanunóo Agriculture: A Report on an Integral System of Shifting Cultivation in the Philippines*. Forestry Development Paper 12. Rome: Food and Agriculture Organization.
  1959 Population–Land Balance Under Systems of Tropical Forest Agriculture. *Proceedings of the Ninth Pacific Science Congress* (Bangkok, 1957) 7:63.
  1963 The Oceanic–African Hypothesis and the Sweet Potato. In Jacques Barrau, ed., *Plants and the Migration of Pacific Peoples*, 129–136. Honolulu: Bishop Museum Press.
Cranstone, B. A. L.
  1961 *Melanesia: A Short Ethnography*. London: Trustees of the British Museum.
Curry, L., and R. W. Armstrong
  1959 Atmospheric Circulation of the Tropical Pacific Ocean. *Geografiska Annaler* 41:245–255.

Darby, H. C.
  1962 The Problem of Geographical Description. *Transactions and Papers, 1962, Institute of British Geographers*, 30:1–14.
Dow, D. B., and F. E. Dekker
  1964 *The Geology of the Bismarck Mountains, New Guinea*. Report No. 76, Bureau of Mineral Resources, Geology and Geophysics, Department of National Development, Commonwealth of Australia.

Egler, F.
  1958 The Nature of the Relationship Between Climate, Soil, and Vegetation. *Proceedings of the Ninth Pacific Science Congress* (Bangkok, 1957) 20:50–56.
Evans, F. C.
  1956 Ecosystem as the Basic Unit in Ecology. *Science* 123:1127–1128.
Eyre, S. R., and G. R. J. Jones
  1966 *Geography as Human Ecology*. London: Edward Arnold.

Fosberg, F. R.
1958   Introduction. *Proceedings of the Ninth Pacific Science Congress* (Bangkok, 1957) 20:1–3.
1961   Qualitative Description of the Coral Reef Atoll. *Atoll Research Bulletin* 81:1–11.
1962   Nature and Detection of Plant Communities Resulting from Activities of Early Man. In *Symposium on the Impact of Man on Humid Tropics Vegetation* (Goroka, Territory of Papua and New Guinea, 1960) 251–252. UNESCO Science Co-operation Office for South East Asia, Djakarta.
1963   The Ecosystem Concept. In F. R. Fosberg, ed., *Man's Place in the Island Ecosystem* 1–6. Honolulu: Bishop Museum Press.
1965   The Entropy Concept in Ecology. In *Symposium on Ecological Research in Humid Tropics Vegetation* (Kuching, Sarawak, 1963). UNESCO Science Co-operation Office for South East Asia. Djakarta.

Fosberg, F. R., ed.
1963   *Man's Place in the Island Ecosystem.* Honolulu: Bishop Museum Press.

Fosberg, F. R., B. J. Garnier, and A. W. Küchler
1961   Delimitation of the Humid Tropics. *Geographical Review* 51:333–347.

Frake, C. O.
1962   Cultural Ecology and Ethnography. *American Anthropologist* 64:53–59.

Freeman, J. D.
1955   *Iban Agriculture.* Colonial Research Studies, 18. London: Her Majesty's Stationery Office.

Geertz, C.
1963   *Agricultural Involution: The Process of Ecological Change in Indonesia.* Berkeley: University of California Press.

Glacken, C. J.
1967   *Traces on the Rhodian Shore; Nature and Culture in Western Thought from Ancient Times to the End of the Eighteenth Century.* Berkeley: University of California Press.

Greenland, D. J., and P. H. Nye
1961   Does Straw Induce Nitrogen Deficiency in Tropical Soils? *Transactions of Seventh International Congress of Soil Science* (1960) 2:478–485.

Gyldenstolpe, N.
1955   Notes on a Collection of Birds Made in the Western Highlands, Central New Guinea, 1951. *Arkiv för Zoologi* 8:1–181.

Harding, T.
1967   Kunai Men: Horticultural Systems of a New Guinea Community. Mimeographed.

Hawley, A. H.
    1950   *Human Ecology; A Theory of Community Structure.* New
           York: The Ronald Press.
Hipsley, E., and N. Kirk
    1965   Studies of Dietary Intake and the Expenditure of Energy by
           New Guineans. *South Pacific Commission Technical Papers,*
           147. Noumea: South Pacific Commission.
Hughes, I.
    1969   Some Aspects of Traditional Trade in the New Guinea
           Central Highlands: A Preliminary Report. Paper delivered
           at the 41st Congress of the Australian and New Zealand
           Association for the Advancement of Science, Adelaide.

Ivinskis, V. *et al.*
    1956   A Medical and Anthropological Study of the Chimbu Natives
           in the Central Highlands of New Guinea. *Oceania* 27:143–
           157.

Keleny, G. P.
    1962   Notes on the Origin and Introduction of the Basic Food
           Crops of the New Guinea People. In *Symposium on the
           Impact of Man on Humid Tropics Vegetation* (Goroka,
           Territory of Papua and New Guinea, September 1960) 76–
           85. UNESCO Science Co-operation Office for South East
           Asia, Djakarta.

Langness, L. L.
    1964   Some Problems in the Conceptualization of Highlands Social
           Structure. In James B. Watson, ed., *New Guinea: The
           Central Highlands* (Special Publication, *American Anthro-
           pologist,* vol. 66, no. 4, pt. 2), 162–182.
Lauer, W.
    1952   Humide und aride Jahreszeiten in Afrika und Südamerika und
           ihre Beziehung zu den Vegetationsgürteln. *Bonner Geogra-
           phische Abhandlungen* 9:15–98.
Laurie, E. M. O., and J. E. Hill
    1954   *List of Land Mammals of New Guinea, Celebes and Adjacent
           Islands 1758–1952.* London: British Museum.
Lea, D.
    1964   Abelam Land and Sustenance: Swidden Horticulture in an
           Area of High Population Density, Maprik, New Guinea.
           Ph.D. dissertation, Australian National University.
    1969   Some Non-nutritive Functions of Food in New Guinea. In
           Fay Gale and Grahan H. Lawton, eds., *Settlement and
           Encounter: Geographical Studies Presented to Sir Grenfell
           Price* 173–184. Melbourne: Oxford University Press.

Leach, E. R.
 1949 Some Aspects of Dry Rice Cultivation in North Burma and British Borneo. *Advancement of Science* 6:26–28.
 1961 *Pul Eliya, A Village in Ceylon; A Study of Land Tenure and Kinship.* Cambridge University Press.

Leeds, A., and A. P. Vayda
 1965 *Man, Culture, and Animals—The Role of Animals in Human Ecological Adjustments.* Pub. 78, American Association for the Advancement of Science, Washington, D.C.

Lévi-Strauss, C.
 1961 *A World on the Wane.* (French editon and some English editions, published as *Tristes Tropiques.*) New York: Criterion.

Lowman-Vayda, C.
 1968 Maring Big Men. *Anthropological Forum* 2:199–243.

McKenzie, R. D.
 1926 The Scope of Human Ecology. *Publications of the American Sociological Society* 20:141–154.

Malinowski, B.
 1921 The Primitive Economics of the Trobriand Islanders. *The Economic Journal* 31:1–16.

Markgraf, F.
 1951 Gnetaceae. *Flora Malesiana*, ser. 1, vol. 4:336–347.

Massal, E., and J. Barrau
 1956 Food Plants of the South Sea Islands. *South Pacific Commission Technical Papers* 94. Noumea: South Pacific Commission.

Mayr, E., and E. T. Gilliard
 1954 Birds of Central New Guinea. *Bulletin of the American Museum of Natural History* 103:311–374.

Meggitt, M. J.
 1962 Notes on the Horticulture of the Enga People of New Guinea. In *Symposium on the Impact of Man on Humid Tropics Vegetation* (Goroka, Territory of Papua and New Guinea, September 1960) 86–89. UNESCO Science Co-operation Office for South East Asia, Djarkarta.
 1964 Male-Female Relationships in the Highlands of Australian New Guinea. In James B. Watson, ed., *New Guinea: The Central Highlands* (Special Publication, *American Anthropologist* vol. 66, no. 4, pt. 2) pp. 204–224.
 1965 *The Lineage System of the Mae-Enga of New Guinea.* Edinburgh: Oliver and Boyd.

Merrill, E. D.
 1917 *An Interpretation of Rumphius's Herbarium Amboinense.* Manila: Department of Agriculture and Natural Resources, Bureau of Science.

Mikesell, M.
    1967   Geographic Perspectives in Anthropology. *Annals of the Association of American Geographers* 57:617–634.

Nishiyama, I.
    1963   The Origin of the Sweet Potato Plant. In Jacques Barrau, ed., *Plants and the Migrations of Pacific Peoples* 119–128. Honolulu: Bishop Museum Press.
Nye, P. H., and D. J. Greenland
    1960   *The Soil Under Shifting Cultivation.* Technical Communication 51, Commonwealth Bureau of Soils. Farnham Royal, Bucks, England: Commonwealth Agricultural Bureaux.

Odum, E. P.
    1959   *Fundamentals of Ecology.* 2d ed. Philadelphia: W. B. Saunders.
    1962   Relationships Between Structure and Function in the Ecosystem. *Japanese Journal of Ecology,* 12:108–118.
    1963   *Ecology.* New York: Holt, Rinehart Winston.
Oomen, H. A. P. C., and S. H. Malcolm
    1958   Nutrition and the Papuan Child. *South Pacific Commission Technical Papers* 118. Noumea: South Pacific Commission.

Palmer, C. E.
    1951   Tropical Meteorology. In Thomas Malone, ed., *Compendium of Meteorology* 859–880. Boston: American Meteorological Society.
Panoff, F.
    1970   Maenge Remedies and Conception of Disease. *Ethnology* 9:68–84.
Park, R. E.
    1936   Human Ecology. *American Journal of Sociology* 42:1–15.
Pelzer, K.
    1945   *Pioneer Settlement in the Asiatic Tropics.* Special Publication 29. New York: American Geographical Society.
Phillips, J.
    1960   *Agriculture and Ecology in Africa.* New York: Praeger.
Popenoe, H.
    1959   The Influence of the Shifting Cultivation Cycle on Soil Properties in Central America. *Proceedings of the Ninth Pacific Science Congress* 7:72–77.
Pospisil, L.
    1963   *Kapauku Papuan Economy.* Publications in Anthropology 67. New Haven: Yale University, Department of Anthropology.

Pouwer, J.
    1961   New Guinea as a Field for Ethnological Study: A Preliminary Analysis. *Bijdragen tot de Taal-, Land- en Volkenkunde,* 117:1–24.

Rand, A., and E. T. Gilliard
    1967   *Handbook of New Guinea Birds.* London: Weidenfeld and Nicolson.

Rappaport, R.
    1967a   Ritual Regulation of Environmental Relations Among a New Guinea People. *Ethnology* 6:17–30.
    1967b   *Pigs for the Ancestors: Ritual in the Ecology of a New Guinea People.* New Haven: Yale University Press.

Read, K. E.
    1954   Cultures of the Central Highlands, New Guinea. *Southwestern Journal of Anthropology* 10:1–43.

Reynders, J. J.
    1961   Some Remarks about Shifting Cultivation in Netherlands New Guinea. *Netherlands Journal of Agricultural Science* 9:36–40.

Richards, P. W.
    1962   Plant Life and Tropical Climates. In S. W. Tromp, ed., *Biometeorology* 67–75. Oxford: Pergamon Press.

Riesenfeld, A.
    1952   Tobacco in New Guinea and the Other Areas of Melanesia. *Journal of the Royal Anthropological Institute of Great Britain and Ireland,* 81:69–102.

Robbins, R. G.
    1959   Montane Formations in the Central Highlands of New
    (?)   Guinea. In *Proceedings of the Symposium on Humid Tropics Vegetation* (Tjiawi, Indonesia, December 1958) 176–195. Publication of the UNESCO Science Co-operation Office for South East Asia, Djakarta.
    1962   The Anthropogenic Grasslands of Papua and New Guinea. In *Symposium on the Impact of Man on Humid Tropics Vegetation* (Goroka, Territory of Papua and New Guinea, September, 1960) 313–329. UNESCO Science Co-operation Office for South East Asia, Djarkarta.
    1963   Correlation of Plant Patterns and Population Migration into the Australian New Guinea Highlands. In Jacques Barrau, ed., *Plants and the Migrations of Pacific Peoples* 45–59. Honolulu: Bishop Museum Press.

Royen, P. van
    1963   The Vegetation of the Island of New Guinea. Lae: Department of Forests, Division of Botany. Mimeographed.

Salisbury, R. F.
    1962   *From Stone to Steel.* London and New York: Cambridge
            University Press.
    1964   Despotism and Australian Administration in the New Guinea
            Highlands. In James B. Watson, ed., *New Guinea: The
            Central Highlands* (Special Publication, *American Anthro-
            pologist* vol. 66, no. 4, pt. 2), pp. 225–239.
Sauer, C. O.
    1952   *Agricultural Origins and Dispersals.* New York: American
            Geographical Society.
Schmidt, F. H., and J. H. A. Ferguson
    1952   *Rainfall Types Based on Wet and Dry Period Ratios for
            Indonesia with Western New Guinee.* Kementerian Perhu-
            bungan Djawatan Meteorologi dan Geofisik (Djakarta), Ver-
            handelingen 42.
Sherman, G. D., Y. Kanehiro, and Y. Matsusaka
    1953   The Role of Dehydration in the Development of Laterite.
            Pacific Science 7:438–446.
Simmonds, N. W.
    1959   *Bananas.* London: Longmans, Green.
    1962   *The Evolution of Bananas.* London: Longmans, Green.
Slater, K. R.
    1961   Reptiles in New Guinea. *Australian Territories* vol. 1, no. 5:
            pp. 27–35.
Souter, G.
    1963   *New Guinea, The Last Unknown.* Sydney: Angus and
            Robertson.
Spate, O. H. K.
    1968   Environmentalism. In *International Encyclopedia of the
            Social Sciences.* New York: Macmillan.
Spencer, J. E.
    1966   *Shifting Cultivation in Southeastern Asia.* (*University of
            California Publications in Geography,* vol. 19). Berkeley:
            University of California Press.
Sprout, H. and M.
    1965   *The Ecological Perspective on Human Affairs: with Special
            Reference to International Politics.* Princeton: Princeton
            University Press.
Steenis, C. G. G. J. van
    1958   Tropical Lowland Vegetation: The Characteristics of Its
            Types and Their Relation to Climate. *Proceedings of the
            Ninth Pacific Science Congress* 20:25–37.
Steward, J.
    1955   The Concept and Method of Cultural Ecology. In J. Steward,
            Theory of Culture Change 30–42. Urbana: University of
            Illinois Press.

Stoddart, D. R.
  1965 Geography and the Ecological Approach. The Ecosystem as a Geographic Principle and Method. *Geography* 50:242–251.
  1967 Organism and Ecosystem as Geographical Models. In R. J. Chorley and P. Haggett, eds., *Models in Geography* 511–548. London: Methuen.
Strathern, M.
  1965 Axe Types and Quarries: A Note on the Classification of Stone Axe Blades from the Hagen Area, New Guinea. *Journal of the Polynesian Society* 74:182–191.
Street, J.
  1969 An Evaluation of the Concept of Carrying Capacity. *Professional Geographer* 21:104–107.

Tansley, A. G.
  1935 The Use and Abuse of Vegetational Concepts and Terms. *Ecology* 16:284–307.
Territory of Papua and New Guinea
  1963 Unpublished Report of the Malaria Service Department of Public Health, Territory of Papua and New Guinea. Port Moresby.
Thomas, W. L., ed.
  1956 *Man's Role in Changing the Face of the Earth.* Chicago: University of Chicago Press.

Vayda, A. P.
  1961a Culture and Environment in the New Guinea Rainforest. Research Proposal submitted to the National Science Foundation. Mimeographed.
  1961b Expansion and Warfare Among Swidden Agriculturalists. *American Anthropologist* 63:346–358.
  1965 Anthropologists and Ecological Problems. In A. Leeds and A. P. Vayda, eds., *Man, Culture, and Animals: The Role of Animals in Human Ecological Adjustments,* 1–5. Washington: American Association for the Advancement of Science.
  1968 War: Primitive Warfare. In *International Encyclopaedia of the Social Sciences.* New York: Macmillan.
  1971 The Pig Complex. To be published in *Encyclopedia of Papua and New Guinea.* Melbourne: Melbourne University Press.
Vayda, A. P., and E. A. Cook
  1964 Structural Variability in the Bismarck Mountain Cultures of New Guinea: A Preliminary Report. *Transactions of the New York Academy of Sciences* ser. 2, 26:798–803.
Vayda, A. P., A. Leeds, and D. B. Smith
  1961 The Place of Pigs in Melanesian Subsistence. In Viola Garfield, ed., *Proceedings of the 1961 Annual Spring Meet-*

    ing of the American Ethnological Society, 69–77. Seattle:
    University of Washington Press.
Vayda, A. P., and R. Rappaport
    1968   Ecology, Cultural and Non-Cultural. In James A. Clifton, ed.,
            *Introduction to Cultural Anthropology: Essays in the Scope
            and Methods of the Science of Man.* Boston: Houghton
            Mifflin.
Vicedom, G. F., and H. Tischner
    1943–1948   *Die Mbowamb: Die Kultur der Hagenberg-Stämme
            im Östlichen Zentral-Neuguinea.* 3 vols. Hamburg: de
            Gruyter
Village Register, Gunts
    1961   Entry 20 August 1961, Village Register of Gunts, Jurisdic-
            tion of Simbai Patrol Post, Madang District, Territory of
            Papua and New Guinea.

Waddell, E. W.
    1968   The Dynamics of a New Guinea Highlands Agricultural
            System. Ph.D. dissertation, Australian National University.
Warner, J. N.
    1962   Sugar Cane: An Indigenous Papuan Cultigen. *Ethnology*
            1:405–411.
Watson, J. B.
    1964   Introduction: Anthropology in the New Guinea Highlands.
            In James B. Watson, ed., *New Guinea: The Central High-
            lands* (Special Publication, *American Anthropologist* vol. 66,
            no. 4, pt. 2) pp. 1–19.
    1965a   From Hunting to Horticulture in the New Guinea High-
            lands. *Ethnology* 4:295–309.
    1965b   The Significance of a Recent Ecological Change in the
            Central Highlands of New Guinea. *The Journal of the Poly-
            nesian Society* 74:438–450.
Watt, B. K., and A. L. Merrill
    1963   *Composition of Foods.* (U.S.D.A. Agricultural Handbook
            8.) Washington, D.C.: U.S. Department of Agriculture.
Went, F. W.
    1959   Photosynthesis. In Martin Huberty and Warren Flock, eds.,
            Natural Resources, 221–232 New York: McGraw-Hill.
Wilson, E., K. Fisher, and M. Fuqua
    1965   *Principles of Nutrition.* New York: John Wiley.
Wurm, S. A.
    1964   Australian New Guinea Highlands Languages and the Dis-
            tribution of Their Typological Features. In James B. Watson,
            ed., *New Guinea: The Central Highlands* (Special Publica-
            tion, *American Anthropologist*, vol. 66, no. 4, pt. 2), pp. 77–
            97 and Map II, f. p. 308.
Wynne-Edwards, V. C.
    1962   *Animal Dispersion in Relation to Social Behavior.* Edinburgh:
            Oliver and Boyd.

Index

Agriculture. *See* Climate; Cultivated plants; Economic organization; Gardening practices; Gardens; Orchards; Soil

Animals: wild and feral, 89–92; listed, 241–248. *See also* Birds; Cassowaries; Dogs; Fishing; Fowl; Gathering; Hunting; Pigs

Bark cloth, 119
Big men, 32–33, 93, 171
Birds, 16, 90–91, 119, 168; listed, 241–242. *See also* Cassowaries
Bismarck Range, 2, 37
Bomagai-Angoiang clan cluster: rusticity of, 2, 8; meets Europeans, 3, 5; language of, 7, 184; origin of Bomagai, 8, 184; physical anthropology of, 21–22; social ties of beyond Ndwimba Basin, 33–35, 93; heartland of, 51; daily life of, 132–136; effects of Westernization on, 191–196. *See also* Big men; Communication; Cultivated plants; Diet; Disease; Economic organization; Funeral practices; Gardening practices; Gardens; Houses; Land; Land tenure; Marriage; Material culture; Ornamentation; Population; Reciprocity; Resources, spheres of; Settlement pattern; Social organization; Territory; Trade; Travel; Warfare
Boundaries: interclan "marks," 9–11; functions of, 10–12; orchard, 81; intragarden "marks," 123–124, 152; mentioned, 51, 52

Carrying capacity. *See* Ecosystem
Cassowaries, 56, 89–90
Central Highlands, 1, 7, 8, 193
Climate: wind, 39, 40, 48; water budget, 35; relative humidity, 47; clouds, 47–50; effect of cloud cover on plant growth, 48–49; radiation, 48, 49, 50; effect of slope aspect on microclimate, 50; mentioned, 12–13

—rainfall: seasonality of, 39–45 *passim*; annual in Ndwimba Basin, 40; daily, 41; intensity of, 41; variability of, 42–43; effect of variability on gardening; dry spells, 43–45; effect of on daily life, 117, 132n

—temperature: annual range, 45–46; daily pattern, 46; elevational zones (*kamunga* and *wora*), 46–47, 80; people's response to minimum, 47

Clothing, 119
Communication: shouting, 4, 16, 100. *See also* Travel
Containers: net bags, 114–115; leaf packages, 115; bamboo stems, 116, 165; gourds, 116; eggshells, 116; wood, 116; pottery, 116
Crops. *See* Cultivated plants
Cultivated plants: ritually important species, 10, 75, 82, 108, 110, 121, 123; as a resource, 74; incidence of major crops, 78–79; semicultivated species, 82–84; diseases and pests of, 92, 164; effect of sweet potato on, 98n; "male" and "female" crops, 124; maturation periods, 162–163; sugar cane, 183; introduction of *Xanthosoma* and maize, 189; tree planting in grasslands, 194; cash crops, 195; listed, 225–240. *See also* Gardening practices; Gardens; Orchards

Diet: adequacy of, 24; protein deficiency, 24–25; sources of protein, 90, 91, 92, 94, 178–182; food consumption, 177–183; seasonal changes in, 182
Disease: dysentery epidemic, 5, 102; incidence and types of, 22–24; absence of leprosy, filariasis, venereal disease, 24; tooth decay, 25; cretinism, 25–26; affects settlement pattern, 102; and sorcery, 102
Dogs, 84, 86–88, 89
Drums, 118–119